W9-BKE-378

ADDITIONAL PRAISE FOR *THE BIG TRUCK THAT WENT BY*

"A top-notch account of Haiti's recent history, including the January 2010 earthquake, from the only American reporter stationed in the country at the time. Katz broke the story of how the deadly cholera outbreak, which spread in the months after the earthquake, was brought to the region by infected Nepalese UN peacekeepers and spread by inadequate sanitation. In his debut, the author chronicles his many investigations during his years living in and writing about Haiti. Unlike coverage by other writers on the island's recent history, Katz's recounting of the earthquake disaster, and the international mobilization that followed, is part of an ongoing story. . . . His contacts and local knowledge gave him special insight into the way the relief operation developed. . . . An eye-opening, trailblazing exposé."

—*Kirkus Reviews* (starred)

"Katz was the only American reporter on the ground when the devastating earthquake struck Haiti on January 12, 2010. . . . Debunks the assumption that a disaster leads to social disintegration or rioting and observes how media sensationalism prompted unwise giving."

—*Publishers Weekly*

"Beautifully written, brave, and riveting, *The Big Truck That Went By* tells the devastating story of the post-earthquake reconstruction effort in Haiti. Weaving together his personal experiences with the knowledge gained from his intensive investigative report, Katz offers us an autopsy of a global relief effort gone wrong. But the book also offers us a moving portrait of the courage, humor, and vision of the Haitians he worked with, offering a glimpse of the possibilities for a different future. Anyone seeking to understand Haiti's current situation, as well as the broader impasses of our current model of aid, should read this book."

—Laurent Dubois, author of *Haiti: The Aftershocks of History*

"The horror of the catastrophic Haitian earthquake of 2010, the adrenaline rush of being a reporter in the middle of dramatic events, the frustration of watching local politicians and poorly informed outsiders combine to paralyze the recovery effort, and the joy of finding love in the midst of the ruins: It's all here. Katz, the only American journalist on the scene when the earthquake struck, gives us unique insights into the plight of a close neighbor whose fate is vitally connected to our own."

—Jeremy Popkin, author of *You Are All Free:*
The Haitian Revolution and the Abolition of Slavery

"Jonathan M. Katz has a passion for the truth. He has shown respect for the people of Haiti by seeking that truth throughout the earthquake and the aftermath. . . . This is an important book, and a page-turner!"

—Mark Doyle, BBC correspondent

"Jonathan Katz's strength is his unique combination of heart, history, and solid reporting, brilliantly married in *The Big Truck That Went By*. Readers experience the country through his personal roadmap, one that is both sympathetic and yet sharply critical of all that could have gone right, but didn't."

—Kathie Klarreich, author of *Madame Dread: A Tale of Love, Vodou, and Civil Strife in Haiti*

THE BIG TRUCK
THAT WENT BY

THE BIG TRUCK
THAT WENT BY

HOW THE WORLD CAME TO SAVE
HAITI AND LEFT BEHIND A DISASTER

JONATHAN M. KATZ

palgrave
macmillan

Quotations from conversations are either taken verbatim from recorded
interviews or reconstructed from the author's contemporaneous notes. In
certain cases, names and identifying characteristics have been changed.

First published in 2013 by PALGRAVE MACMILLAN® in the U.S.—a division
of St. Martin's Press LLC, 175 Fifth Avenue, New York, NY 10010.

Where this book is distributed in the UK, Europe and the rest of the world,
this is by Palgrave Macmillan, a division of Macmillan Publishers Limited,
registered in England, company number 785998, of Houndmills, Basingstoke,
Hampshire RG21 6XS.

Palgrave Macmillan is the global academic imprint of the above companies
and has companies and representatives throughout the world.

Palgrave® and Macmillan® are registered trademarks in the United States, the
United Kingdom, Europe and other countries.

ISBN: 978-0-230-34187-6

Library of Congress Cataloging-in-Publication Data is available from the
Library of Congress.

A catalogue record of the book is available from the British Library.

Design by Letra Libre

All maps courtesy of Rick Orlosky. Reprinted with permission.

First edition: January 2013

10 9 8 7 6 5 4 3 2 1

Printed in the United States of America.

To Clide, Prince, Chris Owen Sanon,
and a new generation in Haiti

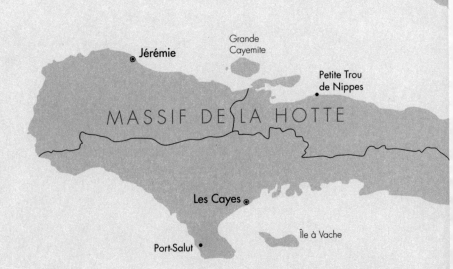

CUBA

← To Guántanamo Bay

Windward Passage

Môle
Saint-Nicolas

Gulf
of
Gonâve

CARIBBEAN SEA

Île de
la Gonâve

Grande
Cayemite

Jérémie

Petite Trou
de Nippes

MASSIF DE LA HOTTE

Les Cayes

Île à Vache

Port-Salut

CARIBBEAN SEA

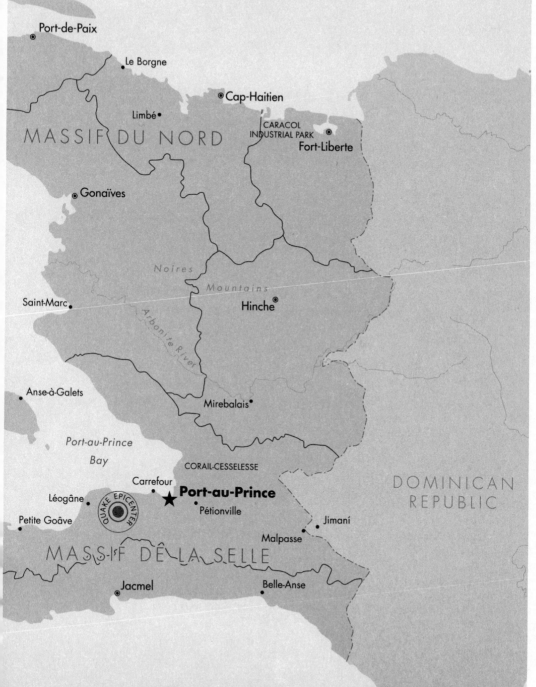

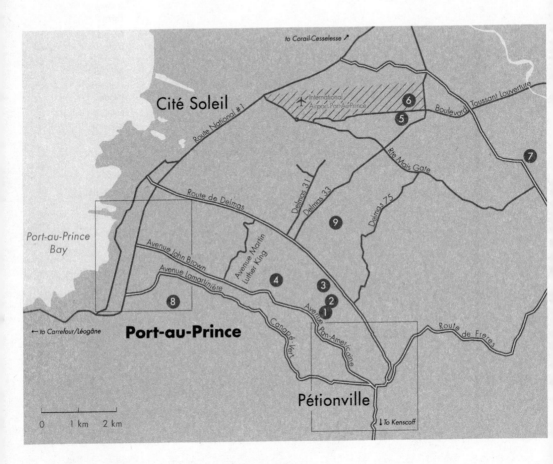

1. US ambassador's residence
2. Pétionville Club
3. Golf Course
   (postquake IDP Camp)
4. Hotel Christopher
   (UN-MINUSTAH Headquarters)
   (destroyed in quake)
5. UN Military Hospital
   (Argentina)
6. UN Logistics Base
   ("Logbase")
7. US Embassy
8. Pacot
   (neighborhood)
9. Pierre Family's House
   (Evens' Step-Family)

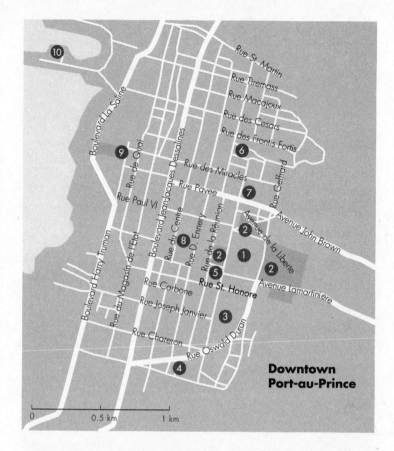

Downtown Port-au-Prince

1. National Palace
   (destroyed in quake)
2. Champ de Mars Plazas
3. Hospital of the State University of Haiti (General Hospital) *(damaged in quake)*
4. National Soccer Stadium (Stade Silvio Cator)
5. Palais de Justice *(destroyed in quake)*
6. Notre Dame de l'Assomption Catholic Cathedral *(destroyed in quake)*
7. Ste. Trinite Episcopal Cathedral *(destroyed in quake)*
8. National Penitentiary *(damaged in quake)*
9. Parliament building *(destroyed in quake)*
10. Main port *(damaged in quake)*

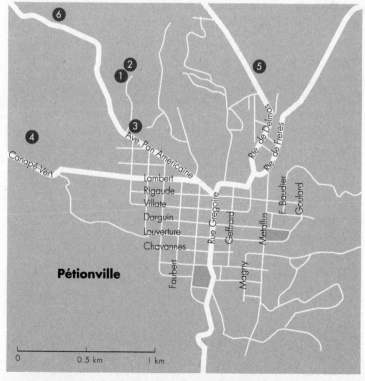

Pétionville

1. Hotel Villa Creole *(damaged in quake)*
2. Old AP House *(destroyed in quake)*
3. Dominican Embassy
4. Karibe Hotel and Conference Center (Juvenat)
5. Caribbean Supermarket *(destroyed in quake)*
6. Hotel Montana *(destroyed in quake)*

CONTENTS

Eight pages of photographs appear between pages 146 and 147

INTRODUCTION

"WHY HAITI?" HILLARY RODHAM CLINTON ASKED IN EARLY 2010, SPEAK-
ing on behalf of a bewildered world. The earthquake that leveled
Port-au-Prince and much of southern Haiti had defied logic, imagination, even superstition. How did a magnitude 7.0 temblor—a
huge release of energy, but not necessarily catastrophic—prove
to be the deadliest natural disaster ever recorded in the Western
Hemisphere? Why did an earthquake, of all calamities, strike at
the heart of a nation already reeling from so many others? And
why, three years after so many countries and ordinary people sent
money and help, hasn't Haiti gotten better?

I wrote this book in part to answer those questions. When the
earthquake struck, I had been living in Haiti for two and a half
years. I had already seen a lifetime's worth of disasters, both political and natural. Two centuries of turmoil and foreign meddling
had left a Haitian state so anemic it couldn't even count how many
citizens it had. Millions were packed in and around the nation's
capital, living in poorly made buildings stacked atop a fault line.
People could not rely on police, a fire department, or schools.
Even the rat-infested General Hospital charged so much for basic
medicine that few Haitians could afford care. Nearly everything—
water, gas for generators, hungry relatives from the countryside—
was delivered by truck. Each day, big eighteen-wheelers rumbled
down the narrow streets, shaking homes as they passed. When the
shockwave surged through Port-au-Prince, just fifteen miles from
the epicenter, many of us thought at first that it was a *gwo machin*,
a big truck, going by.

I wanted to understand how people could endure not only the catastrophe that befell Haiti on January 12, 2010, but also the hardship and absurdity that followed. The aid response was marked by the best intentions: an international outpouring for Port-au-Prince, Carrefour, Jacmel, Léogâne, and other cities in the disaster zone. The numbers were astounding: The world spent more than $5.2 billion on the emergency relief effort; private donations reached $1.4 billion in the United States alone.[1] Thousands of doctors and nurses performed lifesaving surgeries. When it came time to plan for the future, governments pledged about $10 billion more for Haiti's recovery and reconstruction, promising to build a better, safer, more prosperous Haiti than before. "We need Haiti to succeed," Hillary Clinton told a donors' conference, as she answered her own question. "What happens there has repercussions far beyond its borders."[2]

But today, Haiti is not better off. It ended its year of earthquakes with three new crises: nearly a million people still homeless; political riots fueled by frustration over the stalled reconstruction; and the worst cholera epidemic in recent history, likely caused by the very UN soldiers sent to Haiti to protect its people (that story, and my investigation, appear later in the book). Those few who were fortunate enough to leave post-quake camps—an estimated 400,000 still lived under tarps as of mid-2012—usually settled in houses no safer than the ones that collapsed in the earthquake. Though by the time you read this book, the ruins of the devastated National Palace might finally have been cleared, rubble, some mixed with human remains, still chokes much of the city. At last count, more than half the reconstruction money that was supposed to be delivered as of 2011 remains an unfulfilled promise. For many of my Haitian friends, some of whom you'll meet in this book, the legacy of the response has been a sense of betrayal.

I wanted to write this book to understand how a massive humanitarian effort, led by the most powerful nation in the world—my country—could cause so much harm and heartache in another that wanted its help so badly. The United States and Haiti have long had a special relationship, though not an easy one. Founded only decades apart, the first republic in the Western Hemisphere at first refused to recognize the second, then brutally occupied it, and finally spent decades meddling in its affairs. The extreme centralization of people and services in Haiti's capital, Port-au-Prince, which proved so deadly in the earthquake, was in large part a legacy of U.S. policy and actions.

But Haitians admire the American people, and many dream of coming here one day. Haitian Americans have prospered and play major roles in American life while sustaining millions on the island with money sent back (remittances make up more than a quarter of the Haitian economy).[3] Many Americans, meanwhile, are fascinated by a close neighbor whose apparent poverty and dysfunction can be used to affirm our wealth and strength, where good deeds can be performed and theories tested, framed by a culture of Vodou and zombies that entices the imagination. Several officials I talked to for this book spoke of a widely held "romanticism" of the black republic among their colleagues.

One of Hillary Clinton's first acts as secretary of state was to order a review of U.S. policy toward Haiti. That review was finished on the afternoon of January 12, 2010, barely an hour before the earthquake struck.[4] The Americans shifted focus quickly and led the response, providing the largest sums of money and huge numbers of personnel—22,000 U.S. troops alone at the height. In many ways, the response's legacy, good and bad, is an American legacy. We owe it to ourselves to find out what happened.

It's worth considering Haiti also because of what its experience means for all of us. We are living in a time of record-setting hurricane seasons, droughts, wildfires, blizzards, earthquake clusters, and disease, many reaching places that long ago thought they had developed their way out of trouble. In 2010, natural disasters cost $123 billion and affected 300 million people.[5] Understanding how to deal with these crises in the future means understanding what has been done so far. Rescue workers, officials—and, yes, journalists—still approach crises unprepared to think beyond the hoary, illogical clichés that gird disaster response. For instance, that people will panic, riot, or turn on each other after a disaster; typically, they don't. Or that in fashioning solutions to disasters, doing something is always better than doing nothing, no matter how poorly thought-out it is; it's not. And, for anyone who gave money to a major aid group, that they were going to be able to spend your $20 donation on actual survivors of the actual disaster you intended; for the most part, they were not. Part of the reason I wanted to write this book is to find out where your $20 went instead.

Haiti's earthquake struck at a time when Western countries were reconsidering the whole idea of how to give foreign aid. For decades, policy makers had argued against giving to local governments because they were irresponsible, feckless, and, especially, corrupt. New thinkers, many of them in the U.S. government, argued that only by building strong local and national institutions could countries like Haiti prepare for future disasters or deal with the crises they have now. This book explores that debate and the effect it had when the last big truck, the aid response, rolled into post-quake Haiti.

I finally wanted to share my own story of survival. When the earthquake struck, my house in the hills above Port-au-Prince rocked and shattered. I was inside. As I rushed out of the building with the help of my brave colleague and friend, Evens Sanon, I found myself with a bifurcated identity: a journalist responsible for getting information out as quickly as possible and a survivor trying to figure out what had just happened. That experience perhaps made me less objective than the ideal reporter. Less clear-headed, too: Shot nerves gave way to PTSD over time. In writing this book, I have also wrestled with whether the world really needs another American's personal account of living in Haiti, a country whose people are more than capable of speaking but struggle to be heard.

But I believe my experience, in the earthquake and as I remained in Haiti for more than a year after the quake, granted a unique perspective. It allowed me to understand both sides of the divide, between those who seek to improve how aid is given and those who have been trying to improve their own lives for so long.

—*January 2013*

PROLOGUE

NOVEMBER 2008

THE PRESIDENT KEPT GOING TO THE FALLEN SCHOOL, OVER AND OVER, until no one cared that he was there. Sometimes he was driven in one of the big gold SUVs that seemed like the only things his government invested in, could afford, or both. Leaning forward to peer through the tinted windshield, he'd race down the precipitous curves, past the gated mansions of Haitian and foreign elites— food importers and sweatshop owners, heads of aid groups and young diplomats. Then he'd keep going, deep into the slum on the edge of a ravine, where the housekeepers and handymen who cleaned those estates built their brittle cinder-block homes.

At the edge of the site, the president would step out, in his shirtsleeves and slacks, crunching the scattered rubble with sneaker-soled, brown wingtips. He'd rub his bald head, grimace through his salt-and-pepper beard, and gaze at the pile of concrete sliding down into the chasm below.

The school was called Collège La Promesse Evangelique, "The Promise," and that's what it represented to the parents who sent their children to it. Most had fled the floods and gutted farms of Haiti's desiccated countryside to seek better lives in Port-au-Prince. They came to this ravine below Pétionville, a suburb of wealthy Haitians and foreigners in the mountains south of the capital, so they could clean mansions, guard gates, or wait tables. Others serviced the servicers, selling them rice and beans, hawking clothing from blankets along the road, or ferrying them on motorcycles and covered pickup trucks to save walks under the brutal sun.

Most Haitians live off less than $1 a day, which barely covers a small can of rice and a round trip in a group taxi. Yet from those tiny pools of cash, augmented by gifts from relatives overseas, neighborhood parents scraped together hundreds of dollars for tuition so at least some of their children could go to school.

La Promesse had been built by a Protestant preacher named Fortin Augustin. Even the less literate mothers and fathers suspected that its teachers did not know their subjects well, and the students complained that their books were falling apart. But this only made the school typical. Although the Haitian constitution guaranteed universal education, the government had neither the staff nor the budget to maintain a list of schools in the country, much less regulate them. There were fewer than 1,500 public primary schools in a nation with an estimated 4 million children under the age of 15.[1] The vast majority of families depended on fly-by-night, for-profit private schools. In a district of storefront schools in the downtown slum of Bel-Air, students peed in open troughs dug into the classroom, and bored teens could snap pieces of concrete off the worm-eaten support columns. A third of Haiti's teachers hadn't completed the equivalent of ninth grade. Like its people, the government depended on money from overseas— mostly foreign aid—but in a country where each year brought new floods, riots, or political coups, donors never made education a priority. The diplomats never had to worry about such things. While in Haiti, they sent their children to high-end academies such as the English-language Union School, where high school tuition and fees came to more than $10,000 a year.

La Promesse's tuition was exorbitant to those who paid it—at about $200 a year, it represented a substantial portion of its students' families' income. But it was worth it, the parents believed. Education was the surest path out of poverty. If their children could read, write, and do math, learn some French and perhaps a bit of English on top of their native Kreyòl, they might even make it out of Haiti altogether to support their families back home. The Reverend Augustin converted that desire into profit. In the summer of 2008, hoping to cash in on the slum's growth, he added a third story. To save money, as he had with the floors below, he instructed his crew to use low-quality concrete made of sand blasted from hillsides. The workers mixed it with extra water to stretch the material. Augustin also skimped on the iron rebar that reinforced load-bearing walls. The parents living along the ridge could see what was happening, but they were in no position to complain. Most had built their homes the same way.

On the morning of Friday, November 7, during a class party, La Promesse imploded. The news surged up the hill through Pétionville, where I lived in a house rented by my employer, the Associated Press. I raced over, reaching the turn-off to the slum just as police closed the road. As I walked toward the collapse, men pushed the other way, carrying broken bodies of children, some already dead. One boy's head was sliced open to the brain. I picked up my cell phone and called the AP Caribbean bureau in Puerto Rico. Then I forced my way through the crowd until I saw the school's entrance.

At first I hoped the rumors had been wrong—part of the first-story facade remained upright, a hand-painted Mickey Mouse smiling through the dust. Then I looked around the side. Down the precipitous slope, two and a half stories' worth of concrete keeled toward the ravine. Hundreds of men dug with sledgehammers and their bare hands, pulling out whomever they could find. At the entrance, parents charged recklessly at the building's remains, concrete chunks still dropping off the walls. Clearer-headed neighbors blocked the door. One jumped and grabbed the loosened crossbar, swung backward like a gymnast, and kicked a howling father back into the crowd. The stunned man cried out, picked himself up, and rushed the door again.

René Préval, the fifty-fifth president of Haiti, visited that afternoon. Haitian reporters circled the five-foot six-inch leader in a ring of mismatched cameras and twenty-year-old cassette recorders. Préval shouted his sympathies for the victims and promised action to prevent such disasters from happening again. The reporters demanded to know how the Reverend Augustin would be brought to justice. (Fearing for his life from vigilantes as the death toll climbed toward one hundred, Augustin had already turned himself in.) But the more the reporters pressed for specifics, the less the president had to give, and eventually, they let him be.

But Préval didn't leave. He stayed beside the collapse, pacing. There was little else he could do with a meager budget and an incomplete staff. Finally, the president left. But a few hours later, as I was walking back to the office, he raced past me down the hill again, this time piloting the gold SUV himself.

IT HAD ALREADY BEEN A LONG YEAR IN HAITI—after a long decade, after a long century. Four months before the school disaster, in August and September 2008, four hurricanes and tropical storms struck in as many weeks, flooding much of the country and killing an estimated 793 people. People drowned in their living rooms as Gonaïves, the main port city in northwestern Haiti, flooded past its rooflines. In the mountains of the southeast, farmers' children died of malnutrition when washed-out roads kept their parents from reaching markets. Countries whose donations kept Haiti functioning, barely—principally the United States, Canada, and France—pledged millions in aid. Ships and helicopters carried American rice, bottled water, and relief workers in khaki vests and color-coded T-shirts. Those donors had spent years promising engineering projects and long-term investments to keep the rivers from flooding again, but only a small percentage of the pledged funds had been delivered, and much of it had been committed to reports, pilot projects, and overhead. In the end, the same exact rivers flooded in the same exact way they had flooded a few years before, and the aid workers simply came back.

At the end of September 2008, three weeks after the storms and six weeks before the collapse of La Promesse, Préval traveled to New York for the opening of the General Assembly of the United Nations, which features addresses by presidents and representatives of every member nation. When the leader of a major country speaks, the room overflows. But as the second speaker on the fourth morning, the sixty-five-year-old president of Haiti climbed the marble dais and peered at an expanse of avocado carpet and mostly empty beige-and-blue chairs. He wore a dark suit too big in the shoulders and a blue tie decorated with light blue ovals that looked like fish climbing a waterfall.

Préval was born in Haiti's rice country, son of a minister of agriculture. After the tyrant François "Papa Doc" Duvalier rose to power in 1957 and began hunting down members of rival regimes, the family scattered. The future president wound up in Belgium, where he studied agronomy. Years later, after stints as a waiter in Brooklyn and a bureaucrat in Haiti, Préval opened a bakery that sold bread to an orphanage run by a charismatic priest named Father Jean-Bertrand Aristide. A brash liberation theologian, Aristide was a stalwart opponent of the Duvalier dynasty. The baker and the priest became close friends. When Aristide won the presidency in 1990, he made Préval prime minister. Through the coups and attempted coups that followed, Préval proved to be, above all, a survivor. Elected twice to the presidency himself, in 1995 and 2006, he avoided being overthrown and killed, like so many of his predecessors, by forging quiet alliances, speaking softly, and making as few enemies as possible. Préval was not above mucking around with elections or standing idly by while parliamentary terms expired, leaving him to rule by decree. But his chief characteristic, for better or worse, was absolute stubbornness—a quality he was about to display at the UN.

Préval smoothed his tie and began to describe the hurricanes' toll. He thanked the nations that had sent money, experts, and food. Then he glanced around the nearly empty room, looked down, and took a deep breath:

"With all recognition of this huge wave of generosity toward my country, I cannot fail to draw your attention to the concerns that it raises for Haitians."

His eyes rose from the podium.

"I am worried, because I dread that once this first wave of solidarity and human compassion has dried up, we will be left, as always, alone but truly alone, to deal with new catastrophes and to see restarted, as if in a ritual, the same exercises of mobilization."

Someone in the delegate seats coughed.

Humanitarian aid was delivered in all the wrong ways, Préval continued, gaining confidence. Rich countries focused on setting trade regulations that benefited themselves. Few engaged in long-term reform that would make aid unnecessary. Few helped build functioning institutions that could lead to functioning societies. The major donors did not approach Haiti's poor on their own terms, recognizing their simple homes and informal jobs as assets, or showing them respect as potential partners rather than targets for instruction. Free trade could be a good thing, Préval reassured his scattered listeners, but only if conducted "on the basis of clear, transparent rules which are the same for everyone," not rigged to favor powerful nations or a few wealthy elites. In place of temporary relief, Préval called for systematic reconstruction, so his country could build its own safety net and produce its own wealth and food.

From 1998 to 2008, donor countries spent at least $4.8 billion on Haiti aid.[2] Per capita, Haiti was getting more than double the world average and more than much of sub-Saharan Africa, including Somalia and Sierra Leone. Donors were also spending upwards of $500 million a year on a UN peacekeeping mission installed after Aristide was overthrown in a 2004 uprising stoked by gangs, former officers of the military he had disbanded, and some of Haiti's most powerful business leaders. Yet Haiti was still ranked 158 out of 187 countries on the UN Human Development Index and lurked at or near the bottom of nearly every social and economic indicator in the world.

Part of the problem was that, appearances to the contrary, little of the money marked as aid was actually spent in Haiti. Donors made it notoriously hard to track where aid went and how it got spent, but of the $683 million given in 2007, only about 9 percent went directly to the Haitian government as budget support. Between $307 million and $604 million of that $683 million was spent through nongovernmental organizations, commonly known as "NGOs," and foreign private contractors who may have delivered some of that money to Haiti in the form of local subcontracts, or material, or not at all.[3] Large quantities were spent on short-term fixes, such as free food, and supplies whose purchase benefited suppliers and corporations in the donors' home countries, not Haiti.

"*Charity,*" Préval emphasized from the marble podium, "has never helped any country escape underdevelopment."

At the end of his speech, there was a sprinkling of polite applause.

THE DAY AFTER LA PROMESSE COLLAPSED, the foreign responders returned. The U.S. Agency for International Development mobilized firefighters from Fairfax, Virginia; the French dispatched a firefighting team from Martinique. They arrived decked in fluorescent helmets, brandishing floodlights, rescue dogs, and penetration cameras. UN soldiers set up a perimeter to keep out the school's neighbors, who had done nearly all the rescue work so far. CNN flew in a small crew to broadcast the rescues sure to follow. But by the time the firemen arrived, there were hardly any survivors left. So they used their equipment to look for the dead.

By the third morning, you hardly needed special equipment. You could smell the entombed bodies from the top of the hill.

When the sky darkened for a third night, René Préval returned. Without the throng of reporters around him, he looked smaller than usual, the Americans' floodlights reflecting off his bald head. He smiled distantly and looked at the firefighters rappelling down the school's collapsed roof, slumped over the wreckage like a folded sheet.

I greeted him.

"Evening," he nodded, and started to walk away.

"There's all this talk about the school," I pressed on. "The parents say parts of it fell before, that people who were living behind it abandoned their homes because they were afraid it would collapse." The president stopped walking and turned around. "Why can't you make a building code," I continued, "a construction code, so something like this doesn't happen again?"

"There is a code already," he answered quietly. "But they don't follow it." The president watched my eyes to see if I'd ask the obvious follow-up.

I did. "What would make them follow it?"

"What we need," he replied, "is *political stability*." He punctuated the last two words with thrusts of his index finger.

The school fell, Préval was saying, because it was not built properly. It wasn't built properly because there was no agency to compel the owner to follow a safety code. (In the end, there was not even a court system clean or competent enough to prosecute him.) There was no stable government to maintain such an institution or enforce such a code, because Haiti had spent the last century being torn apart by political factions, a bloody U.S. occupation, dictatorships, and disasters. The foreign aid that had rushed into that void had seldom concerned itself with maintaining or even encouraging a government that could manage itself.

"Alone but truly alone, to deal with new catastrophes," Préval had warned the UN six weeks before. By Haitian standards, even at around one hundred dead, this was a moderate tragedy. One big building and a small house behind it destroyed could be the toll of a standard storm. But more was bound to come. Just a few days later, in a macabre coincidence, a second, smaller school cracked on its foundation down the hill in Port-au-Prince. Mercifully, few were injured, but now students across the country began to panic. Port-au-Prince's mayor told me that 60 percent of the capital's buildings were unsafe and should be razed. If a widespread disaster hit a city like that, I thought—and the thought burned itself out.

"*Poli-ti-cal sta-bi-li-ty*," Préval repeated, punching the syllables. He smiled, content that he had made his point, and turned back toward the rubble.

"But what will you do until then?" I called out.

The president walked back toward me. Like an annoyed teacher, he raised an eyebrow, grabbed my left hand, and slapped the back of it.

CHAPTER ONE

THE END

THE PHONE WAS NEXT TO ME ON THE BED, NOT RINGING. IGNORING this was proving difficult. It was a hot, slow January afternoon, just past 4:45 P.M., in the hills above Port-au-Prince, and the newless pall that fell between Christmas and Carnival offered few distractions. AP House, my bureau and residence in Pétionville, was quiet. My lone housemate, the staff photographer, was on home leave in Spain. Evens, our main translator and driver, was finishing some phone calls in the large first-floor office space before heading down the hill to his stepfamily's place, where he'd been living since his divorce. The only other person around was Widler, a hardworking, taciturn Haitian mechanic, who was outside replacing the brake pads under my hopeless, thirteen-year-old Geo Tracker. I was upstairs in my room.

The call I was waiting for was from someone at AP telling me that I could ship out. After two and a half years of disasters and riots—of personal and political intrigue, money-pit cars, and not one utility I could count on—I was done with Haiti. My friends were great. The house was terrific: a two-story with creek-stone walls on the first floor and a big terrace, set back among hibiscuses and lime trees beside the Hotel Villa Creole. From the slum rising behind it, the sounds of children playing filled the day, and I'd fall asleep to hand-clap hallelujahs from the church at night. But AP had long talked about getting rid of the house, and my foreign friends, done with their two-year rotations, had mostly shipped off to the next crisis. AP's international editor in New York told me I could pick my next position, so long as it was Kabul, Lagos, or Baghdad. I chose Afghanistan. It sounded like a good place for a break. All that was left was for the phone to ring.

To kill time, I played online trivia against a friend in the States. I was sitting on my bed in gray boxers and a sleeveless undershirt, sweating out the last of the Tuesday heat. We started a new game: Name a human body part for every letter of the alphabet, in a minute or less.

"I didn't know jejunum was spelled like that," I typed into the chat window as time ran out. "You win."

I heard a loud rumbling outside. I looked out the window, but the yard was empty. Must be a water truck, I thought.

Then the bed started to vibrate. I heard plates rattling in the kitchen downstairs. The wooden mask from Mexico I'd always worried might fall started to sway. Medicine bottles, suntan lotion, and bug spray shimmied on the round black table I always left cluttered because I'd never counted on staying in Haiti long enough to need a dresser.

There had been a rumble on the island before, a little one, when I was the correspondent on its other side in the Dominican Republic. This couldn't be one of those. I stood up from the bed, bare feet against the wooden floor, but felt nothing. The roar outside got louder. Then the floor started to move. The vibrations got thicker. Christ, maybe it *is* one of those, I thought. What do you do in one of those? A doorway. Something about a doorway. I walked toward it but for some reason kept going into the hall. Then everything shoved.

I lowered myself, or maybe I fell. Then a shove came the other way. Then another, and another. Suddenly the house was an airplane in a storm. Everything was falling. A framed photo from Jerusalem barely missed my head and cracked on the floor. Everything was flowing now, blasts coming through the walls, waves through the floor. There was a contest between the up and down and the side to side. Who was going to shove harder, the up and down or the side to side? They were both winning. There was a mechanical roar.

I answered: "No no no no no no no no no. . . ."

The world turned gray and everything blurred, things falling long after there should have been nothing left to fall. The horizontal slats of the crank-out windows shot from their frames and burst across the floor. I watched the front wall crack in two, daylight pushing through the throbbing dust. With every heartbeat, the floor disappeared from under me and reappeared and was gone.

It was going to fall. I was going to fall.

I heard a sound like trees being mowed down in a forest. It was the house next door collapsing. Seconds to go. I thought about running through the shattered glass and tumbling down the stairs, but there was no time. When the second floor went, I could either be under it or ride down on top of it. I went with on top and braced for the pain.

I MOVED TO HAITI IN 2007 from the Dominican Republic on what was billed as a temporary transfer by AP. As the bus crossed into the desert that stretches from the Dominican southwest into Haiti, I opened an old *New Yorker*. My eyes landed on a short story by Junot Díaz, a Dominican American writer. As we neared the Haitian border, I flipped to the next. It was by Edwidge Danticat, a Haitian American. That felt like a good sign.

It was raining an hour later when the yellow coach bus pulled into Port-au-Prince. We had left the Dominican capital, with its tutti frutti–colored high-rises and oceanfront boulevard, for a city of drab, gray cinder-block shacks. In place of Burger Kings and walk-in sandwich shops I saw open-air markets with women crouching on blankets and shouting to customers, or gritting pipes in their teeth. People walked up and down hills, some carrying impossible loads on their heads or stuffing themselves into the psychedelically painted pickup truck taxis I'd learn were called *taptaps*. Blue-helmeted United Nations soldiers splashed through a puddle in their white armored personnel carrier. I took a picture.

The next morning, I walked into the kitchen of my new house to find a large Haitian man pumping water from a blue jug. He turned, looked down at me, and flashed a 100-watt grin.

Evens Sanon is what journalists call a fixer—sort of a combination tour guide, driver, translator, interview arranger, culture explainer, and bodyguard. This brave, invisible fraternity of misfits working from Fallujah to Michoacán make covering the news possible. Six foot five and three hundred pounds, with a smile that could get him out of anything, Evens was born for the role. His Kreyòl had the same New York growl as his English, each syllable ground into a smooth rumble. His clothes were loose too: Evens preferred wearing polo shirts a size bigger than his ample frame. It was a fashion tic he'd picked up as a teenager in Queens in the 1980s, where he once took two bullets in the back at a party. Evens came back to Haiti in 1993, arriving just in time for a U.S. invasion to kick out a junta that had seized power in a coup. Suddenly he was surrounded by Americans all over again. He took a job with Kellogg Brown & Root, translating Kreyòl into jarhead for the occupying Marines. When they left, he met a journalist and found his calling: driving crazy white boys into the worst places in town, at the worst possible times, and getting information. When the next coup took place, in 2004, Evens landed a full-time job with the Associated Press. Three years later, he landed me.

I depended on Evens for everything. He got the call when there was trouble or I needed advice, and seven times out of ten he had the answer. After the broken-down jalopy I inherited from AP died in a flood, he was my only reliable transportation, driving me to murder scenes in the slums of Fontamara and to meet dates at the Lebanese restaurant in Pétionville. When I finally gave up on the company shelling out for a new car, Even found the broker who sold me the 1997 Geo Tracker for $6,000 cash, plus bribe. The car wasn't worth a tenth of that—CARFAX listed it as "salvage"—but the broker wasn't gouging me by much. Unwanted things have a way of finding value in Port-au-Prince.

Evens and I spent our time together, went into the shit together, laughed together, and frustrated the hell out of one another. Our relationship reminded me of a line from a bluegrass album: There wasn't a thing he wouldn't do for me, there wasn't a thing I wouldn't do for him, and that's how we went through Haiti, doing nothing for each other. For a few weeks after I talked to the international editor in New York, I resisted telling Evens I had volunteered for Afghanistan. But he sensed the end was coming, as he always did when trouble was near. One evening we finally had a long talk in the driveway of AP House. He asked if I thought the next correspondent would keep him on staff. I assured him the new person would. We both knew I had no idea.

PINK LIGHT PUSHED THROUGH the widening crack in the wall. Nuggets of glass skittered across the galloping floor. As the house crumbled around me, I pictured myself with my back broken in the basement. When I wake up, I thought, I'd have to find a phone, I must find a—

And then it stopped. I could hear my heart whaling against the walls of my chest. Was it over? Was the floor going to hold? I was still there. *How was I still there?*

I did the only thing I could think of. I shouted for Evens. I expected no reply. There was nothing. Then, through the dust, I heard a bellow back. It got louder, approaching.

"I'm here, man. Are you OK?"

I almost laughed and cried. "I'm OK! Are you OK?!" I shouted.

"I'm OK!" he echoed. *"We've got to get out of the house."* Good idea. But the top step was littered with drywall and glass. Below that was a billowing sea of white dust. I remembered that I wasn't wearing shoes. Or pants. I couldn't see past the top step. I tried to shout but it came out as coughing. I could hardly breathe.

"Are the stairs there?" I forced out. "Can you see them?"

"I see them, they're there. Let's go."

Evens could make out only the bottom stairs. If the middle had fallen, I reasoned, it would still be a shorter fall than leaping from the second floor. I closed my eyes and entered the fog. The stairs wobbled, but held. Evens was at the bottom. I reached him, he turned, and we ran. The first floor was a ruin, rocks blasted out from the forward wall, another wall fallen on the desk where Evens had been sitting. The front door of glass and iron had fallen in like a Chinese screen. "Can't go right," Evens yelled—there were rocks jamming our usual exit to the driveway. We ran to the backyard. I'd taken this course on hundreds of jogs before: around the back wall of the house (now cracked open), under the clothesline (T-shirts scattered on the ground), toward the retaining walls on the far side of the backyard (now collapsed), to the back end of the circular driveway, where we stopped to catch our breath.

Evens pointed up to the ridge above our house, where the neighborhood of cinder-block houses had stood. In its place was a long gray cloud stretching past sight. The night before, a restless Monday, I'd stayed up to record the singing and drums from the church. Now the voices coming from that direction made another sound—a sound I knew only from Haiti. It exits the lips with a consonant tone, a childlike note on top as the voice behind it breaks into a squeak or a near cry. Then comes an element of negation, almost a "no" but unarticulated, a denial, a sound of the voice pushing back against itself. Then it explodes like a crack of thunder, spreading like oil through the air: *whoah, whoooah*. The chorus grows, pausing for breaths as each pass grows louder. I had only ever heard Haitian women make that sound and only ever standing before the worst thing in the world: the collapse of a home, the death of a child. Now it came from everywhere. It resounded from the dust cloud, along the ridge, and up from the ravine. The sound echoed across Pétionville, coming down from the hills, up from below, and from the direction of the hotel. It seemed to come from inside.

We stood and listened. Evens looked at me. "Thousands of people are dead," he said.

I had to call in the story. I didn't expect the cell phone towers to have survived, but maybe the landline at the Hotel Villa Creole, a hundred feet away, had. I ran up the driveway, which climbed a small hill and connected to the hotel. Part of its retaining wall had blasted out, and I climbed over the rocks on my hands and feet. The roof had caved in, and dust poured out of the hotel's entryway. No use looking in there. I shouted at the survivors milling, dazed, in the parking lot: "Potab genye?" "Do you have a cell phone?" "¿Tienes teléfono?" "Avez-vous un téléphone?"

A bald white man came stumbling out of the hotel, talking on a gray BlackBerry. I must have made quite a sight running up to him in boxers and a sleeveless undershirt, still clutching my gray-metal laptop. I told him I was a reporter. To my shock, he nodded, uttered something to the person on the line, and handed it to me. His pale hands quivered as they pulled away. I had never used a BlackBerry before. Where were the numbers? On the left.

Miraculously, it rang.

"AP, this is Danica," answered the line editor in the AP's Caribbean bureau, in San Juan.

"Danica, it's Jonathan."

She started to say something—after years of cutbacks and attrition we were two of just five staffers in a region that used to have dozens, so we often bantered on the phone.

"Danica," I interrupted, "I have an urgent. I don't know how long this phone is going to last. File the urgent while I'm talking to you, OK? Don't wait."

"OK," she responded, confused. "OK—go ahead."

I'd used the wrong word. AP has breaking news down to a science, and there's a formula to follow: A big story gets a one-line news alert, then a 150-word version marked "urgent," then progressively longer versions roll out. But I couldn't remember any of that. I was just staring, transfixed, at the massive crack bisecting the front of the house I had just escaped, as shouts and prayers echoed around me.

"Jonathan?" Danica asked. Her keyboard clacked in the background.

I took a hard breath. "There has been an earthquake in Port-au-Prince."

AN HOUR LATER, WE WERE IN EVENS' beat-up Nissan Pathfinder, scaling concrete and rock up the side road that led from the Villa Creole to the Pétionville grid. At the top of the hill, where the side street met the main road, a seven-story doctors' office, apartment building, and day school for children with disabilities had stood. A backhoe from the state-run construction company was pawing at the pile that remained, trying to reach those trapped inside. A man in a construction hat ran out to wave us into another lane, but there was nowhere to go. The earthquake had struck at rush hour. Cars were coming and going in every direction, including perpendicularly. People on foot carried their injured through the gaps.

Port-au-Prince was built between mountains and the sea. Pétionville is partway up one of those mountains, and just four steep roads connect it with the central capital, each dropping a thousand vertical feet over fewer than five miles: Avenue John Brown, Canapé-Vert, Route de Frères, and Route de Delmas. Even on an ordinary day at nearly 6 P.M., every road down the mountain would be an insane matrix of nongovernmental organization (NGO) staff and Haitian businessmen in big SUVs, their cooks and housekeepers in bumper-dragging sedans and taptaps, herds of goats, impromptu police checkpoints, and stalled water trucks. Now there was hell. Evens swerved left and gunned the engine over a concrete slab, but we were stopped by another wall of cars and pedestrians. Everyone, it seemed, was trying to get somewhere else.

An AP bureau chief had nicknamed Evens' previous car "the Beast," so we called this one "the Beast II." It rattled and hummed up the Port-au-Prince mountains, Evens' seat stunned into a permanent over-recline. With his size-13 Nikes on the gas pedal, it could move pretty fast, especially when there was shooting, after a couple beers, or both. We'd have serviced and gassed it if a hurricane or riot had been imminent, but there's no warning before an earthquake. The gas needle hovered just above empty. The workers at all the nearest gas stations had already shut off the flow to prevent explosions, then left. But we had to push on somehow, to get down the hill if we were going to see how the capital had fared.

The Beast II was filled with everything Evens and I had managed to grab out of the house. The backseat held our makeshift survival kit: a five-gallon jug of water, a first-aid kit, a sleeping bag, a few cans of pineapple slices, and my passport. (In the adrenaline-soaked confusion, Evens had also filled a rolling suitcase with Mardi Gras beads.) Beside Evens was an SLR camera—in a bid to make himself more indispensable to AP, he was training as a backup photographer. I now had pants with no belt, shoes with no socks, and a T-shirt from a Jesus revival that had somehow been on the clothesline. I also had two Haitian cell phones without chargers and four hours of battery life left. We couldn't find our satellite phones.

In the middle of this backseat haul was Widler, the mechanic. A bleeding gash swept across the right side of his face. When the Earth roared, my Geo Tracker had lunged off its jack toward his head. At the last second, it bounced off the wheel he had serendipitously placed next to him, but not before the undercarriage slashed his cheek. Widler's family was on the other side of Port-au-Prince, up a whole other mountain. With the cell phone networks down, he had no way of knowing what had happened to them. We promised to take him as close as possible.

The most important thing for me was to work. The Caribbean bureau put out a news alert with the information I had called in: "PORT-AU-PRINCE, Haiti (AP)—A strong earthquake has hit the impoverished country of Haiti. . . ." My job now was to stay alive and find a way to keep updating the story and send in photos. That was what we always did when there was a crisis. It was why I had been there in the first place. It was the only thing I wanted to do.

It was more complicated for Evens. Like me, he had duties to AP. Like Widler, he was a man from Port-au-Prince with family, friends, and lovers all over the city. As he punched the car into a gap and pushed his way toward the top of Canapé-Vert, it was obvious which side was winning.

Evens' son Chris was supposed to be turning one year old at the end of the coming week. Evens and the boy's mother had split up just before Chris was born, but Evens had eventually stepped in to support them. Since then he had changed, drinking less and talking about preschools instead of wild get-rich schemes. The boy was, Evens' friends would say, a *fotokopi* of his dad, pudgy and confident. Evens would bring him to AP House and make the photographers take pictures of the two together. Chris lived with Evens' ex-wife in the Pétionville neighborhood of Juvenat, reachable by a turn off Canapé-Vert.

As the cars inched forward in both directions, drivers called out to the opposing traffic for reports from down the road. "*Pa gen wout,*" the response would come: There is no road. But Evens ignored the cries. He pushed and jabbed the car forward, fighting for space on both sides of the pavement, even as others were trying to turn back. As he made the right turn off the side street toward Juvenat and downtown, a man coming the other way slammed on his horn: "Canapé-Vert is blocked!"

"I'm only going as far as Juvenat!" Evens yelled back.

"Juvenat is blocked!"

"My boy is in there."

The man nodded gravely. "*N'ap kenbe,*" he replied. We're hanging on.

The Beast II jerked forward. Then, abruptly, Evens swerved wildly to the right and rolled onto an embankment. My heart stopped. I thought the earth had erupted again, or someone was shooting. Evens leaned hard out the window and waved over a man carrying a wooden box: "COMME IL FAUT ROUGE!"

"You're buying cigarettes?" I shouted in disbelief. "Now?"

He grabbed a pack, pulled one out, and lit it. "If I don't smoke," he said through the nicotine, "I ain't getting through this shit."

About a hundred yards from the turn-off to Juvenat, it became clear we could go no farther. Every car in front of us was turning around. After half an hour of driving, we'd gone half a mile. Evens jumped out; he was going to walk the rest of the way.

I looked down the street. Some survivors were wandering aimlessly, others hurried with fixed gazes. The frightened eyes of young men met mine. "You are here, I am here, and this has happened," their gazes seemed to say. I nodded back. There was palpable shock and grief, and searching for help, but no sign of chaos. I had reported from enough disasters to know that expectations of social unrest are usually misguided. But few alive had seen anything of this scale. I wondered what might happen that night, when some of the shock wore off. People who spend enough time in Haiti know that there are sometimes "days without rules."[1] I'd witnessed my share: days when police sat resigned in their trucks as a mob smashed windows, looted stores, and set buildings on fire. I'd ridden through streets while bullets flew and kidnappers of opportunity pulled drivers from their cars. But I'd also spent enough time to know that while those days would stick in your gut like overcooked goat, they were rare, and that sometimes when you thought one inevitable, you would end up with a silly, sotted quiet. Which way would this night go? The sun had already spread into a lazy orange band behind the dust cloud covering the city. In an hour, it would be dark.

I ran some bar mitzvah Hebrew through my mind. Shouting outside the car pulled me back to the moment, and I switched to Kreyòl to talk to Widler.

"Have you ever seen anything this bad?" I asked.

He shook his head. "God will protect us," he said, blood caking on his face. "We should pray." I told him I was.

After a while, Evens came back. He told us his ex-wife Marika and Chris had been inside their small concrete house when the earthquake struck, but it stood. "Thank God," I said. He nodded and lit another cigarette.

It was time to get back to work. We needed phone and Internet. But we couldn't exactly ride around knocking on doors: There was barely half a gallon of gas left in Evens' guzzling Pathfinder. We batted around ideas: the United Nations headquarters. The presidential press office at the National Palace. Or the posh Hotel Montana, with the fastest Internet in the country.

Then we hit on it: the U.S. Embassy. The $75 million compound had been completed two years before on a low dusty plain east of the capital. Unlike nearly everything else in the country, it had reliable twenty-four-hour electricity, a steady supply of food, and running water. More important, it had satellite dishes—at least one, I was certain, would be working. By far the most imposing structure in Haiti, boasting more than twice the square footage of the National Palace itself, the embassy was built in the set-back, blast-proof style that followed the 1998 bombings of the American legations in Tanzania and Kenya. If the U.S. Embassy hadn't survived the earthquake, nothing had.

"OK," Evens said. "I'll get you to the embassy." He turned the Beast II and headed east toward the wide, steep thoroughfare of Route de Delmas.

WE WERE NEARING THE BIG BOULEVARD when I lost my bearings. I felt my throat closing, sore in the back of the mouth. The enormous dust cloud continued to hang in the air no matter where we went, and I labored to breathe. Each gasp of concrete powder put me back in the falling house. Then my mind would zoom back to the Beast II, dizzy, tired, and confused. I spat into my hand to check for blood.

"I'm starting to panic," I told Evens, tapping his leg with my fingers to make sure he was still there.

"No, you're not," he corrected calmly. "Here's what we're going to do. We're going to drink some cool water, and we're going to chill." Widler held the water jug up from the back, and Evens directed the spout toward my hands, the water splashing through my fingers and into the fabric of the seat. "Don't waste it!" I protested, but he only said, "Jonathan? We're going to drink and we gonna *chill.*" I washed the dust off my hands and drank from the next pour, as I'd seen kids in the slums do a thousand times. The water opened the back of my throat and went down cool. I drank some more and managed to breathe clean.

Evens was the man for the moment. His life was about staying two moves ahead of danger to protect the people in his charge. In protests he could always tell the difference between a warning shot ("Don't run, don't panic") and bullets fired in our direction ("Get in the car, let's go"). As the first shockwave hit, Evens had felt dizzy and noticed bits of mortar falling from the walls. Although he had never experienced a major earthquake before, something told him to get up and walk outside, seconds before the wall collapsed on his desk. When the shaking stopped, he watched Widler crawl from under the Tracker, bloodied but alive. Then he ran inside to get me.

Suddenly, Evens managed to make a local call, reaching his stepcousins, the Pierres. The Pierres had fed and housed Evens when he had returned to Haiti in the 1990s, and it was their house on the side street called Delmas 41 that he had lived since his divorce. I heard Evens' end of the conversation: "What? Where? Calm down, cherie. *Calm down, cherie.*"

I saw the look muddling his eye and knew what was coming. "Evens, we have got to get to the embassy," I tried as he hung up.

"They said family is hurt," he said. He looked over at me. "I'm sorry."

I waved away his apology. A bleeding man carried another bleeding man past the car. "Don't worry about it. All of this is work."

Twilight deepened as we made our way down Delmas. Whole office buildings had tumbled onto the road. Telephone poles leaned drunkenly, their lines splayed out like long black strands of hair. In a disaster movie, this would have been when wanton looting began, but that's not how it goes in real life. Some of the roadside walkers did have telltale bulges under their shirts—a box of cereal, a loaf of bread—essentials to get through the next days, when markets surely wouldn't be open. Were they stealing things they needed or protecting things they owned? Both would have made sense.

"Fraaaaaaaanz. Fraaaaaaaanz," a wild-haired woman wailed on the side of the road, followed by pleas I couldn't make out. I asked Evens for a translation.

"*Franz*," he said after listening to the keening. "*You were my strength. You were all I had.*"

At one point, I thought I had caught a wireless signal, but in the fleeting seconds it took Evens to skid to a stop and for me to run out of the car in search of the source, the signal flickered and disappeared. As I walked back, dejected, I looked down and saw a teenage boy motionless in the ripening dark, blood rushing out of his head into a deep brown puddle. I stepped around the body, dodging traffic and a downed power line, back into the car.

Soon it was night, though considering the capital's electricity problems, it was only slightly darker than usual. Those who had generators fired them up. As we moved down the steep boulevard, Evens had to steer around whole buildings that had tumbled into the road. Finally he made the right turn onto the winding cross-street of Delmas 41. There seemed to be no working generators here. Night deepened into Stygian black. At last, the headlights fell on a family in folding chairs. As one, the Pierres rushed to greet Evens.

An older woman in a dress spoke to him low in Kreyòl, her eyes filling with tears and her arms hung around his wide neck. Across the street was the two-story home in which the entire family had lived. It had collapsed. One stepcousin, whom Evens called Fat Boy, had escaped with a deep wound on his right leg. The stepcousin's father, sister, and two-year-old niece had not.

Evens dug in the backseat for a flashlight and took off across the street. Leaning with his whole body, he shouted their names: "Jean Pierre!" "Natasha!" "Carla Janvier!" Nothing came back. We needed more light. I realized I could illuminate the wreck with the flash of my point-and-shoot, but there was still no sign of those inside. I walked back down to the street. A bulldozer emerged from nowhere, its lights illuminating the houses one by one—this one standing, the next fallen, that one badly cracked. It didn't even pretend to stop when I tried to flag it.

Evens took the front steps back down.

"We're going to take Fat Boy to my mother's."

"We're going to what?" I asked.

"He's injured."

My gaze narrowed. It had been hours since my call to AP. Evens and I had reams of material now, descriptions that could help start rescues and convey needs. But I needed a phone to get that out. Evens' mother, who was visiting from New York, was staying in Pacot, five miles west. The U.S. Embassy was five miles to the east. It had taken us nearly three hours to go four miles so far. "Evens— what is he going to get at your mother's house that he isn't going to get here?"

"It's quick," he said.

"Goddammit, Evens!" I shouted, forgetting the people around us.

He put a hand on my shoulder and promised that after this one last stop, we would go straight to the embassy. Sheepishly, I realized that he wanted to check on his mother too.

On our return trip up Delmas 41, we passed a six-story apartment building that had collapsed. Evens stopped, a small concession to work. Inside the gate, a girl in a clean pink-collared shirt, jeans, and sandals, barely any dust on her, stood on the trunk of a crushed Honda sedan, staring into the pile. She told me, her voice soft but steady, that her whole family was inside.

"I'm sorry," I said helplessly. "Can you hear anyone in there?"

She shook her head and kept staring.

Evens and I joined some men trying to move the blocks, but without tools, it was impossible. He pointed to an unmoving foot visible in the rubble. I walked around the side, using the flash on my camera to light up the pile. I got nothing but shadow and rubble.

It was only long after that night, when I examined the images on my computer, that I saw what I had recorded. In a photo taken at 9:20 P.M., deep in the dark expanse, a hand is reaching forward. A head, covered with blood and dust, is visible just behind it. Both look frozen, as if their owner had almost made it out when the building fell on top of him and he died. The next photo, taken one minute later, tells a different story. In this one, the same head is facing the camera. Its mouth, under a black mustache, is open. It is the mouth of a man who is very much alive, but in terrible pain, and trying to say something.

At 9:21 P.M. on January 12, 2010, that man was alive.

I didn't see or hear him. I don't know what I would have done if I had. I have thought a lot about those hours after the earthquake, my responsibilities in that moment. I knew people who made different choices: A freelance photographer friend, an American named Ben Depp, had left his cameras for a pickax. That night I believed that my greatest responsibility was to report the news, so the outside world might comprehend the scale and urgency of the crisis and send help. It was a duty I thought important, maybe noble, even if fulfilling it meant my career would advance too. I thought I would be of more use that way to the people around me. In hindsight, I'm not sure. And that's the one great truth revealed in moments like that one: You always have to choose, and you will never know.

THE INTENSE LATE TWENTIETH-CENTURY MIGRATION from the country-side, which made Delmas and other once-peripheral districts into urban centers, had created a barrage of styles unified only by their stark utilitarianism: hand-poured concrete boutiques, one-story houses with iron bars for windows, and brutalist four-story office buildings towering too close to the road. Zoning wasn't a priority in those tumultuous times, much less the enforcement of build-ing codes. Architects and engineers, poor and unscrupulous, many with no training, built how and where they wanted. Haitian au-thorities called the result "anarchic construction." Many of those buildings, perched on unstable earth along a road that plunged nearly seven hundred feet in just over two of its miles, had now crumbled to their foundations.

Thousands thronged the streets and medians near downtown Port-au-Prince. Whole neighborhoods had emptied and come to-gether, singing long, low hymns. In the first twenty-four hours af-ter the quake, the U.S. Geological Survey's distant sensors would register at least fifty-four aftershocks greater than 4.0, including five greater than 5.6. Each time the soil moved, and it felt like it moved every few minutes, arms rose in prayer. "Jesus Christ is returning!" one man shouted from atop a concrete block as we reached the edge of Pacot. I was in no position to argue.

Soon, the detours caught up with us. The Beast II choked and sputtered. Widler told Evens there were fueled-up cars in his boss's garage nearby. Evens stretched the fumes until the machine wheezed to a halt, and then we rolled the car to the edge of a rubble-blocked street. While Evens and Widler went off into the darkness, I helped Fat Boy dress his bleeding leg. Then Evens and Widler came back, beat-up plastic jugs filled with siphoned gasoline and a hose in their hands. We improvised with sticks and plastic until gas flowed into the tank. It would have to be enough for now. Pushing through the thinning but still onerous traffic, we delivered Fat Boy to Evens' mother on another dark and decimated street. She hugged and kissed her son, then hugged me. When he told her he had to go, she smiled and said she understood. We drove a little farther up the mountain and dropped Widler at the end of an unpaved road. He had a long walk ahead and still no idea whether his family was alive.

I had been trying my phone every several minutes and—yes!—managed to get through to Danica again. I dictated as fast as I could. I told her about churches that looked as if they had been bombed from the sky, people praying, aftershocks that were sending us running from the car like lunatics, and the people trying to rescue one another. Before the line cut, I asked her to call my mother. She said my mother had been calling the bureau all night.

By then midnight was approaching. Seven hours after the quake, traffic had dissipated. Drivers had either abandoned their cars in the middle of the road or reached wherever they were trying to go. As Evens tried to trace the circuitous paths that crossed the city south of downtown, mounds of debris forced us to turn back and try new routes. Eventually we found ourselves in the center of the city, and the country, on the national mall of the Champ de Mars.

Across the lawn, where plazas, parks, statues, and stone monuments surround government buildings, stretched a crowd without end. People had come from every part of the city—walking, driving, carried—to the great plaza at the foot of the National Palace. The presidential mansion, with its three white, tapered domes, had been the symbol of power and sovereignty in the nation for nearly a century. Some had come in the hope that the president would emerge with advice, a prayer, or word of when organized help might arrive. Many had nowhere else to go. There were hundreds of thousands of them, perhaps half a million, but they made barely a sound. There was only the shuffle of a million feet and a silvery glow from the moon over acres of heads. Evens and I drove into the plaza. People wandered in and out of our path as if moving in a dream. I looked past them and froze.

The great white dome on the rightmost side of the National Palace appeared to be bowing forward in the moonlight. I looked away and then back again, certain the illusion would disappear. It did not. At the center, the largest of the domes, said to be modeled on the U.S. Capitol, had fallen at least a story, crushing the wide portico beneath. Nearly all the windows were blown out. It was gone.

I tried to talk, but a bark came out. There was a hollowness in my stomach. I was dizzy. This was the destruction of the White House, the collapse of Westminster. The substance and symbol of the state itself was under those fallen domes and ceilings. As flawed an institution as the Haitian presidency had been, at least at times it had been an institution, a national institution, in a country that had so few.

I plugged furiously at the send buttons on my cell phones to call back the Caribbean bureau, but there was no signal. "We have to get to a phone, Evens," I shouted. "Holy shit. We have to get to the embassy."

Evens wound around the plaza into the emptiness of La Ville, the commercial center. The only sound came from our wheels crushing rock, then the squeal of the brakes, and, occasionally, echoes of men yelling down the street. Bodies flickered into view in the shadow of small fires along what appeared to be the Grand Rue, the main commercial thoroughfare. I could only guess what streets we tried after that. Rue des Miracles. Rue Eden. Rue de L'Enterrement—Burial Street. Suddenly Evens slammed on the brakes. There was another corpse in the middle of the road. We had come within a few yards of running it over. Then the body rolled over and sat up, turning into an old drunk. The man threw his hands in the air and started hollering. Evens and I looked at each other and burst out laughing.

Eastbound on the airport road that led to the embassy, traffic reappeared. The reason was clear: The UN peacekeeping mission's military hospital was on the right and its airport base farther down on the left. UN soldiers from Jordan had created a blockade that stretched hundreds of yards, cutting the road in two. Haitians knew that, in a crisis, the Argentine-run military hospital was the island's best. People on motorcycles, in group taxis, and on foot were pushing past each other toward the hospital gate, loved ones in their arms. Trying to keep the crowd at bay, the soldiers ran at anyone who slipped through, waving assault rifles and shouting in Arabic. The Haitians shouted back in Kreyòl. Some of the families had deposited their loved ones on the ground in the hope the soldiers would take pity and bring them inside. The soldiers were frantic. As an armored personnel carrier lurched to seal a gap, Evens saw an opening and charged through it. He slowed as we neared the guns.

I summoned up the little Arabic I'd learned in hopes of getting back to the Middle East. "*Marhaba!*" I yelled. "*As salaam aleikum!*"

A Jordanian soldier spun around. "*Aleikum salaam?*"

I pointed at my chest. "*Ana sahafi.*" I am a journalist. I ventured a Palestinian word for "go" and gestured down the road to show I had no interest in going to the hospital. I had no idea how to say embassy. When in doubt, go to Spanish. "*Al-embajada . . . amrika?*"

He stared blankly. Then he turned and waved for the tank-like carrier to back up and let us through. "*Shukran!*" I yelled. Thank you. But he was turned around, waving his gun again at the people in the crowd.

Evens made one more stop after the checkpoint. On the way to the embassy, under a working light beside a standing building, a woman was selling cooked food. The portly matron, still finding plenty to laugh about on that catastrophic night, was offering rice, plantains, and fried pork that she had cooked up that morning. People with pocket change were lining up to have some. I had rice and plantains. Evens had some of everything. It was good. He paid, and we moved on.

In the weeks to come, to those overseas, the quake zone would be seen as a helpless zoo, its anguished victims awaiting salvation from elsewhere. But mere hours after the disaster, I had seen backhoes and bulldozers working, and here, as with the cigarette man in Pétionville, commerce continued to function in spots. There was no sign of violence or a "day without rules." In the midst of near-total disaster, people were trying to go on.

Soon it was on the horizon, tall as the day it had opened two years before, radiating its electric glow into the shattered night: the Embassy of the United States of America. Ahead lay a task completed, a place to lie down and, if one could dream, a shower. We'd made it. The Beast II rolled into the parking lot, and a Haitian security guard came over to wave us away. I fished out my U.S. passport and explained our situation. The guard seemed sympathetic but unsure.

At that moment, for the first time since the earthquake, my phone rang. It was Ben Fox, AP's Caribbean bureau chief, and both Danica's and my boss in San Juan, calling for an update. I told him what we'd seen, and he sent out a new alert: "PORT-AU-PRINCE, Haiti (AP)—AP journalists: Haiti capital largely destroyed in quake; casualties severe and widespread." He asked me to send photos as quickly as possible and to try to get comment from the embassy. We hoped this would not be too difficult. After all, I was the sole American correspondent of the sole American news organization in the country.

I heard someone shouting my name. I hung up with Ben and spun around to see Dominic Randazzo, a consular officer and one of my poker buddies, emerging from the security guardhouse fronting the embassy; he had seen us pull up via the closed-circuit. For a moment, the terror melted away. We hugged, laughing, and traded stories. "Do you want to talk to the spokesman?" he offered. "Perfect," I said. He went inside, reappeared, and led us into the guard shack.

We waited among the X-rays and metal detectors until Jerry Oetgen, the counselor for public affairs, arrived. A small white man with a bright white beard, he looked as tired as I felt. It was sometime after 1 A.M. Evens and I were about six miles from where we had started and had probably driven twenty-five or thirty miles in all. It had taken eight hours.

After we exchanged greetings, I asked Jerry if he knew how many Americans had been killed.

He didn't. Injured? Couldn't comment. How many were being evacuated? That he couldn't say. Did he have a statement? No, not yet. He seemed weirdly unaffected, as if I'd called to ask for the ambassador's travel schedule.

"All right, Jonathan." He started to walk back.

"Jerry?" I called out. He turned back. "I was wondering if we might be able to come into the embassy."

He looked at me.

"My house collapsed. Both of our houses, actually." I pointed to Evens.

"What are you looking for?"

"Not much, you know. Just some coms—we'd like to use the Internet. If I can get on the computer, we have some photos to send." Evens started gathering up his camera equipment. "And then, if it's possible, just a place to lie down. Some water or food."

He paused. "No."

"No to . . . which part?"

"All of it."

I took a second. "These photos. . . . They're for the Associated Press."

"We can't do that," Oetgen said in the same toneless tone. "Security protocol."

I processed this. "Phone? E-mail?"

"Sorry."

"To my mother?"

He shook his head. "Sorry."

My head hurt. Security protocol? Had he been outside? I scrambled for ideas. "What if I write out an e-mail by hand on notebook paper? Could you type that into your e-mail and send it? One to my mother. One to AP." That he agreed to. I wrote two short messages and handed them to him. I asked again if there was a place to sleep.

"Well," he said, taking a moment to assess. "You're welcome to sleep in the parking lot." Then he walked into the embassy.[2]

Eventually, Dominic returned to say we could stay in the guard shack. There were Band-Aids and antiseptic on the counter beside the X-ray machines, and I put them on the gash on my leg. A helpful passerby punched in a phone code that enabled international calls, and I called my parents. After a while I was allowed to go into the main building, where I received some rations and, after an hour of negotiations, permission to sleep inside the main building.

But not Evens. "Not a U.S. citizen," the staffer explained. So I took the rations and walked back out to the guard shack.

The big man was sprawled on the floor, his body blocking the right side of the security counter. He snored like the truck I thought I'd heard that afternoon. I put the food and water down and lay my dusty sleeping bag on the hard floor a few feet away. I looked at the granite countertops, wondering if they would withstand the shaking I knew would come again in the night. But I forced my eyes to close and concentrated on falling asleep. We would be going back into the streets at sunup, and that was coming very soon. My snoring brother would need me to be on my game. Almost as much as I needed him.

CHAPTER TWO

LOVE THEME FROM *TITANIC*

PORT-AU-PRINCE WAS NEVER AN EASY PLACE TO LIVE. SIXTY MILLION years ago, the land under it was caught in the middle when the buoyant continental crust of North America crashed into the Caribbean Plate. The two plates had been pushing against each other for ages, forcing up from the seabed an arc of islands that would one day be known as the Greater Antilles. Then came a jolt so violent that it changed the plates' direction, catching the arc in a sideswiping collision that would slowly tear each island to splinters. On the second-largest island of the Greater Antilles, these shearing forces forged the highest mountains and deepest troughs of the archipelago. On its northern half rose the Massif du Nord; in the southwest, the Massif de la Hotte and Massif de la Selle. Between these mountains, at the foot of where the Caribbean was being pushed over the volcanic terrane, was a solitary lowland depression just seven and a half miles wide. That is where Port-au-Prince would be built.

Over thousands of years, several groups of people migrated across the archipelago without leaving evidence of large settlements. That changed around fifteen hundred years ago with the arrival of the Taíno, potters and weavers who organized themselves into chiefdoms.[1] At the western edge of the lowland depression, one chiefdom built a capital called Yaguana. The Taíno's reasons for choosing that spot are lost to time; after a Genovese sea captain ran aground on the island's north coast in December 1492 and found evidence of gold on behalf of the Spanish crown, the first wave of European colonists murdered and enslaved the Taíno, working them to death with such industry that after a century their civilization was wiped out. Only their words remained: *tobacco* for a roll of leaves to be smoked and *hurricane* for the mighty windstorms that rose from the sea. The Taíno had many names for their island too, but one, best befitting the western half, where four-fifths of the splintered land jutted at least six hundred feet and rose to peaks more than eight thousand feet, was pronounced *Hay-iti,* meaning the "mountainous place." The Spanish used different names: Hispaniola, or little Spain, for the island as a whole; and Santo Domingo, after the Catholic saint, for their colony.

Other European empires attacked the island, first because of rumored gold, then for access to the rest of the Americas, and finally just because they were fighting for everything in the world. A 1697 treaty ending an unrelated war in Europe divided the island, with the Spanish retaining control of the east and France gaining dominion over the west. Mapmakers simply translated the existing colony's name into the two languages: Spanish Santo Domingo's capital was on a protected bay off the island's southeast. French Saint-Domingue was ruled from a city on the northwest coast called Cap-Français, close to where the Europeans had first arrived. No one cared as much about the plain adjacent to the former Yaguana, which took several more days to reach by ship from Europe.

That began to change in the mid-eighteenth century. Having killed the Taíno and given up on gold, the Europeans found a new source of wealth. Sugarcane and coffee grew like weeds in the island's fertile soil, and the French imported thousands of kidnapped African men, women, and children each year to cultivate the crops. The labor was deadly, but it made Saint-Domingue the French empire's greatest engine of wealth. Pirates and English privateers menaced Cap-Français, the rich colony's de facto capital, from the north; the plantation owners sought a more protected port in the south. There was a promising spot along the lowland depression a few miles east of La Yaguana, which the French pronounced Léogâne. The spot was shielded from foreign armies and hurricanes by high mountains to the north and south. Its founders laid out a rectilinear grid by the sea and established a new port, which some say they named for an early visiting ship called *Le Prince*.[2] In 1749, France's King Louis XV declared the Port-au-Prince the capital of Saint-Domingue.[3]

With mountains at its back and the sea at its throat, there was little space for the new city to grow. Still outshone by Cap-Français, Santo Domingo, and the magnificently productive countryside, Port-au-Prince remained a backwater. Then, over the course of the twentieth century, the city's population exploded. Given what happened just two years after it was founded, the city's fathers would have found this an exceedingly bad idea.

IN 1751, A SERIES OF EARTHQUAKES RATTLED HISPANIOLA. They culminated on November 21, when a massive temblor razed the brand-new city of Port-au-Prince to the ground. Everyone was stunned. In the century and a half since that Genovese captain, Christopher Columbus, had stumbled onto the island, the ground had been still. There had been no equivalent earthquake in France in memory; the massive temblor that would transform Western philosophy and science by destroying Lisbon, Portugal, on the seemingly inviolable date of All Saint's Day, 1755, was still four years away. Whatever the Taíno knew about earthquakes, they weren't around to tell. The colonists, noticing that flexible wood structures withstood the quake better than rigid masonry, briefly outlawed the latter. But the order was soon forgotten.

That bill came due again on June 3, 1770. At roughly 7:15 P.M., the earth unleashed a magnitude 7.5 earthquake, destroying prisons, hospitals, churches, government buildings, and homes. At least two hundred people died.[4] Many slaves responsible for food production escaped into the mountains, and a famine broke out in the city, killing thousands. Tainted meat bought from rival Spanish colonists sparked an anthrax outbreak that killed thousands more.[5]

The upheaval that formed the Caribbean islands had also made the lush chain one of the world's most volatile earthquake zones. But while small earthquakes erupted with regularity on other islands, such as Puerto Rico, in western Hispaniola, the ground tended to erupt massively and then go still for decades, or even centuries. After destroying the new city twice in its first twenty-one years, the fault under Port-au-Prince locked in place. But those who had learned the island's secret would not be around for long.

Over a century of rule, the French had brought nearly a million African slaves to Saint-Domingue. But their lives were short. Some 10 percent died each year, hacked, crushed, or scalded to death in the sugar-making process, sickened by horrid living conditions, or murdered.[6] Since it was cheaper for the masters to buy new people than keep alive the ones they had, two-thirds of the colony's slave population at the start of the 1790s had been born in Africa, nearly all arriving after the last great earthquake on Saint-Domingue.[7] The white masters refused to educate slaves, if they could communicate with them at all. Many of the enslaved retained their native tongues; others were developing a mixture of French and those languages into a new vernacular called Kreyòl.

In 1791, as revolution tore through metropolitan France, slaves, former slaves, and the mixed-race descendants of slaves and plantation owners rose up. Even while declaring commitment to the rights of all men, the French Republicans fought to keep their most valuable colony, the bedrock of their national wealth. The Spanish, who still controlled the eastern two-thirds of the island, invaded Saint-Domingue, as did the British. The black insurgents, many led by a former slave named Toussaint Louverture, played the invaders off each other, defeated them all, and ended racial slavery in the colony.[8] When Napoleon tried to invade to reinstate the vile institution a few years later, the people stood up to an expeditionary force of the most powerful army in Europe and, through strategy, fierce combat, and some help from yellow fever, won independence. The new nation's first leader, Jean-Jacques Dessalines, reclaimed the Taíno word for the jagged land, Haïti, and on New Year's Day 1804 declared an independent republic. Cap-Français was rechristened Cap-Haïtien, and Port-au-Prince became the national capital. What memory of earthquakes might have remained had been swallowed by decades of war.

An earthquake and tsunami would rock northern Haiti in 1842, killing thousands, but it ranked low on the agenda of a president fending off rivals and insurrections. A massive earthquake and aftershock would strike off the northern coast of the Dominican

Republic, long since the name of Haiti's Spanish-speaking neighbor on eastern Hispaniola, in 1946, but few died: It was a holiday, and most people were outdoors. Haitians didn't spend much time worrying about such things. Earthquakes were urban disasters. And, at heart, Haiti was a nation of farmers.

The new nation faced trouble from the start. The United States and Europe relied on slavery to drive their economies. A nation not only ruled by black people but forged by former slaves who had overthrown and carried out violent reprisals against their former masters was an intolerable exception. The new nation was embargoed and denied recognition, most importantly by the young United States. Cut off from an unwelcoming world, the young republic developed as a place where free people provided for themselves without having to answer to much authority.

Those first generations stayed out of the cities, building their new nation in the countryside, which they called *peyi andeyò*—the "land beyond." They raised manioc and pigs on the mountains and planted rice in the valleys. Difficult to reach and harder to govern, this forbidding land was where the nation's culture, language, and religion were forged. It would take quite a force to make people leave.

IN JULY 1915, THE UNITED STATES INVADED HAITI. The island nation was already in turmoil: Six presidents had been overthrown in four years, and a peasant militia was preparing to march on the capital and toss out another. Because the rebel leader opposed widening U.S. commercial and strategic ties, the armored cruiser USS *Washington* steamed into Cap-Haïtien on July 1, ostensibly to protect the American consulate. Weeks later, the sitting president, Vilbrun Guillaume Sam, ordered the killing of political prisoners thought loyal to the rebels. An enraged mob pursued him to the French Embassy and hacked him to death with machetes. President Woodrow Wilson ordered the *Washington* down to Port-au-Prince. By evening the Marines controlled the capital, then went to war against the rebels. Per a treaty signed by a new, U.S.-installed Haitian president a month later, the Americans took control of Haiti's finances, security, and government.[9]

The United States actually had been planning such an occupation for years. It had spent decades grabbing territory from

Hawaii and the Philippines to Panama to create markets for U.S. businesses, check the territorial ambitions of European empires, and spread American-style democracy. The construction of the Panama Canal between 1904 and 1914 led to a string of U.S. invasions across the Caribbean basin, including Honduras, Nicaragua, Mexico, and the Dominican Republic, while bolstering an occupation of eastern Cuba that had begun in 1898. Haiti was suddenly important real estate: The new U.S. naval station at Guantánamo Bay protected the west side of the Windward Passage, an essential trade route from the U.S. mainland to the canal; on the east side was the Haitian settlement of Môle Saint-Nicolas. The invasion allowed Wilson to ensure American control of the passage and of the island itself, while Germany and other rival powers were otherwise engaged in World War I.

The Haitian political turmoil that was America's avowed reason for intervening was caused in part by crippling debt. Haiti had been bankrupted through the nineteenth century by an indemnity France had forced the country to pay—reimbursement for what French planters considered their lost property of land and Haitian bodies. Haiti's leaders hoped meeting that debt would mean recognition by the world's powers, but the price was political and economic stability, as they had to take out loan after loan to pay down the imposed debt. Seven months before the assassination of President Sam and the start of the U.S. occupation, U.S. Marines had gone ashore to seize the gold in Haiti's national bank and take it to the National City Bank of New York (now Citibank), on the pretext of securing payment on those mounting debts.[10] That embarrassment had stoked the rebels' anger and destabilized Haiti's politics. Now, with the country under total U.S. economic and military control, the United States could try to shape Haiti as it saw fit.

The Americans remained in Haiti for nineteen years and five U.S. presidential administrations. They rewrote the constitution, forced chain gangs to build roads, and brutally suppressed rebellions. An estimated fifteen hundred to three thousand Haitians died in combat, many tortured in the process. "In Haiti the reality of American actions sharply contradicted the gloss of [American leaders'] liberal protestations," the historian Hans Schmidt has written. "Racist preconceptions, reinforced by the current

debasement of Haiti's political institutions, placed the Haitians far
below levels Americans considered necessary for democracy, self-
government, and constitutionalism."[11]

The occupiers weren't just wreaking wanton havoc; they were
trying to create a Haiti that they thought would be better for its
people. U.S. commanders envisioned flourishing fruit, sugar, and
coffee plantations; schools; and ascendant Haitian cultural and
professional classes, all made possible by instruction in "good governance." The catch, the historian Laurent Dubois has written, was
that "they also wanted to make sure that the Haitian government
was compatible with American economic interests and friendly to
foreign investment." Where these interests conflicted, U.S. economics always won out. For instance, the primary goal of rewriting
the constitution was to abolish a prohibition on foreign land ownership that had been a cornerstone of nationalism since independence. When parliament refused to approve it, the United States
dissolved the legislature and forced a sham national plebiscite to
ratify the change.[12]

Like any occupying force facing an insurgency, the Americans
knew it would be easier to control the country from a single locus
of power. The rebels were mostly in the north. Port-au-Prince was
to the south and had a good harbor and a compliant merchant class.
The Americans helped construct a new National Palace, its domes
and white walls inspired by the White House and U.S. Capitol. They
formed a new Haitian army that disarmed peasants and broke up
pockets of resistance. The Americans also made the capital their
economic center, using their new land ownership to enrich U.S.-
bankrolled, export-focused companies such as the Haitian American
Sugar Company (HASCO) and the Haitian Pineapple Company.

The anthropologist Michel-Rolph Trouillot has dubbed this
concentration of political, economic, and military power "the Republic of Port-au-Prince," and its legacy was still felt in the early
twenty-first century.[13] If you lived outside the capital and wanted
a passport, you had to get to Port-au-Prince. If you wanted to go
from northeastern Haiti to southeastern Haiti, the roads first took
you west to the capital.

Haitian presidents under the occupation liked the power they
drew from centralization. After the United States left in 1934,

their successors continued bolstering the capital's control over rural politics, expropriating peasant land for factories that produced commodities for the United States and stifling dissent using the army the Americans had created. But neither presidents nor the generals who enjoyed that concentration of power, nor the United States that helped create it, would be able to control the monster it was about to unleash.

HAVING SAT OUT WORLD WAR II and enjoying investment from a booming postwar U.S. leisure economy, Port-au-Prince enjoyed something of a golden age in the 1950s. The city became a Caribbean hot spot that competed for tourists with Havana and San Juan. It boasted fountained tropical plazas, gleaming Beaux-Arts buildings, and an International Casino pier where glass-bottomed boats set out for tours of a coral reef. Among the hundreds of thousands of tourists who visited in those days were my grandparents, who docked at Port-au-Prince on a Holland America cruise. The ship's guide recommended the pristine city beaches, taking in a "Voodoo rite" or an art excursion five miles out of town to Pétionville—"one of the island's most picturesque villages."[14]

Yet on the margins of the capital and in the countryside were signs of an economy on the brink. Overpopulation, deforestation, and a decline in crop prices—particularly coffee—were driving down agricultural production. Ex-farmers streamed into *bidonvilles,* urban slums that spread along the capital's shoreline. The military-run government was ultimately done in by a natural disaster: When the generals proved unable to cope with the toll of 1954's Hurricane Hazel and were accused of stealing aid meant for storm victims, antigovernment protests forced a new national election in 1957.

Many voters backed a University of Michigan–educated physician named François Duvalier. Known in rural Haiti for his service with a U.S. medical mission, his former patients called him Papa Doc. Duvalier was also an intellectual father of *noirisme,* a philosophy that argued for replacing the light-skinned power class installed by the U.S. occupation with darker-skinned Haitians.

Although he was new to politics, he showed cunning and ruthlessness in gaining the nomination of an influential populist party.

The election was bloody. The army, furious over a plan by one of Duvalier's opponents to disarm its soldiers, backed Papa Doc. The United States, wary of black nationalism but convinced that a strong hand would prevent communist infiltration, stood aside.[15] Support for the former country doctor in *peyi andeyò* proved another powerful force: At a critical juncture, northern farmers loyal to him cut off food shipments to the capital.[16] Duvalier's victory would in many ways be a triumph of peasants over the growing capital. It also ensured that that triumph would be their last.

Papa Doc spent the rest of his life consolidating absolute power through terror, bringing the smallest mountain municipality under the control of his National Palace through the appointment of loyal "section chiefs." In what he called the Duvalierist Revolution, he declared himself president for life, destroying or taking over any institution that operated outside his reach. Rivals were killed. Even the army was largely neutralized, replaced by Duvalier's secret police, the *tonton makout*.[17] Journalists were assassinated, and newspapers critical to Duvalier were shut down. A sign in Port-au-Prince spelled out in glowing neon: "I Am the Haitian Flag, One and Indivisible— Dr. F. Duvalier."[18] Even the United States cut off much of its aid. Soon the only institution left in Haiti was Papa Doc.

In 1971, facing death from heart disease, Duvalier forced parliament to lower the minimum age for the presidency so his nineteen-year-old son, Jean-Claude, could succeed him as president for life. At first "Baby Doc" seemed like a figurehead, racing cars and throwing parties while his father's cadres continued their oppression. Then the economy, bolstered by resumed U.S. aid and higher commodity prices, unexpectedly grew. Duvalier took credit for the boomlet and promised more. At the country's lone major airport—François Duvalier International, which Papa Doc had fittingly built in the center of the capital—the young dictator put up a picture of himself with the message:

> *My father made the political revolution.*
> *I will make the economic revolution.*[19]

The analogy was all his.

Baby Doc's economic plan was to enrich his coterie with state-funded projects while courting U.S. investment. Washington believed that Haiti could become a "Taiwan of the Caribbean"—a hub of cheap manufacturing close to Florida.[20] Eager to secure the good graces of the Carter and Reagan administrations and happy to bolster industry in his capital, the young Duvalier offered American companies tax exemptions, full repatriation of profits, and a 100 percent nonunion workforce.[21] "Economic processing zones" were built to house low-wage factories where cheaply made clothes and other goods would be assembled for the U.S. market. At one point, all the baseballs in the U.S. Major League were sewn in Haiti. Manufacturing grew from 17 percent of the economy and 25 percent of exports in 1970 to 25 percent of the economy and 58 percent of exports in 1985.

But the economic revolution's result was economic collapse. The lucky gains of Baby Doc's early presidency were squandered by destructive policies, including the export processing zones in Port-au-Prince. The tax breaks that made these zones possible meant that little went back into state coffers. As agriculture faded due to neglect and the focus on urban industrialization, the factories' meager wages drew thousands from the countryside. Migrants overflowed nearby slums, but few could land or hold onto the low-paying jobs. Haiti's already paltry real income fell.[22] Inflation rose. The country went from relative fiscal stability to running huge budget deficits while spending more on imports than it earned on exports. Even Baby Doc had to admit that the factory zones "remained enclaves with a weak level of integration into the economy."[23]

After three decades of poverty and terror, the people had had enough. Protests grew too big to suppress, and Duvalier's allies quietly distanced themselves. On February 7, 1986, Jean-Claude Duvalier drove his wife, three-year-old son, and one-year-old daughter to the airport in a silver BMW and boarded a U.S. Air Force cargo plane for France, leaving the army in charge.

As news of Baby Doc's flight spread, the capital exploded into a carnival of joy and revenge. People poured into the streets to dismantle symbols of the dictatorship, kill makout, and restore democracy. But the euphoria would last only as long as the fumes from Baby Doc's plane.

Haiti was arguably in the worst shape of its tormented history. The Duvaliers had stolen aid money and plundered state coffers. Baby Doc was said to have pocketed as much as $800 million in his 15 years in office.[24] As his father had reduced the country's political institutions to a single, all-controlling National Palace, Jean-Claude's factories had sucked what little economic power remained in Haiti into the capital. The Duvaliers also drove out generations of professionals, businessmen, and leaders needed to run the swelling metropolis: One in six Haitians fled the country in their three decades of rule.[25]

Port-au-Prince was becoming what geographers call a "primate city," a metropolis so big that its mere size distorts the balance of economy and power. The cycle of urban growth and national decline would now propel itself, like a zombie careening down a mountain.

WITH DUVALIER EXILED AND THE MAKOUT DISMANTLED, army officers battled for power. In 1987, an elected assembly created a new constitution that banned cults of personality, mandated decentralization, and barred Duvalierist officials from government. But army-backed thugs massacred voters in the first attempt at a presidential election, and the provisional government canceled the vote. Puppet presidencies and coups followed. Export manufacturers, showing as little tolerance for political uncertainty as they had for high wages, bolted. Rawlings moved its baseball assembly plant to Costa Rica. HASCO closed its occupation-era sugar refinery. The chaos laid bare the consequences of a centralized state with an export-focused economy and its failure to invest in education, healthcare, agriculture, and food production for the country's fast-growing population.

The United States, insisting on a semblance of democracy, pledged to withhold aid until elections were held. After yet another factional coup in 1990, the hobbled military government finally held a constitutional vote. Inhabitants of the massive urban slums came out to vote for one of their own: a short, sharp-witted former Catholic priest named Jean-Bertrand Aristide who had risked his life preaching against the Duvaliers and the army in urban bidonvilles.

Aristide promised social equity and a redistribution of land and wealth and, above all, *bo tab la,* a place for the disenfranchised at the decision-making table. The people rewarded him with an overwhelming 67 percent of the vote. Haiti's small but powerful business elite, many of whom had interests in the garment factories, saw him as a threat and backed army and Duvalier loyalists eager to again join forces and reclaim power. It took them less than a year to exile the ex-priest. Another junta seized control, murdering Aristide's supporters. Refugees escaped on rafts to Florida. The United States rounded them up into new migrant detention centers at Guantánamo Bay before sending most back home.[26]

The George H.W. Bush administration had little love for Aristide's populism and rabble-rousing speeches, which were discomfitingly leftist for Washington. At least some members of the junta had been on the Central Intelligence Agency's payroll before the coup, the *New York Times* revealed while the putschists were still in power.[27] But the White House soon became fed up with the junta and its abuses. Bush instituted a limited embargo. The next president, Bill Clinton, made the embargo hurt: He enforced trade restrictions and froze the U.S. bank accounts of businessmen who had supported the anti-Aristide coup. The move, however idealistic, had disastrous consequences: Privation spread, and most of the remaining export factories closed. Finally, in 1994, Clinton ordered a U.S. invasion to return Aristide to office. The coup leaders, outgunned and promised asylum or amnesty, backed down without a fight as U.S. Marines and soldiers again landed on Haiti.

Aristide was back, but hobbled. He eliminated another institution: the army that had overthrown him. It was replaced by an undermanned police force, bolstered by a series of UN peacekeeping missions. Still, his supporters were jubilant. Clinton went to Haiti to celebrate in person. *"Kenbe fem, pa lage,"* the American president told the Port-au-Prince crowd. It means: "Hold on tight. Don't let go."[28]

IN THE 1980S, WEALTHY WESTERN COUNTRIES, aid groups, and multilateral banks began promoting policies to spur development in impoverished nations. "Structural adjustment programs" convinced target governments to make abrupt changes—lowering of trade barriers, cutting of deficits, deregulation of private business, privatization of state functions, and emphasis on foreign investment—by promising hundreds of millions of dollars in grants and loans in return.[29] Economists called it shock therapy.

In preparation—some say in exchange—for Aristide's return, his government in exile agreed to just such a program, authored by a group that included the World Bank, the U.S. Agency for International Development (USAID), and the Organization of American States (OAS).[30] For a short time the economy rebounded. Inflation slowed, and the Haitian gourde stabilized against the dollar. But shocks would quickly undermine that progress.

One of the worst shocks ran through *peyi andeyò*. For decades, import tariffs had made international food artificially expensive, protecting Haitian farmers. Western economists hated this. They argued that big U.S. farms could produce rice more efficiently than Haitian smallholders, so Haitians should buy cheap American food while maximizing their own advantage: the willingness to work in assembly factories for pennies on the dollar. In his acquiescence to making Haiti a "Taiwan of the Caribbean," Jean-Claude Duvalier had agreed to chip away at Haiti's protective tariffs. Now Aristide bottomed them out, and the imported food came flooding in.

This was not really "free trade": U.S. rice was cheap because American farmers were supported by government subsidies averaging $1 billion a year.[31] The subsidized U.S. rice, much of it grown in Clinton's home state of Arkansas, took over the Haitian market. Unable to compete, Haitian farms shut down. Peasants cut the last of their trees to sell as cooking charcoal. Others uprooted crops whose long roots once stabilized the soil and planted quick-yielding, short-rooted beans, hastening landslides and floods. More people fled to the capital. But the foreign-owned garment factories had already closed and moved elsewhere. The Haitian factory owners had been hit disproportionately hard by the embargo because many of them personally supported the anti-Aristide coup. The cycle of dependency was fatal: Ex-farmers were now rice buyers, so the government had little choice but to keep allowing imports cheap enough for them to buy. That shut down more farms, which created more poverty, which drove more people into the city, which meant more people than ever needed to buy cheap foreign rice in order to survive.

Washington and its allies placed another condition on Aristide's 1994 return: He would have to step down as scheduled in 1995, despite having spent nearly his entire term in exile. Under the Haitian constitution, he also could not run again immediately. In the next election, Aristide backed his former prime minister, a man he told voters was his *marassa*, or "twin": René Préval, who won in a landslide. Because the two leaders were close and many Aristide loyalists remained in positions of power, the ex-president was widely seen by supporters and opponents as the power behind the palace.

The turn of the twenty-first century saw deepening poverty, Haitian infighting, and disintegrating relations with the United States. Préval was soft-spoken but deeply opinionated—and known for his fondness for rum. He dug in against an opposition parliament that refused to approve his choice of prime minister and, in 1997, dissolved it altogether. The international community cut off access to $500 million in aid it had promised in exchange for reforms. Opponents alleged fraud in a 2000 Senate election that was dominated by Aristide's Lavalas party, and the U.S. Congress refused to resume assistance until a do-over election was held. Préval refused. Haiti's opposition parties boycotted the scheduled presidential election that fall, and the OAS refused to send observers. Pre-election bombings hit Port-au-Prince. Aristide was reelected.

In his second term, the former priest watched the lingering support he'd enjoyed from the Clinton White House evaporate. Another Bush came to office, his advisors viewing Aristide as a would-be Fidel Castro inherited from the Democrats. In Haiti, the business elite and factory owners again funded a social movement against Aristide. A coup attempt failed. The United States continued withholding aid, and the faltering government shrunk further.

As poverty worsened, dissatisfaction spread. A growing number of opponents accused the president of becoming as power-mad as his predecessors, concerned more with intimidating enemies than managing national affairs. In early 2004, a small band of well-armed rebels led by former Haitian Army officers burst across the Dominican border and sped toward the capital. Aristide resigned (coerced by the Americans, he said) and found himself on yet another U.S. plane, this one bound for Africa. The United States helped form an interim government, which approved a U.S. military incursion followed by a UN peacekeeping mission to forestall conflict between the rebels and Aristide loyalists. The rebels went into hiding as the thousands of soldiers with the UN Stabilization Mission in Haiti—known by its French initials, MINUSTAH—killed, arrested, and disarmed Aristide's partisans.[32]

A new presidential election was finally held in 2006. Préval, now reportedly sober, entered the race, strongly backed by Aristide supporters who believed he would return their leader from exile. He came up just shy of the 50 percent needed to avoid a runoff, but the Aristidists rioted until foreign observers agreed to stop the election and declare Préval president. The partisans cheered and waited for the new president to bring back his twin. They would be waiting for a while.

WHEN JEAN-CLAUDE "BABY DOC" DUVALIER had been president, four in five Haitians had lived in the countryside. On the eve of Aristide's final departure, nearly half the population lived in cities. A third of Haitians still in Haiti, nearly 3 million of a population approaching 10 million, were trying to carve out space in and around Port-au-Prince. The pattern fit a global trend: In 2008, for the first time in human history, most people on earth lived in urban areas. Social scientists said this could make for a positive development because cities generate jobs and income, deliver social services efficiently, and relieve pressure on the environment.

Port-au-Prince is what happens when that all goes wrong. By the first decade of the twenty-first century, the capital was a place with little privacy or discretion. Sex, health crises, and arguments often took place in the open. Merchants jostled for space, pushing each other's market stalls into crowded streets. Travelers wore each other's sweat in the backs of taptaps. There was no protection from each other or the elements. Haiti's capital was a place so naked it had no skin. The shoreline slums grew, encroached on the National Palace, and climbed the surrounding mountains. Because there was no regulatory body to oversee construction, the masses built shacks of crumbling sand-based concrete supported by a few strands of rusted steel wherever they could find space. After a few days of heavy rain, some would slide into oblivion.

As the capital's population exploded, the state disappeared. The country's $1 billion budget in 2009 was smaller than that of Florida's Miami-Dade County, although Haiti had four times more people.[33] Haiti meanwhile owed $1.8 billion in external debt.[34] The little money that the state collected came mostly from duties on imports and exports, which businessmen had long since learned to avoid. UN soldiers were everywhere, but in their daily lives, Haitians could rely only on a tiny, underfunded national police force. Firemen showed up late to fires because their trucks didn't have gas. Doctors and nurses at the General Hospital went months without pay.

Horrendous traffic became a symbol and source of civic and national gridlock. Driving from one neighborhood to another, you might have spent hours stuck behind the swinging 50-caliber gun of a UN peacekeeper, watching a kid on a bike hitch a ride up the mountain on the bumper of a taptap or a family of four maneuvering on an overtaxed motorcycle. Since the city didn't provide decent plumbing or electricity, exhaust-belching private trucks carried every basic good you can imagine. The water trucks played a music-box version of "My Heart Will Go On"—the love theme from *Titanic*. You would hear their song, then the ground would rumble, and the walls and roof of your house would shake.

The state's functions were supplanted, but never replaced, by an ad hoc system of foreign aid groups and NGOs. Saying they had learned their lesson from Duvalier-era kleptocracy, foreign governments resisted giving money or power to national authorities and funded NGOs and private contractors instead. There were anywhere from three to nearly ten thousand such aid groups in the country—one for every thousand Haitians. Diplomats, aid workers, and adventure-seeking misfits flocked to a city where the culture was fascinating and the pay was great. Many drew hazard bonuses, tax breaks, and free rent on top of a competitive salary. Their homes were cleaned by housekeepers whose going day rate was less than half the $10 we forked over for a box of Rice Krispies at the high-end Caribbean Supermarket. It was an unpretty discrepancy, but few came to run wild or slum in luxury. Most foreigners arrived with good intentions: to help the poorest people in the hemisphere, people who could never seem to catch a break. But the aid groups' power to act without oversight or accountability was almost absolute. There was no way for Haitians to appeal an NGO decision, prosecute a bad UN soldier, or vote an unwanted USAID project out of a neighborhood. The Republic of Port-au-Prince had given way to a republic of NGOs.

HAITI IS A DIFFICULT PLACE. No one, not even the rich, is fully insulated. You knew Christmas was near in Port-au-Prince because the kidnappings started—gang members want to buy presents too. Their targets were usually Haitian, and when the families couldn't scrape together a ransom—sometimes even if they did—gangs often tortured and killed their captives. The foreigners and wealthy Haitians were more difficult but also more valuable prey. Anyone who came to Haiti intending to help "those poor people" quickly learned that this place had no fewer—though also no more—murderers and thieves than any other. The police and courts were at best unreliable. Justice was more often handled by a machete-armed mob. Poverty is no baptism.

Life was a trial by paper cuts. Even getting cash was a headache in a city with few reliable ATMs. And I was one of the lucky ones, with cash to withdraw. Living on an island that produced little meant most things were imported and expensive. A gallon of gasoline hovered near $6 in a country where most people lived on $1 a day. But though nearly every Haitian faced hardship, most people I knew were kind and profoundly courteous, if also possessed of a wicked sense of humor. I could hardly ask for directions from a stranger on the street without being roped into a conversation about what a fine morning it was, and who my family was, and then a long description of landmarks and turns that may or may not have led to where I was trying to go.

The hardships mounted, though. Days after I arrived in October 2007, a storm that would have barely slowed traffic in Miami killed a dozen people in a town north of Port-au-Prince in a flood caused by deforestation. A few weeks later, Tropical Storm Noel flooded the capital's largest slum, Cité Soleil. The following winter and spring, global food prices spiked, a devastating turn for people with no savings and little means of finding additional income.[35] By April, food protests turned into riots that toppled the prime minister, leaving the country in an all-too-familiar power vacuum. That fall, four consecutive storms ravaged the country: limping Tropical Storm Fay, the torrential Hurricane Gustav, Tropical Storm Hanna—the most brutal, with its massive, city-swallowing floods—and the Category 5 Hurricane Ike. La Promesse, the school behind my house, collapsed a few weeks later.

In 2009, nature seemed to take a break. No hurricane hit. There were street protests, and protesters were killed, but the country seemed to have settled into an uneasy lull. Bill Clinton became the UN Special Envoy for Haiti, pledging, in a slogan borrowed from his work after the 2004 Indian Ocean tsunami, to "Build Back Better" from the storms. The stakes, everyone knew, were high. President Préval, ever more resented by a people whose lives were getting harder by the day, became fixated on the memory of the school collapse in Pétionville, haranguing foreign envoys to deliver metal classroom trailers to replace all three-story concrete schools he was convinced were on the brink of collapse. Diplomats wondered openly if he'd started drinking again.

If we had only looked, we might have known. In May 2005, a 4.3-magnitude temblor had struck Port-au-Prince. The newspaper *Le Nouvelliste* spent all of fifty-seven words on the *tremblement de terre,* noting no damage and scant information from the interim government. A few days later, the U.S. Embassy sent a more detailed memo to Washington. The temblor was a reminder, the anonymous diplomat wrote, that a catastrophic disaster was possible in the capital. After two centuries of struggle, Haiti had a third of its population packed into an overcrowded city on a fault line. We lived, worked, and ate in poorly made buildings. There were no good public hospitals and few responders ready to help. There was nowhere for people to go. "The last thing Haiti needs now," the memo concluded, "is an earthquake."[36]

CHAPTER THREE

BLAN AND NÈG

FIRST LIGHT FOUND ME STIFF-BACKED ON THE LINOLEUM FLOOR OF THE U.S. Embassy guard shack. In groggy flashes it all came back: the casualties piling up at the UN checkpoint, the destruction of the National Palace, the damage to AP House, the women's cries. There were now other castaways in the room, grumbling about aftershocks and debating their chances of getting out. Most were from an American Airlines flight, the last from Port-au-Prince the previous day, which had been boarding when the quake struck.

Evens, already awake, was gathering our things. "Morning, Jon!" he half sang when he saw me stirring. He gave me an eyebrow-raised, exaggerated smile as he collected the vinyl-wrapped ration packs I'd stacked on the floor.

"Morning," I grumbled.

He slung his wide-lens camera over his shoulder and cradled a lopsided pyramid of rations. "I'm gonna put these things in the car," the big man said, narrating his movements as he often did, in an overly enthusiastic singsong he meant to sound encouraging. "And then it's time to go to work!"

My funds came to two crumpled bills totaling 100 gourdes, about $2.50, and our possessions and supplies to what was piled in the back of Evens' car. But he was right—all we could do now was work and hope that, by day's end, we'd have somewhere to sleep, something more to eat, and a way of getting out information.

AS WE DROVE WEST, BACK TOWARD THE CITY, the scenes got worse. Cracked houses gave way to fallen roofs and then city blocks obliterated in full. Mounds of concrete, rock, and twisted rebar bore no sign of the barbershops and boutiques that had stood eighteen hours before. A man wheeled a black suitcase past a school, now a two-story pile of concrete and kindling. A classroom poster of Haiti's former presidents dangled like a Christmas-tree star atop an interior wall, yet the building behind it had barely fissured. Logic had fragmented in the assault from the ground. Even the mountains beyond the city looked violent.

By radio and word of mouth, news was starting to trickle in from across town. Most of the ministries—including finance, the foreign ministry, communications, education, and the central tax office, had *effondrée*—returned to their foundations. The white-walled Palace of Justice, built in the Beaux-Arts style of the neighboring National Palace, followed its sister into oblivion, its shattered domes and roofline ornaments lying atop a mountain of gravel and sand. Both the Episcopalian and Roman Catholic cathedrals imploded. Multistory masterpieces of naïf art had been lost forever in the destruction of the Episcopal Sainte-Trinité. The spires of the Cathédrale Notre-Dame de L'Assomption, visible from almost anywhere in the city half a day before, were missing. Word came that the main building of the Hotel Montana, the luxury hotel where we'd thought about looking for Internet, had tumbled with hundreds of guests and staff inside. Untold neighborhoods simply *kraze net*—broke completely. At barely 7 A.M., the streets were full of people, but there was a strange and unkind quiet.

What had been concealed by the darkness was now impossible to ignore. Bodies were everywhere. Bodies laid in rows, bodies piled atop one another on street corners, bodies extending acrobatically out of broken walls. They were covered with whatever was at hand: bed sheets, cardboard, their own clothes. On one corner, four girls, none looking older than ten, lay in a row, their silent, restful faces turned toward the sun, as if they were enjoying its warmth. Some bodies had been torn into pieces and rested in pools of blood; others had been left whole. With the sun back up, men were rushing into the rubble with sledgehammers, trying to find survivors.

Evens slowed the car when we reached the UN hospital. The Jordanian checkpoint from the night before was gone, but the bodies of victims, now covered by white plastic sheets, were still lined along the road. Evens grabbed his camera and got out. I watched him in the side mirrors as he trod through the knee-high grass until he found the right shot. Then he pulled away the camera and did something I rarely saw a photographer do: He just stood there, looking at the body with his own eyes.

In nearly every previous calamity in Haiti, one's chances for survival came down to one's means, which were inevitably bound up with family status, nationality, and race. In a hurricane or riot, the wealthy and foreigners retreated to their concertina-topped estates. But for the millions who could afford to build homes only on a silty hillside or ravine, even a heavy rain could prove deadly.

But this time, great government ministries and posh hotels had crumbled alongside the meanest cinder-block homes. The houses and apartments of embassy workers had collapsed along with the supermarkets and gyms they had frequented. Spain's ambassador was pulled out of the rubble of his home with serious injuries. Children whose parents had scraped together tuition to put them in afternoon classes died at their desks. So had any young bureaucrat or executive in training diligent enough to be working at 4:53 P.M. on a pre-Carnival Tuesday. Hundreds of government workers died in the National Palace and the ministries, or at the Provisional Electoral Council, which had been busy planning an upcoming election. Their bosses, who slipped out early, had for the most part survived.

Whether you had been in Haiti for fifty years or an hour, whether you were in the most broken-down slum or the best hotel, survival came down to the strength and flexibility of the columns, ceilings, and walls surrounding you at the instant the fault gave way. But then, earthquakes had always been that way. The Haitian historian Georges Corvington wrote of the 1770 quake that smashed colonial Port-au-Prince, one of history's most rigidly stratified civilizations: "Blacks, soldiers, settlers rich and poor were all turned into mere people, leveled by common misfortune."[1] That colonial leveling had not lasted long; the first stirrings of revolution came a few years after. Two hundred forty years later, the leveling happened again, and again, it would not last. Barely fourteen hours after the disaster, those with means were trying to leave the country, while the vast majority of the population tried to hold on until help found them.[2] How you fared had everything to do with whether you were a *blan* or a *nèg*.

BLAN COMES FROM *BLANC,* the French for "white," but it does not refer to skin color alone. A better definition would be "foreigner." *Peyi blan* means something like "foreign country" and can describe any place outside of Haiti, including the entire world beyond it. If you come from a peyi blan—whether Canada, Japan, India, or even Cameroon—you are most likely a blan, no matter the color of your skin. The opposite of blan is *nèg,* which in turn derives from "nègre," an archaic and now generally offensive French word for "black person," but in Kreyòl it means, simply, "person." Many use it the way Americans use "guy." *Sa nèg la* means "that guy over there." But those words would seldom describe me. If I was "over there," I would be *sa blan la.* I was something different.

Lots of cultures have words for "us" and "them." In my grand-parents' creole, Yiddish, we were yid and others were goy, which was generally an insult. But blan doesn't have to be an insult—in fact, it's often used with affection. In contrast, it's a putdown for someone who considers himself *nèg* to be called *blan* by another Haitian, the ambivalent reference meant to associate the target with the wealthy Haitians whose lighter skin and features derive from European and Middle Eastern ancestries. Nearly every group of Haitian boys seems to include a coffee-skinned boy nicknamed Blan. I saw it as a double joke: mocking him once for looking like a blan and again for not being privileged like one.

Although only a few thousand foreigners live in Haiti at any time, you could argue that blan and nèg is the cardinal division of Haitian society. It is the first divide between "us" and "them," before the "us" gets subdivided again by gender, local origin, or class. Nèg and blan hang out, dance, become friends and lovers, and marry, but as a blan, you will continue an existence apart because you have things others want. Things that a nèg might ask for, either subtly, through a text message about a medical bill or a passing mention of school fees, or via a direct plea, say, for a U.S. visa—people often hoped I could procure one with a phone call. The very young, very old, and most desperate would simply blurt out on the street: "Hey, Blan. Give me one dollar."[3]

The way that many blan viewed nèg revealed something even more fundamental. Where nèg saw on the other side the possibility of a windfall, the blan saw danger, often far in excess of reality. There were kidnappings and crime, to be sure, but many organizations took measures fit for a war zone, curfews and tight restrictions on what neighborhoods staff could enter. The employees of the Irish cell phone company Digicel were given on-call drivers and bodyguards to shuttle them between their mansions and an approved list of restaurants. The NGOs, embassies, and UN pushed their employees to live in just a few neighborhoods, principally Pétionville and the former Duvalierist stronghold of Pacot. The rest of us followed. This invisible barrier was known, inside and out, as the Blan Bubble.

The irony was that blan in Haiti had for the most part come to help—any who were ostentatiously callous, profiteering, or racist were held up for derision by the rest of the crowd and usually didn't last long. A critic's argument that an aid project was paternalistic or wrongheaded didn't just irritate; it offended. "What you don't understand, Katz," a longtime aid worker once snapped after I'd written a critical article, "is that there are a lot of people out there working really hard. Really hard. And they are trying." He was right. They were trying, and they did care. They wanted life to get better for Haitians, and to make that happen, they were deploying the best lessons of years in international affairs and public health programs at some of the world's top universities.

The problem often was that these individuals were merely the vanguard of distant, massive organizations whose managers seemed less interested in nuances or painful lessons on the ground. And their—our—ability to report back those nuances was inhibited by the fact that we were viewing life through a bubble, separated by language, class, and divisions that stretched back farther than Haitian history. Even for the most enlightened soul, it was too easy to see the people passing in the window of an air-conditioned SUV as creatures on exhibit, performing feats of strength and unintended comedy. We could have fun, enjoy the beaches and mountains, and spend our weekend nights in the clubs. Then on Monday, everyone went back to work, reporting to headquarters and foreign capitals about the irredeemable other that was Haiti.

WHILE EVENS AND I WERE STILL SLEEPING in the guardhouse, a shard of moon dangling in the placid sky, a motorcycle sputtered on the waterfront road near downtown. Only a faint headlight illuminating their way through the dust, the pair aboard turned up a side road. A crowd had formed up ahead, staring into a darkness flecked with torn paper and sheet metal. "How many were inside?" the second rider asked, dismounting.

"At least ten, Mr. President," someone answered. "And many staffers as well."[4]

Préval and his wife had been next to his residence in the hills when the earthquake struck, knocking the mansion to the ground. For hours the president, in shock, met with advisors on his lawn. Then, at 2 A.M., he had jumped on a motorcycle to tour the damaged city. He saw the toppled ministries and the ruined Palace of Justice. He saw that the twelve-inch-thick plaster domes of his National Palace had plunged two stories into his office and rooms of state. The four-column portico had crumbled, its pediment ripping down the pole from which the national colors flew. Préval had seen his people, the tens of thousands who had fled their wrecked homes, staring through the palace gates and waiting for some sort of reassurance. But he had no reassurance to give them.

Things looked no better at the parliament building. The earthquake had caught the deputies and senators in an argument over electoral law. No sooner had the senators stormed out than the deputies' chamber shuddered, heaved, and staggered to one side. When the dust cleared, the Senate wasn't there anymore. An impossibly small mound of bricks and papers was in its place, the chamber's leaders buried inside.

The survivors now began gathering around Préval. They told him about the young job seekers who regularly loitered outside parliament. The parliamentarians called them *chimère*, gangsters. (The young men referred to the politicians the same way.) But when the columns snapped and the upper chamber fell, the surviving senators admitted in hushed and grateful tones, the chimère were the first on top of the pile, pulling out by the suit arm anyone they could find. They said the young men had even found and handed back wallets full of money and cell phones lost in the debris.

Soon rays of the rising sun fell over the heap. Préval's slight build seemed to sink deeper in his billowing white dress shirt and slacks. As the people of the capital slowly roused themselves to face the fullness of the destruction, their president kept watch at the parliament for four and a half hours.

The president spoke softly to those bleeding around him. He watched as the Senate president was lifted, stunned, from the rubble, and he conferred with Senator Youri Latortue, a bitter foe accused by newspapers and the U.S. Embassy of everything from "brazen" corruption to drug trafficking (which he denied).[5] It was Latortue who would confirm to me, a few hours later as we crossed paths in downtown traffic, that the president had survived. There was no other way to know: By the time the city awoke, Préval had gone back into hiding.

Although tragedy often touched him personally, Préval's default response to crises had long been to shrink from the public eye. Some of it was his strategy for political survival: Knowing that any declaration had the power to alienate or disappoint, Préval had kept his mouth closed through riots, protests, and past disasters. The president's friends joked that he was Haiti's Lao Tzu, a political Taoist who preferred inaction to action and always took the path of least resistance. In a nation whose political discourse had been defined by the high-squeal dementias of Papa Doc Duvalier and the winding electric fantasias of Father Aristide, the prototypical Préval speech was an awkward, measured silence.

But this time the silence stung. Even Préval's friends would not forgive that after the worst catastrophe in his country's history, he made no national speech at all, even if only to say, "I am alive, and we will struggle on." Only when an arriving CNN crew spotted him at the airport did he mutter a few disoriented words. "My palace—collapsed," he told correspondent Sanjay Gupta, who responded as if expressing sympathy to a child: "So you don't have a home?" Préval's dazed expression and embarrassment of speaking English in public did not succeed in making him look presidential, or even sober.

And yet, it may be that no one understood better than Préval what had just happened or what was to come. He had stood before the collapsed school in Pétionville a year and a half before and warned of anarchic construction's danger in an unstable state. Like Cassandra, he had predicted at the UN that the humanitarian effort then under way would soon dissipate and that when the next catastrophe arrived, the nation would see, "restarted, as if in a ritual, the same exercises of mobilization." He had known, he had warned, and he had been powerless to stop it.

PAST THE SHUTTERED AIRPORT, at the bottom of the Delmas side road called Delmas 33, a sister, three brothers, and their mother and father were searching for a place to camp. Tired hands held a few remaining plastic packets of water and some swaths of multicolored cloth to stitch together as a makeshift tent.

Like many in the capital, the Cherys were rural migrants. They hailed from a mountainous Haitian island off the coast of Hispaniola called Île de la Gonâve, a quiet place where farmers grew plantains, corn, and peanuts. In fact, the island was shaped like a peanut, protected not by a shell but the azure sea. The water kept out the tumult of the mainland, with its politics and coups d'état, but also much of the commerce and aid. The people's affect was thus gentler but their poverty more severe. The Cherys' parents, full of hope, had come to the capital two decades earlier, when the siblings were children, joining the crush in search of urban opportunity. The family had long since become accustomed to new types of struggle and want. The family had first settled on Delmas 33, where it crossed the airport road. But business on the street was slow, and soon the Cherys, low on cash, found themselves pushed to the outskirt slum of Croix-des-Missions.

The only daughter, Rosemide Chery, had been there alone on the afternoon of January 12, late for church as usual. Services had already started, but the twenty-six-year-old was still fixing her braids and humming a hymn. Rose hated that house. She hated the neighborhood, and the crackheads, bandits, and vagabonds who lived in it. Some ran protection rackets, forcing her and her mother to hand over what little they made selling sneakers, rugs, and secondhand apparel in a little stall near the U.S. Embassy in Tabarre. She dreamed of being able to afford to move back to Delmas 33. She thought about becoming a laboratory technician and took classes in one of the overpriced local schools until tuition money ran out. Then she thought about following her uncles and aunts into the national police force—she had the shoulders for it, and with her big clear brown eyes, she could put on a stare to boil ice—but a policeman's salary was far too low; an embarrassment, she sometimes remarked, beside the better-paid and -equipped UN police and soldiers who were the real power in her country.

So she was stuck. As long as she worked in commerce, Croix-des-Missions was all her family could afford, and as long as the Cherys lived among the bandits of Croix-des-Missions, they would never make enough to move. Only Jesus could get them out. It didn't hurt, Rose figured, that she called on Him from a church in Delmas 33.

Rose was about to leave when she felt a rumbling under her feet. She moved to find steadier ground, but the spot she was aiming for suddenly was no longer there. She fell and got up, then tumbled again. On her hands and knees, she managed to crawl into the street. People ran madly, slipping, knocking their heads against flying bricks. The world had gone white, as if the afternoon clouds had turned into bags of flour and exploded. Rosemide's heart was beating so hard she feared it would break her jaw. "Jesus!" she screamed. "Jesus is coming! Everyone accept Jesus in your hearts!" Then the ground hushed.

Rosemide's younger brother Twenty was alone at the Delmas 33 house of his girlfriend, a childhood friend named Kettelie, who was back on La Gonâve. Twenty's given name was Wismy, but he had renamed himself in the city, the crisp sound of his English nickname conjuring visions of dark green bills, though Rose sometimes said it with a smirk: Tweh-nee. Twenty, a lyricist in a rap "clique," was the sharpest dresser in the clan. Every flat-brimmed cap popped, and every cap had a shirt—aquamarine for aquamarine, black for yellow; each shirt got the right belt and the right, slightly drooping pants, and the shoes didn't play. If he didn't have the piece he needed, he'd rent it, and if he couldn't afford to rent it, he'd borrow it. And he usually got his way. Twenty had the same deep Chery eyes as Rose, brown islands in pools of white that looked through what you were saying to who you were. A thin scar ran between, from the center of his forehead to the bridge of his nose.

Minutes before the earthquake struck, Twenty was lying on Kettelie's bed, thinking about going to a party for some friends of friends in the music business, which is to say guys who liked to rap. The rap cliques could make it big, or at least a little bigger, by getting a track on a bootleg mix CD and hope to hear it played on radio or TV. The guys throwing this party had just made the biggest gig of all: visas to the United States. But Twenty decided not to go. He only had ten Haitian dollars—about U.S. $1.25—that he had earmarked to repair his pre-Carnival shirt. The light bulb came on, signaling a rare flow of electricity: a sure sign to stay. Twenty put water on the stove and started boiling eight eggs. He could eat two or three, and if anyone came over, he'd share. He lay back down and waited.

Minutes later, the pot overturned and the eggs shattered across the floor. The house splintered, and Delmas howled like a siren. Twenty jumped up and ran out to find the world boulvèse—spun upside down. He reached for his phone and thought better of it—he didn't want to know what had happened to his friends. But soon the word flooded up the street. The house where the visa party was taking place had caved in. Everyone inside was dead.

From across the city, Rosemide and Twenty set out to find family and one another. Twenty tried not to stare at the wreckage, or linger on the cries for help coming from underneath. He had to stay focused on finding his own family. The next day had nearly broken by the time Twenty and Rose found each other and the rest of their household: mother, father, and their youngest brother, Benjy. The eldest, Billy, was still missing. Tears streamed down their dust-covered faces as they fell into exhausted and thankful embraces. That night they lay down on the dirt road beside their home in Croix-des-Missions, which had ominous cracks through the walls. Through the night, their mother passed out little sacks of water from a big bag she sold at the market, then shared more with her neighbors. The family was too distraught to feel hunger.

When the sun rose, the eldest brother, Billy, appeared, and finally the Cherys' hearts could rest. They took stock. Twenty had an idea. "Forget this place," he exclaimed. The night before a friend had mentioned to him there was open land where people were setting up camp, away from the collapsed buildings and power lines, and it was right off Delmas 33, near the turn off for the airport.

Rosemide's eyes lit up. "That's right next to the church!" she thought, and uttered a little prayer. The Cherys gathered what they had and set out down the road.

THE CELL PHONE SIGNALS WERE GETTING STRONGER, and as we wound our way through the wreckage of downtown, I was able to get through to the AP Latin American headquarters in Mexico City. A reporter and photographer had been dispatched from San Juan, the chief there said, and were scheduled to cross into Haiti overland from the Dominican Republic at any moment. He asked if we could meet them at the Villa Creole—the hotel beside my cracked-up house, back up the mountain. I barely had time to agree before the call ended. My phone was prepaid. I'd run out of credit.

The road to Pétionville was thick with traffic. Every so often, the side of the mountain would shake, rocks tumbling down and screams going up. As Evens' car inched forward, we passed a small vehicle that looked like it had been going downhill when the quake struck. It had been crushed by slabs of rock. Two hands still gripped the steering wheel. I looked at the slabs hanging onto the unstable hillside and wondered who would be next.

"I can't take this," I announced, unfastening my seat belt. "I have to get out." Evens wished me a nice walk.

An old man was threading among the bodies along the road, lifting the stained cloths that hid their faces, sighing in relief when he did not recognize a face, then saying a small prayer. Finally I arrived at the source of the traffic: abandoned cars. All-white UN bulldozers were pushing them into the gully, clearing the road at the entrance to the peacekeepers' headquarters at the old Christopher Hotel. A scoop crushed the hood of a diplomat's pristine SUV, its tires popping like balloons.

Then I saw someone I knew, alive.

"Patrick!" I shouted.

Other people turned around, but he kept walking.

"PATRICK!" I shouted again, running toward him. A political advisor to both Haitians and the blan, most recently Bill Clinton's liaison office in Haiti, he was built like a point guard. He saw me, and we embraced like brothers.

"It's really good to see you," he said. He looked as if he hadn't slept in a day.

I answered in kind.

"You know, I was just with Caroline," he said, referring to a Belgian friend who worked at the UN. I was closer friends with her fiancé, a German named Jan Olaf Hausotter, who was a rising political star at the peacekeeping mission. I remembered the day he told me over a game of pool that he'd proposed to Caroline, and that she would be moving to Haiti to live with him.

I looked at Patrick with worry.

"She's fine, she's fine," he assured me, though his voice trailed off. I imagined Jan's relief.

"Where is she?" I asked.

"She's here, at the Christopher." By my blank expression, he realized I hadn't heard. "The Christopher fell," he said.

Six years after the UN took it over, the Christopher still felt like a hotel. Staffers sat for breakfast meetings beside a drained pool, peacocks wandering between the tables. When the earth shook, the five-story building toppled like a wedding cake falling off a table. Hundreds had still been at work.

"You should go to her," Patrick said. "She can use everyone's support right now."

I knew what he meant before he said it, but I didn't want it to be true. In the terror I had simply, quietly, assumed that everyone I knew was dead, until proven otherwise. But I had managed to process that as an abstraction, as something that had happened to others, something impersonal. Unreal. Patrick saw me waver, placed his hand on my shoulder, and said it.

"Jan was inside."

IN THE PARKING LOT OF THE VILLA CREOLE, survivors of the quake bled on the cobblestones and bedsheets hung over them atop rattan chairs from the lobby to block out the beating noonday sun. Those who had already gone *lot bo dlo*—"across the water," in the Haitian phrase—were placed head to toe on the road to the main avenue. I saw a young girl, her closed eyes visible through translucent fabric, the lips slightly parted as if taking a breath. I caught myself watching quietly, as if I might wake her. I had an urge to take her picture, followed by a stronger urge not to.

The owners of the Villa Creole, a family of Dutch, American, and Haitian expats, had decided to turn the parking lot into a triage center. A twenty-something doctors' assistant named Jimitre Coquillon was tending to a woman on the ground. "But I am just an assistant," he said. "There are more doctors coming. Blan doctors."

The woman cried out, writhing weakly. He stroked her arm and said softly, "Cherie. . . ." "I'm sick!" she moaned. "Her house fell on her head," Coquillon explained.

Walking among the injured, I thought about Jan. Why had I just left the Christopher? On another day, had a friend been in mortal danger, I would have exhausted myself trying to rescue him or grieved his loss. But that day I moved on. Was it the enormity of the disaster? The sheer number of friends and colleagues I feared—and soon knew—were dead? A strange ritual began in the following days. The Facebook pages of friends in Haiti from whom no word had come filled with comments from friends: "Hope you're OK. Call when you get a chance, would you? Thinking about you back home." Waiting for a response was excruciating; the comments from friends piled up with increasing anxiety—and, in some idle, glazed moments, once I found a steadier Internet connection, I would refresh their homepages every few seconds. Nothing. Nothing. Still nothing. When news of survival finally posted, fear transformed into jubilation. But sometimes there was no answer. The worried posts became more anxious, the wondering turned into praying, and the praying turned into refusals to give up hope. After bad news or enough time, condolences and remembrances appeared and, finally, silence. Yet the profile pages remained online. Bodies, at least, are buried.

AP's reinforcements still hadn't appeared, but I got word of working Internet at the Dominican Embassy, meters away. Evens told me to go on my own. I recognized the look in his eye. "Everything OK?" I asked. He nodded, distracted. I told him not to disappear. We had work to do. And everything I owned was in his car.

The Dominican soldiers inside the small compound were in a state of siege, pacing, with guns drawn. Most wore face masks, perhaps guarding against some imagined postquake epidemic or attack. Dominicans and Haitians share a long history of mistrust, some tracing to a nineteenth-century Haitian occupation of the whole island, though in recent decades brutal Dominican aggression and state-sanctioned racism were to blame. Tens of thousands of Haitians who crossed the border each year seeking work, and hundreds of thousands of Haitian descendants denied Dominican citizenship by dint of Dred Scott–like rulings by the Suprema

Corte de Justicia, were targets of discrimination there. After a Haitian was lynched by a Santo Domingo mob in 2009, protesters in Pétionville broke the embassy's windows and tore down its national seal. But no one outside the gates was likely to be thinking about that now.

Nor did the sparse, one-story building have much to offer a would-be thief, other than some card tables and an old computer. I used it to dash off an e-mail to my editor asking for a toothbrush, spending money, a working cell phone, and some socks. Then the power went out. The Dominicans were shutting off the generator every few minutes to conserve fuel.

As day turned into night, the AP staffers arrived. The photographer asked for photos to send back to the bureau. All that was with Evens, I explained, and tried in vain to reach his cell phone. Soon, editors in three countries were fuming. A world of media outlets was waiting on these images; Evens' job was to have them ready. I did my best to stall, quietly cursing the big man for taking off.

I made my way down the line of dead, back to the Villa Creole. On the back deck, the hotel workers were grilling food, and there was space to lie down. I staked out a spot on the bricks next to the pool.

Eventually, a familiar shadow appeared over me. I shouted at him. Didn't he know this could cost him his job? The big man rubbed his head. He explained he'd been digging at his stepfamily's house, looking for the three still trapped in the rubble. "We found two of them alive," he explained. "The baby, and my step-sister. I'm sorry, man. I'm sorry. It took all day to dig them out."

CHAPTER FOUR

THE CROSSROADS

AT 10:10 A.M. ON JANUARY 14—41 HOURS AFTER THE QUAKE—BARACK Obama strode into the White House diplomatic reception room. "I've directed my administration to launch a swift, coordinated, and aggressive effort to save lives and support the recovery in Haiti," he declared, his national security team assembled behind him. "Responding to a disaster of this magnitude will require every element of our national capacity—our diplomacy and development assistance; the power of our military; and, most importantly, the compassion of our country."[1] Obama laid out the priorities of the American response: ensuring the safety of U.S. citizens in Haiti; deploying search and rescue teams; and providing food, water, and medical assistance to the affected population. He announced an initial disbursement of $100 million, concluding solemnly: "To the people of Haiti, we say clearly, and with conviction, you will not be forsaken; you will not be forgotten. In this, your hour of greatest need, America stands with you."

That morning, Haiti's once vast and empty sky filled with foreign planes and helicopters, the rolling Port-au-Prince bay with gray warships. The U.S. Army 82nd Airborne dropped from helicopters onto the lawn of the shattered National Palace. The Air Force redirected an RQ-4 Global Hawk drone bound for Afghanistan to survey the Haitian capital.[2] The day before, the U.S. Air Force Special Operations Command had, in its words, taken control of Toussaint Louverture International Airport.[3] They were summoned by the three-star Lieutenant General P. K. "Ken" Keen, the No. 2 at the U.S. Southern Command, or SOUTHCOM, which oversees Latin America. In a feat of good—but could have been exceptionally bad—timing, Keen had been at the U.S. ambassador's residence in Pétionville when the earthquake struck. Over the next few hours, Keen, ex–Special Forces and a Ranger in the 1989 incursion into Panama, became the leader of Joint Task Force-Haiti, in charge of coordinating what *TIME* magazine would call America's "compassionate invasion."

Aid-workers' Land Rovers and military caravans multiplied in the dust. Scores of NGOs, configurations of Red Cross and country chapters of Oxfam and Doctors Without Borders reported to the scene. So did Islamic Relief Worldwide UK and Acupuncturists Without Borders. John Travolta packed his private Boeing 707 with food aid and Scientologists intent on "touching people through their clothes, and asking people to feel the touch."[4] Journalists rushed in, including dozens on two planes chartered by AP. Our colleagues brought an arsenal of food, supplies, communications equipment, and, kindly, deodorant and changes of clothes for Evens and me. It was like our own personal airlift.

The primary purpose of this first wave was to save lives. Mexico, Luxembourg, and Iceland were among those nations that sent search and rescue teams. Doctors and nurses flooded in to perform thousands of surgeries and amputations: A team of about 350 medics from neighboring Cuba already on loan to Haiti were quickly joined by hundreds more.[5] A field hospital set up by Israeli army medics became known as the go-to for trauma cases. The U.S. military helicoptered the injured to ships at sea for treatment while dozens of medical NGOs flocked to the wrecked campus of the General Hospital—the informal name of the Hospital of the State University of Haiti—pitching tents and generators.

The response was made possible by the allocation of $2.21 billion for emergency relief by foreign governments. About half was disbursed by the United States, with significant contributions by the European Community, Canada, and Brazil. Private donors, spurred on by images that ran on a continuous loop on cable news, gave at least $3 billion. Through handheld devices, many could seemingly touch the victims themselves—a novel experience two years after the release of the iPhone—and with the same finger send pledges via text message to organizations such as the American Red Cross. A March 2010 Fox News poll would find that more than half of U.S. registered voters donated to Haiti's relief.[6] Private U.S. donations reached $1.4 billion by year's end—about $6 per American adult. A Colorado artist named Bryce Widom, who donated $180 from sales of his paintings to the medical NGO Partners in Health, spoke for many when he said, "My heart is breaking, witnessing the devastation the people of Haiti are enduring. And I want to help."[7]

Secretary of State Hillary Rodham Clinton landed on January 16 for meetings inside the security perimeter of the Port-au-Prince airport, in which she emphasized the American provision of rescue, water, food, and medical help. The next day, UN Secretary-General Ban Ki-moon watched as bodies of the 102 staffers who had died in the collapse of its headquarters at the Hotel Christopher—the largest single loss of life in UN history—were loaded onto his plane. On January 18, Bill Clinton arrived as UN Special Envoy for Haiti, unloading pallets of bottled water with his daughter, Chelsea, and visiting patients at the General Hospital.

Yet, hard as it is to conceive, the outpouring paled next to the extent of the destruction. Injuries caused by an earthquake are both complex and horrific. Someone crushed under concrete might have several compound fractures and puncture wounds from debris. Broken skin is at risk for infection, especially in Haiti, where few have immunity to tetanus. If a limb turns gangrenous, it may have to be amputated. In the meantime, the survivor may suffer a heart attack, severe dehydration, cerebral injury, paralysis. The longer she stays pinned, struggling to breathe, the more her motionless, crushed muscles will break down, releasing potassium and a protein called myoglobin. If rescuers come and free her, the release of the weight will send those particles rushing into her bloodstream, where they can cause the kidneys to shut down.

Medical units operated at full capacity for ten days, Israel's 121 doctors and nurses treating 1,100 alone. Those who looked too gravely injured to survive had to be turned away. Many of those treated had to be discharged early. Days of arbitrary life-and-death decisions took a psychological toll. "Denying care to some patients for the benefit of others was not a course of action that came readily to physicians," the Israeli mission's leaders would later write in the *New England Journal of Medicine.*[8]

Nobody knows how many died as a result of the earthquake. The foreign powers deferred to the Haitian government, but it had no way to count. It didn't even know how many people had lived in the quake zone. The official death toll ticked upward: 10,000. 50,000. 111,481. On February 10, Préval told my colleagues and me that the figure was 170,000. His communications minister corrected him: "No, no, the official number is 210,000." Irritated, Préval snapped, "She doesn't know what she's talking about." For no apparent reason, the UN stopped matching the Haitian government's count after it passed 230,000. About a year later, a team of researchers financed by the U.S. Agency for International Development (USAID) who carried out a household survey would estimate that no more than 85,000 people could have died; a team of U.S. academics would retort that the real figure was 158,000. The Haitian government kept raising its number until it reached 316,000.[9]

The only funeral I witnessed in those weeks was for an old man who had lived in the countryside: He had died of a heart attack, far from the quake zone, and his relatives processed him to the wailing thump of a second-line jazz band.

There was no time to mourn earthquake victims, given the number of dead and the demands of tending to survivors. It was all families could do to dispose of the bodies. Some were burned to skulls and ribs, eaten by pigs, or carted in state-owned dump trucks to mass graves. Others were trucked to the General Hospital. As the tiny morgue, built to hold about thirty cadavers, overflowed, workers threw bodies into the parking lot. The pavement soon overflowed with thousands of corpses bloating in the sun, encroaching on the tents where high-strung doctors were trying to keep injured patients alive. It was impossible to keep track of the dead. After a few days of digging with sledgehammers at his stepfamily's house on Delmas 41, Evens helped wrap the crushed body of his stepfather, Jean Pierre, in a white bed sheet and followed instructions on the radio to bring cadavers to the national soccer stadium. After laying Pierre in a pile near the goalie box, he asked an official for some kind of receipt. The official just laughed.

Death became unremarkable. When the afternoon sun was strongest, we sought shelter in the closest shade, even if that meant sharing it with a corpse. Three days in came the smell—a sour, meaty thing with an oniony tinge. Sometimes it was even sweet. Many Haitians were convinced the smell was a vector of disease; it wasn't, but breathing it twenty-four hours a day didn't do much for one's mental health. Face masks became a hot commodity—construction grade if you could manage, surgical in a pinch. U.S. soldiers asked their mothers to send Vicks VapoRub, which they smeared under their noses. Those with fewer means smeared thick white mustaches of toothpaste in a line or an artful curve under the nose.

The most hardened journalists and aid workers, many straight from battlefields of Afghanistan and Democratic Republic of Congo, remarked that they'd never seen anything like it. Some broke down and left. "I'm not as tough as you guys," a colleague said tearfully as she zipped up her bag. But I didn't feel tough. I felt numb.

AS IT BECAME CLEAR THAT THE AID EFFORT could not reach everyone, shattered neighborhoods began competing to flag down aid caravans. Up went bed sheets and cardboard signs with messages in Kreyòl, Spanish, and French: "Nou bezwen ed," "SVP nous avons besoin de nourriture et de médicament," "Ayudanos aquí." Soon survivors understood that another language would be more effective: "We need help."

The signs' authors understood they could not rely on their own government. Préval had quickly retreated to a police station beside the airport, thin walls separating him from the jail on one side and the runway on the other—a troubling location in a country whose leaders often ended up in the former or took off for exile from the latter. His communications minister held press conferences under a mango tree, but the president refused to speak. The first time I saw him there, he smiled faintly and said simply, "I'm happy that you are alive. You're lucky." Then he went back inside the building.

SEARCH AND RESCUE WAS THE HIGHEST PRIORITY of the responders. Ban Ki-moon called it "the most urgent need," and Obama noted the six U.S. search teams in all his speeches. General Keen, the head of Joint Task Force-Haiti, informed SOUTHCOM the morning after the quake that "not . . . hundreds, but thousands" would need to be extracted from rubble.[10] The rescue teams' specialized technology and training exemplified the advantages the developed world offered Haiti: sensitive microphones, heat-seeking devices, rescue dogs.

News coverage centered on the rescues. Journalists traded vigils to ensure audiences would not miss a single survivor being pulled from the rubble. A successful rescue was like the earthquake in reverse: from unfathomable destruction, life. The tone of the reporting took on a religious tinge: "A New York rescue squad pulled two miracles from the rubble of Haiti," led the *New York Daily News*. As California governor Arnold Schwarzenegger, a man who knew the power of images, remarked, "Many of us were able to watch the California rescuers live on television, performing all of those miracles."[11]

The first U.S. team to reach Haiti was dispatched to UN headquarters and, after ten hours of sawing, pulled out an Estonian bodyguard with minor injuries. (Ban Ki-moon called it "a small miracle."[12]) Other teams scoured the Caribbean Supermarket, the where we had once bought our $10 boxes of cereal. An enormous effort targeted the collapsed Hotel Montana, which had some two hundred people inside—mostly foreigners—when it fell. General Keen would boast: "The Hotel Montana at one time had six teams alone because of the number of people trapped there."[13]

The places where ordinary Haitians lived and worked—schools, stores, homes, and offices, many with equally ghastly numbers inside—got far less attention. Two days after the quake, one hill over from the Montana, CNN's Ivan Watson watched a team of Haitian rescuers try to free an eleven-year-old girl named Anaika St. Louis, whose legs were pinned under concrete. They could reach her, but they didn't have equipment to dig her out. The buried child, her sunlit braids ghostly with powdered concrete, wailed as the crew debated severing her leg. But without blood for a transfusion, the amputation could kill her. Watson, his voice shaking, told the anchor in Atlanta: "On the neighboring hill, there's a hotel—a posh hotel a lot of foreigners were staying at. There—there are dozens of American, French, and Chilean rescuers there, working to rescue at least one woman named Sarah, who's trapped." Another heartrending scream from the rubble stopped him cold. Even with international attention now on her, it took the rest of the day to find a generator and power saw to pull the girl out. She died of her injuries two days later.[14]

There were many reasons for this disparity. Most foreign rescuers arrived without clear orders where to go. The Haitian government had no reporting mechanism in place for those in need, and there was no formal coordination of rescue efforts, either between international organizations or between General Keen's task force and the Haitian government. Foreign officials knew the UN headquarters, Montana, and Caribbean Supermarket. One of Keen's own men was among the hundreds of foreigners buried at the Montana. Those who ventured into wider Port-au-Prince faced language barriers and security concerns; some imposed curfews for work outside the high-end compounds, retreating based on vague reports of "civil unrest."

The coverage of those few featured rescue sites provided a much-needed uplift for viewers abroad. Their miracles were flotsam hope in a sea of sadness and desolation. The luxury hotels and high-end supermarket thus appeared on broadcasts around the world. When new rescue teams came in, they knew where to go. They had already seen the priority sites on TV.

ON THE THIRD MORNING AFTER THE EARTHQUAKE, scientists were still trying to locate the exact position of the eruption, estimated to be eight miles under a 2,600-foot mountain in the Massif de la Selle. It was hard to imagine a site more devastated than Port-au-Prince, but in fact the epicenter was about 15 miles southwest and there were suburbs and towns even closer to the capital. Under another blue, rainless sky, Evens and I, along with several AP staff, made our way to see for ourselves.

For decades, Haitian governments had sought to prioritize decentralization—moving people and services from the capital back to the countryside. The earthquake had done what politicians couldn't: As we made our way out of town, we passed a parade of families, their possessions stacked in carts and atop their heads. In all, an estimated 600,000 people fled the capital in the days after the quake. It was now critical for responders to follow them. At least in their communiqués, some foreign powers stressed that they understood this.

On the outskirts of Port-au-Prince, we came to a fenced area surrounded by some of the only grass lawn in Haiti. The quake closed gas stations and crippled the port needed to bring in more fuel. But these towering white gasoline storage tanks had been full when the quake hit. And when God closes a door, as they say, other things crack.

Men were on our truck before it stopped: "Hey, chief! I got it! Wey, boss!" They'd gotten quite a business going in the preceding days siphoning the fuel.[15] The gasoline was rosy; the black diesel syrupy and unrefined. "Get back!" one of them yelled at the man next to him and punched him in the head. He howled and cursed the other's mother. Gasoline, in short supply, sold for nearly U.S. $12 a gallon. Diesel was far more reasonable at U.S. $3. After Evens negotiated a rate of about U.S. $100 for a partial tank of diesel, two skinny men with dirt-streaked T-shirts ran over and poured it in through a makeshift plastic funnel. The dizzying smell of fuel washed over the truck.

Our destination was Carrefour, a suburb of nearly half a million that borders the capital. For centuries, competing missionaries had staked out parts of Haiti; Carrefour was strong with Seventh-day Adventists and Jehovah's Witnesses. Collapsed, though, churches all look the same. We drove up the unpaved street, where it seemed like half of what had stood were fallen. A still-hanging banner read: Happy New Year 2010.

It didn't take long for us to be directed to a high school that had fallen. Collège Catherine Flon had consisted of three two-story buildings. Half of one building remained, its nearest wall fallen clear away, leaving two stacked dioramas of scattered chairs and desks. A pair of legs in black jeans and clean blue canvas shoes stuck out from the rubble beside me.

A physics and math teacher named Leslie Lafond hunched on a chair across the street, hands shaking atop his cane. A few hundred students had attended the school. Its owner had built a foundation for a single one-story building, but as tuition money rolled in, he kept adding more levels and then threw up two more hastily built towers. It was an echo of La Promesse, the school that had imploded in Pétionville in 2008. But while fear of reprisals had made La Promesse's owner turn himself into the police—who released him when the heat died down—no one would make this building's owner even flirt with punishment. It was just one tragedy among many.

Three girls who had played hooky the day of the quake were staring at the feet of dead classmates protruding from the rubble. A young man paced helplessly; he had rushed over from his university in the Dominican Republic when he heard that his mother, a teacher at the school, was trapped. Some men were prying at concrete blocks with sticks in a futile effort to push them over.

Where were the search and rescue teams? I asked Lafond, confused.

He said a city worker had come by the night before with a generator light so the teachers could illuminate the debris. They could hear people calling from under the rubble. But without tools, there was no way to get at anyone inside. No police had come, he said. No firefighters. No UN. As little attention as parts of Port-au-Prince were receiving from the search teams, Carrefour was getting none. Five days later, a U.S. team would start making its way toward the epicenter, but by then it was far too late. "Most of my students are dead," Lafond told me, wiping away tears and sweat with the back of his hand.

Just then, a sleek U.S. Navy helicopter hummed high overhead. A group of women sitting beside us looked up and shouted, "Here! We need help here!" But the chopper turned back east toward the capital. The women laughed at the helicopter and at themselves.

YOU CAN TELL THE HOSPITALS IN HAITI by their green walls, the color of surgical scrubs and new growth. Before a cracked green building in Carrefour, a handful of Doctors Without Borders staffers in safari vests shuttled between the victims who limped in or were carried by friends. Inside there was just one operating table, where a Dutch doctor named Hans Van Dillen stood over a pregnant woman. His small team had decided to go to Carrefour on its own because it had heard that there was still no medical aid there, three days after the quake. "We were afraid things were like this," Van

Dillen told me. "They have nothing. If we bring in the materials and the people, we could have it up in a couple of hours."[16]

I asked him about the pregnant woman. He walked me out of her earshot. "If we don't treat her, she is going to die. But there's nothing we can do. We don't have an O.R." He excused himself and went outside.

"*Bonswa*," I said to the woman. I asked her name.

"Gelsaint Celine," she answered feebly. She put her last name first, as Haitians often do.

"How many children do you have?"

"Four."

I didn't ask if that included the baby inside her.

"She was nine months' pregnant," a midwife tending to Celine said in English, maybe so Celine couldn't understand. "The baby was due on the twelfth"—the day of the quake. "It broke the placenta and moved into her body. It's dead."

"But you're giving her medicine?" I asked, pointing to an IV.

The midwife shook her head. "Salt and water."

Celine's condition would have been easily treatable in an equipped hospital. She kept shifting her glance between us, looking for clues on our faces. Not feeling it was my place to say anything, I just smiled. She smiled back.

"*Mési,* Celine," I thanked her.

"Mési," she replied.

CARREFOUR MEANS "CROSSROADS." It was here that the roads to a dozen rice-planting villages met by the sea. In Haiti, a rural country where the population is spread over mountainous terrain and nearly everyone goes by foot, crossroads mean everything. If you live on a mountain, a day's walk from the nearest town, the first word of a new president, a warning of trouble, or news of your faraway cousin's new child is likely to come at the crossroads. They are natural places to gather, or build.

"In the past Carrefour was one of the nicest places," a local journalist named Michel-Ange Ferdinand told me as I squatted on a curb in the dusty center of town. "There were lots of trees and lots of little villages." He told me swank social clubs had appeared along the banks of the cool Rivière Froide, as artists and writers turned the town into a cultural capital in the mid-twentieth century. But as the population swelled and the Duvalier dictatorship shifted into kleptocratic rule, the river filled with sewage. Peasants cleared trees in the hills for charcoal, and the garden city turned into another rundown suburb of concrete stores and low-rise buildings. The natural meeting place became a red-light district where people came for whorehouses and cheap bars.

Crossroads figure in Vodou as well. When practitioners, *vodouissant,* summon the spirits, they first call the *mét kafou,* or master of the crossroads, Papa Legba. He comes all the way from Africa, the mystical Land of Guinée, ambling the undersea passages with his walking stick and keys. Papa Legba is always the first one in and the last one out. At his kafou the past meets the future, the seen the unseen. When people die, their spirits stop at the crossroads on their way back across the water to Guinée. If they haven't done right in their lives, it is there that they will find their reckoning. And when strangers come to Haiti, often they must pass through a crossroads of their own, whether they are looking for one or not.

"EXCUSE ME," A VOICE SAID outside the hospital in halting English. "Can I speak to you?" I turned to see a short young man wearing a white T-shirt and a big smile. "I am from here in Carrefour. I am living since Tuesday at the Jehovah Witness Hall. There are forty families there." He showed me a hand-scrawled list of names.

"I'm sorry," I said. "We don't have any aid. We're journalists."

"There are forty families in the Jehovah Witness Hall," he repeated, the smile stuck on his face. "We do not have blankets. There is no food, and other people are throwing the dead bodies to the door. They leave them at our door."

I had to take a call, but when I finished, the young man returned.

"Good morning," he began again. "Since Tuesday I am living in the Jehovah's Witness Hall of Carrefour. We have forty families. There is no food or medicine. There is no water."

"Brother," I pleaded. But he just kept smiling and again held up the list of names.

I took out my notebook. "OK. What's your name?" Stevenson Belgrade. Age twenty-two. Auto mechanic. House collapsed. "Since Tuesday I am living in the Jehovah's—"

"Right," I interrupted. "Like I said, I'm a journalist. I don't have aid. Just these." I opened my backpack and showed him a bundle of latex gloves. He said he could use them, so I handed him a bunch. "I'm sorry. That's all I can do. I'll put you in my article, and maybe someone else will come help." I slung my backpack over my shoulder.

The young man's smile faded, and he lowered his paper. "But where we are, they will not see us," he said.

THERE WAS SURELY LITTLE FOOD in the Jehovah's Witness Hall, but whether this was evidence of a food crisis was hard to judge. There was not much information circulating on how warehouses and supply chains had been affected by the quake: None of the responders was in touch with the Coordination Nationale de la Sécurité Alimentaire, the Haitian government agency that oversaw food security, which was scrambling to continue its work despite the destruction of its office on Route de Delmas. The Haiti office of the UN World Food Programme calculated that it had enough food stored in Port-au-Prince to provide one full meal to 300,000 people for three weeks. How much more was needed to avoid a full-blown food crisis? Nobody knew.[17]

Some responders worried about famine. But while Haiti suffers chronic malnutrition, it has never had a full-blown famine—and an urban earthquake was unlikely to cause one.[18] The one benefit of the destruction of Haiti's domestic food sector by U.S. trade policies was that there was not much of a farm sector left to disrupt. It was crucial for imported food to keep flowing into the country for the moment, which meant repairing the main port in the capital, which the quake had damaged beyond use. But the costs of that repair ultimately would get passed on to consumers through increased container fees, which would again force prices to rise. Meanwhile, even as supplying free food aid helped temporarily depress prices and fill gaps in supply, it would also deprive income to thousands of food vendors and remaining farmers, further injuring the market at the moment it needed to rebuild. A delicate balance was required.

The water situation was similarly complex. Before the earthquake, fewer than a third of Haitians drew water from public or private taps; the rest came from wells, bottled and bagged water, and cisterns filled by trucks. What was needed after the quake, as before, was a way to filter and purify the water already on hand, rather than expensive new water from abroad. Yet the aid effort offered no image more iconic than its human chains passing along boxes of bottled water, plastic shrink-wrap gleaming in the sun. The U.S. military reported distributing 2.6 million bottles of water, including at least 120,000 gallons of deluxe FIJI Water from "the remote Yaqara Valley of Viti Levu," bottled eight thousand miles away. You can still find the containers in the great plastic dams of debris in the capital, blocking canals when it rains.

Complexity was lost in a media environment that demanded attention-grabbing sound bites. "Not nearly enough food to avoid increased malnutrition in the near term" came out as "no food." "Systemically poor access to water" became "no water." The price of the hard sell was panic. Fearing that Haitians were at risk of immediate starvation, responders loaded planes with whatever they could find. Logjams ensued, especially at the country's lone major airport in Port-au-Prince. A friend who helped manage logistics for the World Food Programme would recall being overwhelmed by haphazard shipments from foreign supermarkets, mixed with unlabeled boxes of rubber gloves and Danish hand puppets, and helicopter sorties showing up with only a few pounds of food and no destination on the log. The urge to help seemed to have overpowered the desire to do so thoughtfully.

Expectations of desperation, near famine, and chaos led responders to expect riots at food and water distributions. To force food out while maintaining distance from crowds, the U.S. Navy threw boxes of bottled water and rations from hovering helicopters until other responders complained that this method was itself causing panic.[19] The U.S. military then experimented with test drops from massive U.S. Air Force C-17 Globemaster III cargo planes. Spiraling tails of food and water packets sprouting olive-green parachutes looked great on TV, but the drops solved a problem that didn't exist. Eventually, SOUTHCOM rejected the airdrops as "not . . . effective or safe."[20]

This left direct food distribution. One afternoon in late January, I watched a streetlight sway on the crowded Champ de Mars as thousands jostled in long, unruly lines for cooking oil and rice stamped with U.S. flags. Some survivors had waited for two hours in the blazing sun, but as they pushed to the front, the soldiers fired warning shots. The crowd, panicked by the soldiers, pushed the other way. One trigger-happy UN soldier kept popping up behind the riot shields to unload cans of pepper spray. Those hit would fall back, screaming and holding their eyes, and others would rush forward to take their place.

"They're just throwing food at people!" Thomas Louis, an unemployed father who had lost his home in the earthquake, exclaimed. He told me food could have been distributed more effectively through existing networks, such as churches. But there was no way to communicate this to the shooting, pepper-spraying soldiers. He began walking back to his two young boys, waiting far from the crowd. "Aren't you going to get any food?" I asked. He waved his hands as if he were clearing smoke. "Too dangerous."

It took a month for aid workers and soldiers to agree on a better system. Food would be handed out at sixteen distribution points around the capital. Coupons were distributed to women, who were considered less likely to start trouble than men.

Looking back, aid workers would say they did the best they could under the circumstances. One aid worker later told me that food distribution had improved once the panic abated.

But people weren't panicking in Haiti, I said.

"Well, people were panicking outside Haiti," she replied.

THE EXPECTATION OF VIOLENCE, coupled with the language barrier, led to some bizarre moments. Nine days after the earthquake, two paratroopers from the U.S. Army's 82nd Airborne Division were manning a checkpoint behind the ruined National Palace. Just across the street, on the plazas of the Champ de Mars, tens of thousands of survivors milled in the hot sun and washed clothes in fetid fountains, in the first stages of building what would become one of the capital's largest shantytowns.

By midmorning, about two dozen Haitian men had assembled in front of the soldiers' post. The men waved their spindly arms and shouted; the Americans—dressed in full battle rattle, a desert-colored Humvee by their side—could only eye the angry-sounding throng warily through sweat-soaked Oakleys. Upon deployment, they had been told to be on guard for a social melt-down, and no doubt they were wondering if that was what they were starting to see.

A great gray sky-chain of U.S. helicopters droned overhead, shaking the ground as hard as aftershocks as they landed. The Haitians, shouting in a mixture of Kreyòl and broken English, raised their voices louder to be heard:

"GIVE ME A JOB!"

"I SPEAK ENGLISH! I CAN DRIVE A CAR!"

"ARE YOU BRINGING MORE FOOD? MY FAMILY HASN'T GOTTEN ANY FOOD!"

"What's up?" Evens asked the men in Kreyòl.

"These blan aren't doing anything!" replied a baby-faced man in his twenties in Kreyòl. "They're just standing there!"

"They are keeping the road open for cars to reach the hospital!" an older man corrected him. "It's a valuable thing!"

A man named Thomas Edouard, who had lost his home near Route de Delmas and spent days touring damage throughout the quake zone, pointed accusingly toward the crushed National Palace. "The people who are running this country, they keep everything for themselves! They keep the people in darkness! It's an organization of corruption! There is no government!" He pressed an index finger into my chest. "I think the Americans should take over this place and put in the same degree of law they have in your country!"

A man named Patrick Mercier rushed from the back, grabbed my hand, and raised it in triumph. "Our hats off to Barack Obama because he is sending his people to take control of the country! Haiti should become part of the United States!"

Now there were deafening cheers, and arguments broke out about the degree to which Haiti should be part of the United States and who among the men deserved to go to Miami first. Applause started in the back, and the shouting crescendoed. The men gave up on me and wheeled back toward the uncomprehending paratroopers, who gripped their assault rifles more tightly and steadfastly stood their ground.

BY THE THIRD DAY AFTER THE QUAKE, the narrative in the foreign press had transformed from postdisaster desperation to burgeoning chaos. On January 15, while I was in Carrefour, a World Food Programme spokeswoman in Geneva reported that desperate Haitians had "cleaned out" stores of food and water and looted WFP warehouses. It took hours for her to walk back the story—her report was mistaken, the food in WFP's warehouses was still there—but the damage was done. Headlines rang out: "HAITI NEARS BREAKING POINT AS AID IS SNARLED, LOOTERS ROAM."[21]

Security was the overriding foreign concern of the response. Forty-two different governments deployed military assets. The United States sent more than 22,000 troops; in the waters off Port-au-Prince, nineteen American ships prowled, led by the 100,000-ton nuclear aircraft carrier USS *Carl Vinson*. The UN Security Council authorized an additional 2,000 blue helmets and 1,500 police, bringing its troop levels to nearly 13,000. NGOs and the UN warned staff in the quake zone to confine themselves to base.

Yet, for decades, researchers have told us that the link between cataclysm and social disintegration is a myth perpetuated by movies, fiction, and misguided journalism. In fact, in case after case, the opposite occurs: In the earthquake and fire of 1906, Jack London observed, "never, in all San Francisco's history, were her people so kind and courteous as on this night of terror." "We did not panic. We coped," a British psychiatrist recalled after the July 7, 2005, London subway bombings. We often assume that such humanity among the survivors, what author Rebecca Solnit has called "a paradise built in hell," is an exception after catastrophes, specific to a particular culture or place.[22] In fact, it is the rule. Just as survivors and witnesses in New York and Washington came together and helped one another in the horror of the September 11, 2001, attacks, above all else, the people of Haiti bound together to find and give solace, as communities, in the midst of the devastation.

"Another common belief is that disasters are usually accompanied by increases in antisocial activity, such as looting, price gouging, traffic violations, and violence," Erik Auf der Heide, a disaster expert at the U.S. Department of Health and Human Services,[23] has written. "Even when looting is not actually observed, that fact is often attributed to the extraordinary security measures that have been taken rather than the fact that such behavior is inherently uncommon." In fact, he continued, what we are often actually observing is people salvaging their own property.

There was definitely looting of abandoned homes and stores in the days after the quake. Whether this represented an increase in crime was harder to say. Certain crimes got a lot of notice. As in New Orleans after Hurricane Katrina, authorities and journalists were on the hunt for signs of social breakdown. When reports emerged of Haitian men and women scavenging wrecked buildings on Port-au-Prince's Grand Rue for bolts of cloth, pots—and, not incidentally, water and food—journalists flocked. Dozens of photographers were on hand on January 19, when a policeman put a bullet through the brain of a fifteen-year-old girl who was carrying paintings she had apparently stolen from a Grand Rue store. Images of her lifeless body ran in newspapers around the world. Some saw a criminal stopped in the act of a crime, others a girl who had risked everything to help her family survive, killed by authorities using excessive force.[24]

Foreigners were mostly focused on a few trouble spots. Haitian police had their own. On January 18, I was dispatched to Cité Soleil, an oceanside shantytown formerly dominated by drug trans-shipping gangs since uprooted by UN soldiers. I watched a man toting a silver revolver rob a motorcycle driver in broad daylight and make off with his sack of rice. Neighbors told us that gangsters who had escaped in a mass postquake exodus from the damaged National Penitentiary had started a nocturnal turf war, and the bodies of hacked-up foot soldiers were showing up facedown in the garbage canals. Haitian police encouraged vigilantes from loudspeakers: "If you don't kill the bandits, they will all come back."[25]

Such incidents were taken as proof by foreign authorities that a security-oriented, command-and-control response was necessary. That chaos on the Grand Rue didn't spread and that machete fights in Cité Soleil never approached generalized unrest were taken as proof that this approach had worked. Maybe that's the fallacy Auf der Heide noted. Maybe not. Although accurate statistics don't exist, some types of crime did seem prevalent in the months after the earthquake—for instance, horrific reports of sexual assault. Authorities did leave huge swaths of the city unpatrolled, and there's no way to know what might have happened had there not been tens of thousands of soldiers waiting offshore, ready to intervene.

But there was also no indication that these isolated crimes constituted a budding civil war, nor a sign that millions of ordinary Haitians were embracing postquake hardship as an opportunity to run wild and steal, embarking on the crimes they'd been waiting to commit if only an earthquake would destroy their homes. Those thinking of Haiti's history of political turmoil—the "days without rules"—conflated strategic action with postdisaster shock, akin to assuming that New Yorkers would react to a major hurricane by occupying Wall Street. In fact, while some Haitians committed crimes after the quake, far more appeared to be doing everything possible to restore a sense of security.

The day after our trip to Carrefour, I headed with another small AP team to what turned out to be the town closest to the heart of the earthquake, Léogâne. We would find its downtown, nine miles from the epicenter, eviscerated as if by a steamroller and nary an aid group or military caravan in sight. The whole area was quiet as a graveyard, with one exception: Just before town we hit a roadblock of rocks and branches piled across the cracked highway. About a dozen men brandished machetes and wooden clubs.

When we stopped the car, they greeted us with smiles. "It's good you're coming to see Léogâne," one man said. Another held a meticulously hand-painted sign: SOS: WE DON'T UNDERSTAND WHY EVERYTHING IS GOING TO PORT-AU-PRINCE BECAUSE LEOGANE WAS BROKEN TOO.

I asked what the weapons were for.

The man told me they were on guard for bands of looters they heard were running wild in the capital.

"Where did you hear that?" I inquired.

"On the news," he replied.

I ENDED EACH OF THOSE DAYS on the bricks of the Hotel Villa Creole, on a deck where most of the press corps bivouacked beside a debris-filled pool. Every time the ground shook, the pool's water level seemed to got lower, and the number of reporters around it rose.

I became convinced that the next major aftershock would send us all flying backward in a pile of cameras and half-eaten Clif Bars.

The Villa Creole was never as famous as its sisters in Port-au-Prince. It wasn't kitschy like the Caribbean-gothic Hotel Oloffson, nor posh like the Montana, nor hip like the shiny, new Karibe Hotel in Juvenat. Anderson Cooper's crew at CNN had rented out the whole Plaza hotel overlooking the Champ de Mars downtown. But the Villa Creole was perfect for the rest of us. It was mostly standing, first of all, and its core functions—an outdoor kitchen, massive diesel generators, and, most miraculously, the bar—had made it through the quake. The hotel was happy to rent its standing rooms, some with horizontal cracks in the walls, to the flood of newcomers and to serve meals culled from a pre-quake stash of coffee, chicken, salmon, and rice. For a discount, you could sleep in a flower bed or beside the pool.

In the evenings the deck filled with shouting TV crews and herds of backslapping Spanish photographers. Radio guys milled with digital recorders, looking for a place to sit. Grizzled Haitian fixers chatted about their families and houses, eyeing younger men who'd snuck in looking for jobs or an opportunity to scam exhausted reporters. Some European wire services and the *Miami Herald* had staked out a spot under a ribbon of standing roof. No one ran faster during an aftershock.

I slept, worked, ate, and pissed outside. If you're not willing to sleep under a roof, I learned, warm bricks can make a fairly soft bed. The bigger problem was the Beeping Thing. We all thought it was a smoke detector or a universal battery backup in its death throes, but it went on for a month. Beep beep beep. (Pause.) Beep beep beep. (Pause.) You could tell who was new around the pool because they'd ask what the beeping was, and then everyone who had managed to block it out would groan and go back to hearing it for hours. Beep beep beep. (Pause.)

The number of doctors and patients in the hotel's parking lot grew. Each night, as the ground shook, I woke with my head bouncing on the bricks and cries of "*Jezi sove nou!*"—Jesus save us—rising from the patients on the other side of the wall. Sometimes intruders—perhaps looking to steal food or medicine—came too close to the camp in the dark, and the Haitian security guards fired their shotguns. Sometimes the interlopers shot back. Bam pop pop. BANG. Beep beep beep. (Pause.)

Down the hill, a hundred feet away, stood what remained of my old home. A security guard in the next house over had not made it out, and the smell of his rotting body wafted in the breeze. One night about a week after the earthquake, I found myself yelling at a hotel worker to go find someone, anyone, to cart the body off. He said he didn't know whose body it was. I asked why that mattered. We both laughed.

Friends who should have been alive were dead. Ones I was convinced were dead showed up by the pool, very much alive. I developed the habit of touching people on the arm while talking to them, as if to make sure they were really there.

Evens St. Felix, a Haitian photographer who often shot for Reuters, showed up two days after the earthquake with a long face. He greeted me and grabbed me in both arms. I asked him how he was. "*Nou la,*" he replied. We are still here. It's what everyone said.

"But you?" I asked.

He looked down. His grandmother and several cousins had died, and his young daughter was gravely injured. "But the problem," he went on, "is that I lost my cameras. I can't work." He looked like he was going to cry. I understood. Losing equipment at a moment like that was a matter of life and death. Haitian journalists depend on the crisis economy; when foreign journalists come to throw around money after a coup or disaster, local shooters and drivers can pull down a years' worth of salary in a few weeks—money St. Felix would need for his daughter's care and to rebuild their lives. I told him we'd do what we could.[26]

Later that day, a reporter from Greek national television came around with a sheet of notebook paper. It was a game. Journalists were putting down a word to describe Haiti. I looked at the paper. "Diseased," someone had written. "Violent." In a big rectangle someone with little patience for spelling had scrawled: "DISQUSTING."

Nou la. I took the paper and wrote: HERE.

IN LOUISVILLE

I stepped from the minivan onto the snowmelt and looked up at the redbrick mansion. In Haiti, its thick high walls and cream plaster four-column portico would have signified someplace important, a government ministry or an ambassador's house. Someplace that would have imploded that day. But here it was just a set of professional offices, on another road in the town where I had grown up. Next door was a salon called Visible Changes.

That's a funny name, I thought. Everything looks the same as ever.

For weeks after the earthquake, I had refused to leave Haiti. I was not about to let go of the biggest story ever to cross my beat, a story that had almost killed me the moment it started. I hadn't stopped working except to address the most elemental needs—sleep, eat, shower, shit, and the occasional beer or rum—and that had kept me from unraveling. I had seen it all around me: The Spanish woman with a deep purple head bruise the width of a Coke can, begging me to tell her where the Spanish citizens were supposed to go; the young Haitian man in a Yankees cap who burst out wailing on a seaside boulevard; the older bourgeois type who spent days wandering around the hotel pool repeating the same thing to anyone who would listen: "Have you heard if the Central Bank was destroyed? If it has been destroyed, the consequences will be grave." As long as I kept working, I was solid.

A hundred feet from the house that had tried to kill me, sleeping on bricks, I was fine. I got used to waking up six times, head bouncing on the bricks as a roar ran through the ground and the jigsaw hotel. I learned to ignore the screaming and running of new arrivals un-accustomed to the aftershocks, the shouts from the trauma patients on bed sheets in the parking lot, and the demonic resilience of the beeping alarm. I just kept going, taking my assignments, going out to the provinces or another fallen capital district, interviewing anyone I could in the incongruous sunshine, churning the atmospherics into news stories on AP's satellite connection when the evening shadows fell. As long as I didn't stop, I didn't have to think about what was actually going on.

After a few days, senior reporters started pressing me to take a break. One in particular, a longtime veteran of Caribbean coups and African wars, began to talk in velvet tones about posttraumatic stress disorder, the hell she'd seen it wreak on lives and families and careers. I thanked her and assured her I was fine, but she put a finger in my face and said, "Don't fuck around." One day, a week after the quake, she simply ordered me to take the day off. But what was a "day off" in the disaster zone? The morning began with a 5.9 aftershock that sent reporters screaming naked from their hotel rooms. But that, I was used to. It was the doing nothing I couldn't stand. All that mental adaptation was being wasted with me sitting by the pool, adrenaline tapering off, nothing to do but stare at the top of my cracked house and listen to inanities and complaints while waiting for the world to end again.

OK, she said. Then you need to go home. This is my home, I protested. No, she said: Home.

I held out another week. But soon even I could see it. At night I no longer slept, and during the day I was never really awake. I became increasingly agnostic on the question of whether I was still alive, looking for tangible signs to prove I had not simply died in some accident in the house and been hallucinating everything since—the groaning of the earth, the faces of the dead, Anderson Cooper. "I'm leaving Wednesday," I told my colleague one afternoon. She smiled.

There were still no commercial flights from Haiti, so Evens took me and a suitcase of drywall-dusted possessions to the Dominican border. I hopped a taxi and negotiated the mile-long traffic jams of NGO cars and an Italian military convoy for the four-hour ride to Santo Domingo, where I caught the first of three connecting flights.

My parents were waiting for me just past security, smiling but misty-eyed, arms open. I told them my goals for the week were simple: sleep, eat, sleep, rest, relax, and resupply. Sleep came first, in my old bed under middle-school posters of Alfred E. Neuman and B. B. King. The relaxing was done at an upright piano in the living room, where I'd bang out blues riffs until I got hungry. Resupplying would come at the end, when my folks took me across the river to the Bass Pro Shop in Clarksville, Indiana—a 280,000-square-foot marvel replete with a faux cave, an aquarium, and three (three!) NASCAR simulators. The *families milling in camouflage and safety orange were surrounded by a fantasyland of postdisaster swag: portable water purifiers, puncture-proof insoles, and an entire department of neoprene waders ideal for urban floods.*

But there was a fourth task, more pressing to my editors and parents. It was why I had come to the redbrick monstrosity. The sign was behind a precision-painted door, down the steps into a beige-carpeted basement: "Therapist."

Journalism has come a long way since the days when dealing with psychological fallout meant having a drink and getting back to work. New research into the long-term effects of workplace stress, greater social acceptance of analysis, and a lot of advocacy have led to a new treatment plan: seeing a therapist and getting back to work. PTSD has even gained a sort of army/navy store cachet among some war- and disaster-zone correspondents, a stamp of unimpeachable authenticity: Not only have you gone—no, done—somewhere dangerous, but you did it so thoroughly that it got to you. This is weird to me. It's like wanting pneumonia.

The first thing I did after walking in was scrutinize the ceiling. It looked sturdy. Then I scanned the walls for cracks. A few small chips in the paint, nothing structural. Around the corner was a waiting area, inhabited by a lone white teenage girl. She looked as if she'd been crying. I sank into one of the upholstered chairs. On the end table beside me, a special earthquake edition of TIME showed a woman in a bright red shirt walking with a bundle on her head, through smoke and debris somewhere around what looked like the Grand Rue. I knew the spot. I knew the guy who took the picture. Even the woman look familiar. It was the tearstained teenager in the seat across from me I felt alien next to.

A door opened, and a voice with the honeysuckle twang of my eighth-grade science teacher called out my name. I walked into a little office, egg-yellow light refracting from the snow through the blinds in the windows. The therapist, a woman with short hair the color of corn silk, sat in a rolling chair. I sat on the couch.

"So I understand you've been in Haiti," she said.

I nodded.

"And you were in the earthquake?"

I nodded again. She nodded back compassionately. "You're an aid worker?"

"I'm a journalist."

"And I understand you'll be in town for a week?" I said yes. "And after this week?"

"Haiti."

Her eyes flashed a subtle concern, but she went on without comment. She started explaining her method, and that she worked with a lot of soldiers from nearby Fort Campbell and Fort Knox, just back from Iraq and Afghanistan. She'd seen good progress with them, even though some of her colleagues said that techniques for dealing with PTSD were a waste of time. She laughed and waved her hands. "I know what it sounds like," she said, assuming I was one of the naysayers. "But it's not some kind of voodoo! It really works!" She laughed. I let it slide.

She asked me to tell her what happened in the earthquake.

As I took her through what was already becoming a well-worn tale, I started to wonder: Was I even affected at all? I wasn't talking to myself or having fits about the earthquake. The opposite, actually. I was increasingly fond of spitting rages about dumb annoyances, like the time the Haitian guys helping me recover things from the destroyed office grabbed broken electronics instead of books. Yet I had not so much as shed a tear for the dead, not even the dozens I had known. When two good friends died in early 2008, in a car crash in the Dominican Republic, I'd been a mess. Even the collapse of Collège La Promesse in Pétionville two years earlier made me sadder than the earthquake. I guess that catastrophe was easier to understand and, in understanding, mourn. On my week of Louisville R&R, I would sit at the piano for hours, pounding the keys and belting: "The water is wide/I can't cross over . . ."—pushing images of the devastation to the front of my mind as hard as I could—"and neither have/I wings to fly . . ."—in hope of feeling something. But I didn't.

Over the following years, I would learn more about what was happening to me. The standard reference manual of the American Psychiatric Association says that for trauma to be categorized as a disorder, there must be symptoms of avoidance (e.g., of thoughts or places), numbing (emotional), hyperarousal (trouble sleeping, overvigilance), or intrusive recollection (thinking or dreaming about the trauma when you don't want to)—and for those to become PTSD, they have to persist at least one month (and for chronic PTSD, as with me, three).[1] The symptoms can leave you almost totally functional or thinking you're *functional when you really aren't at all. But I didn't know any of this then. It wouldn't be until the weeks after my brief visit home, when the dreams really began, and I was grinding my teeth so hard I would wake up with pain in my jaw, and biting my tongue so thoroughly that it was leaving divots that got irritated when I ate, and the long jags of asphyxia anxiety that echoed the terror of not being able to breathe in the minutes the earthquake, that a professional could even officially diagnose me with some issues. At three weeks out, I was just in shock.*

As my story moved past the quake into the day after, I relaxed a little. I tried to make myself open to be helped. I watched the therapist's kind face for signs of trouble. Was I numb or avoiding? Hypervigilant or panicky? I didn't feel like it. I felt like I was there, present, in a carpeted basement under a couple of thousand square feet of brick, gabled roof, and moldings held up by God knows what, feeling it in my spine every time the foundation settled or heavy traffic rumbled by, but relaxed, re-laxed, simply telling the tale, informing her calmly of the fundamental reality of the earth, that the very things that keep us alive also conspire to kill us. That the unwritten agreement between the earth and us is unwritten for a reason, because the earth never agreed to anything. This didn't feel like avoidance. It was the closest thing I had to the truth, a truth I couldn't share with most people and certainly not the readers I was writing for, because it sounded cynical and absurd. But my memo-ries weren't intrusive. I wanted them. In fact, I didn't want anything but them.

I finished the story, and for a few seconds she leaned forward in her chair without speaking. "That's . . . horrible," she finally said.

Oh no, I thought. Not you. "Yes," I replied.

She paused again. "That must have been awful."

"It was awful."

She said nothing. The rose fell off her cheeks. Now I just felt ashamed. "It's OK," I offered. "Not everyone died. I thought I was dead. But I wasn't."

She nodded.

"It'll be OK."

"OK." She looked away.

I didn't think my story was so hard to take. I still don't. I thought most people in Haiti had a story more interesting than mine. My friend who pulled her crushed leg out from the doorjamb of her collapsed kitchen and found her way to safety by the light of an iPod. That could set a therapist on edge. The couple that rappelled four stories down a loosened pipe. That was something. In Haiti, we could sit around and talk about it, or sit around and not talk about it, without feeling strange or ashamed. I didn't blame the therapist for struggling with my story. I had a lot more practice with it than she did. But at that moment, all I wanted to do was go back to somewhere people understood.

She collected her thoughts and started paging slowly through her appointment book. "So you can come in again on Wednesday?"

I had no plans. Sure, I said.

"Then—I would say probably we should meet a third time on Friday." I agreed again.

But in my mind I was already past that to Sunday. I was out the door, beyond the parking lot, on a long silver jet.

CHAPTER FIVE

SPOILED CORN

FOR THE TWO MONTHS AFTER THE EARTHQUAKE, THE CHERYS SLEPT ON hard dirt beside a church where Maïs Gâté, the airport road, crossed Delmas 33. The adult siblings—Billy, Rosemide, Twenty, and Benjy—crammed with their parents under a roof of rags in what Rose called a carnival of colors. The flimsy top was held up by sticks planted in dirt laced with pebbles and broken glass. When it rained, the Cherys got shivering wet. When it was hot, they baked and the rags frayed. But at least they felt safe: They knew most of the other families sleeping beside them in the lot from the old neighborhood.

The Cherys' apartment remained upright, if cracked. Like most people who had experienced the power of the traitorous ground, they preferred to sleep outdoors, especially with aftershocks still rattling nerves. But they had paid the full year's rent in advance, and even if they were able to find a lightweight tin shack somewhere, it would cost more—money they didn't have. The family thought about joining the hundreds of thousands of people who had left the capital for older homes in the countryside, but the Cherys' lives were now here. Twenty had his rap group, Rose her on-again/off-again boyfriend, David Désir, and Billy his girlfriend, Darlene. They just needed a way to make life in the quake zone work.

A week after the earthquake, Rose and her mother, Marie-Ange, had found the courage to check on their market stall in Tabarre. It took all their nerve to dart under the market's looming concrete overhang, but they froze when they hit the dusty shade.

Merchandise was scattered everywhere. Rose raced through the narrow rows of merchants' tables only to find the big market basket they had abandoned in disarray.

"*Vòlè*," Marie-Ange seethed. Thieves.

"They didn't take everything. Just the most important things"—the best housewares, sneakers, sheets, and rugs—Rose would later recall. On the way, she and her mother had watched soldiers and police rumble past, but they were in a hurry to get somewhere else. The prospect of looting at the more visible and prosperous establishments on the Grand Rue brought out the security presence in full force. Impoverished thieves raiding the baskets of impoverished merchants seemed to inspire less urgency.

The Cherys had no insurance for their merchandise, and they could hardly take out a loan: Even before the quake, banks had demanded 100 percent collateral for an interest rate of 20.5 percent; now even street-corner sharks were low on cash. Meanwhile, the importers who used to bring in the plastic-wrapped bundles of secondhand goods that small merchants like the Cherys would buy and resell were now more interested in securing aid contracts. Rose could only put her arms around her mother. "Once it's gone, it's gone," she would later recall, philosophically. "There's nothing you can do about it."

The days after the earthquake had been a battle against death; the weeks after, a struggle to find a new kind of life. By February, the emergency was over. There was no one left to search for in the rubble, and the bodies had been cleared from the streets. Those injured in the quake had died, gotten better, or at least stabilized. Most people had settled into the more familiar slog of finding ways to eat, sleep, and stay as healthy and sane as possible. Millions needed help more than ever, but now this meant something different than a few free days' worth of rice and cooking oil. They needed work to restore their income and, with the spring rains looming, more durable forms of shelter. David, who spoke decent English and had long dreamed of moving overseas, tried to find job as a translator with U.S. troops. He left his resume and was called back for two interviews. But the Americans never called again. "You see what our country has to offer?" he vented. Rose told him to calm down.

Relief organizations sent Haitian workers to the Cherys' camp to assess damage and the help that was needed. At first Rose was happy to chat, but soon the conversations grew stale. "All these questions!" she would recall, sucking her teeth in disgust. 'Which of your belongings were damaged? Are you hurt? Where were you during the earthquake? How much were you making in commerce before?' We were expecting something of it. . . . They claimed they would get us into houses. And we waited, and nothing."

SINCE THE MID-TWENTIETH CENTURY, most Western governments, multilateral institutions, and aid organizations have conceptually divided disaster response into the three Rs: emergency relief, medium-term recovery, and long-term reconstruction. Relief agencies such as the Red Cross and the UN World Food Programme, along with the military and other first responders, would rush in to rescue survivors and mitigate the disaster. Then, they'd hand off responsibility to development-minded agencies that would begin addressing longer-term needs—for instance, temporary shelter and classrooms. Finally, governments and multilateral institutions, the only ones with the massive resources needed to rebuild, would step in to handle the long-term response.[1]

As February arrived, responders continued to focus on relief. Emergency food distributions continued. Medical workers kept going, day and night, but were increasingly treating victims of car crashes and malaria. No system was in place to keep track of the thousands of amputees and other earthquake victims surgeons had saved but left behind; their aid groups and militaries had committed neither the time nor the money to stick around for months of often critical follow-up care. The major aid groups had spent very little of the emergency money they had raised, but people overseas were still pumping in more at the behest of celebrities and CNN. The quake-day image of Haitians waiting plaintively for help etched deeper into people's minds. "It's a big world out there and we all have a lot of responsibility to look out for people who can't look out for themselves," George Clooney had told MTV News, as his all-star telethon raised $61 million for the American Red Cross, World Food Programme, and other NGOs in late January.

But survivors were trying to look after themselves, and their prime concern was shelter. On January 16, there had been at least 107 identifiable postquake settlements in Port-au-Prince. By July, there would be more than 1,500.[2] One of the city's largest formed on an incongruous nine-hole golf course at an exclusive private club between Route de Delmas and Bourdon. The Pétionville Club had been built by U.S. officers during the occupation in the 1930s. In the days after the quake, its owner, still an American, rented it back to the U.S. military, who turned it into the forward operating base for the 82nd Airborne. Some believe the owner was hoping to forestall an invasion by those displaced from surrounding neighborhoods. If so, he experienced a self-fulfilling prophecy: When the paratroopers began handing out rations and bottles of water, people began setting up tents to be closer to the distribution point, until the roughs and greens held a village home to tens of thousands of people.

Other responders faced a similarly self-reinforcing problem. Many recognized that settlement camps could turn into semi-permanents slums, taking land needed for reconstruction. But aid groups, who tend to go by the book, also started referring to the congregations as "internally displaced people" (IDPs)—a legal term for refugees who've remained within their country's borders. With this seemingly procedural insight, Haitians on urban lots were suddenly subject to the same protocols as wartime IDPs who'd fled hundreds of miles across, say, rural Sudan. The NGOs started delivering the camps water, medical care, and food. (The World Food Program, in a major exception, tried to hand out food away from camps to encourage dispersal.) But while in sub-Saharan Africa, the challenge was often to bring remotely dispersed survivors together, in Haiti, many of the homeless were near their old neighborhoods; some even had homes that seemed stable enough to spend the day, if not the night. But who would want to go back when the aid was in the camps? Moreover, the longer small businesses stayed shut down, the fewer people could afford anything but a free, makeshift tent.

The settlements grew also because responders had removed almost none of an estimated 33 million cubic yards of earthquake rubble, first distracted by security concerns and then unable to deal with complicated land tenure issues, including identifying sites where the rubble could go.[3] After the quake, many families had chosen to stay on side streets near their broken homes, in the hope that help would arrive there. When it didn't, these people too had little choice but to join the settlement camps.

Though concerns about security had proved unwarranted, most of the planning by aid groups—organized by area of concern, or "cluster"—was done inside the security perimeter at Logbase, the UN Logistics Base on Maïs Gâté, the airport road.[4] That meant few Haitians could attend. And since nearly all the meetings were held in English, few Haitians could have understood anyway. (This was explained via an International Federation of the Red Cross report with a tautology: "The language of the national cluster remained English because only English speakers attended the early meetings.")

The cluster participants—who met a short walk from where the Cherys had thrown up their shelter of rags—rarely ventured into the city, to say nothing of the countryside, themselves. An early exception was Mike Godfrey, an aid worker with decades of experience who had spent the previous year and a half overseeing a USAID agriculture and watershed management program in the Haitian countryside. Both Godfrey and his rented apartment in Pétionville survived the earthquake, and unlike most participants, he continued to live outside the security perimeter, making the four-hour round trip each day. At first he wasn't quite sure what role he could play. "I've been here," he remembered thinking. "I know what's going on."

What was going on—at the meetings and in the streets—disturbed him. The Logbase bull sessions were dominated by bureaucratic procedure. With aid workers constantly rotating in and out, many staying for only a few weeks, nearly every meeting had to burn time getting newcomers up to speed. The meetings about shelter issues rarely addressed the estimated 600,000 people who had spontaneously decongested the capital by moving to their ancestral homes in the countryside.[5] Thousands more had moved to the relatively open land between the capital and the Dominican border.

Godfrey had overseen CARE USA's operations after the 1998–1999 war in Kosovo, when at least 1.2 million refugees were driven from their homes. Responders in the Balkans made a point of delivering aid to individual families instead of squatter camps, for fear of encouraging people to stay in them, he recalled, and followed refugees' lead when they returned to their homes on their own. If the aid effort in Haiti could similarly deliver resources to people outside of the capital, Godfrey and many others reasoned, this might incentivize them to remain where they were, solving one of the country's biggest problems. In Port-au-Prince, he was convinced, as water, medical care, food, and services were brought directly to the camps, the new settlements would become permanent. He tried to explain this to people working on camp handouts, but they were too busy to listen. As Godfrey watched thousands who'd fled seep back into the capital, he stopped going to meetings all together. At one of his last, the aid worker—whose stout jaw, wavy yellow hair, and groomed white beard could make him a convincing extra in *Julius Caesar*—stood up and asked, "How can you continue to function when there isn't a person who's been here for more than three weeks, and the chairman arrived yesterday?" Most participants agreed but could only shrug.

The Haitian government was at a loss. Two days after the earthquake, Myrta Kaulard, the World Food Programme's country director, who, like Godfrey, had been in-country since 2008, boarded a helicopter with a high-ranking minister to survey the burgeoning settlement camps. She told him, "If you let things go at the outset, it will be so difficult to recover." The minister told her not to worry—the camps were temporary. Just a few weeks later, the new reality was undeniable. On January 25, recognizing the large numbers of people now forced to improvise shelter for themselves, President Préval asked the international donors to provide 200,000 new camping tents for the homeless, with the expectation that thousands more would be needed.

The Cherys prayed they'd get one. A waterproof camping tent with fiberglass poles would be a vast improvement from rags atop dirt. But a few days later, a new rumor went out: The request had been canceled. There would be no tents. Instead, people instead would get some kind of plastic-coated canvas tarp. People were furious at the president for having let them down.

Here's what happened: Three days after Préval had requested camping tents, a U.S. delegation changed his mind. A group of advisors led by U.S. Ambassador to Haiti Kenneth Merten and newly arrived U.S. Special Coordinator for Relief and Reconstruction Lewis Lucke met with the president and told him that previous experience had taught aid workers that camping tents were a bad idea. By virtue of being conical or dome shaped, they created less vertical square footage than tarps hung over poles. They were also more expensive, bulkier, more difficult to replace, and, because of all this, more likely to keep people where they were.[6] Lucke, who had been USAID's first mission director in postinvasion Iraq, referred to this as "thinking outside the tent."[7] The responders also argued that after the Pakistan earthquake of 2005, uncoordinated NGOs delivered poorly designed tents that lacked waterproofing. It wasn't clear why they couldn't simply do better in Haiti. After all, on the campus of the U.S. Embassy and at Logbase, aid workers were living in some very nice camping tents.

For Haiti, the Americans proposed a three-phase plan instead. In the relief phase, now slated to go until at least May 1, every family in the quake zone would get a tarp. Then, during recovery, which would go into force in time for the hurricane season, responders would build 125,000 temporary houses known as T-shelters, generally 193 square feet or fewer, with plywood, particleboard, or larger tarp walls and metal roofs. Finally, during the reconstruction phase—to be funded at an upcoming donors' conference in New York—responders would start building real, permanent housing. What they needed from Préval was land where they could build the T-shelters. Preferably this territory would not be in a floodplain and could hold tens of thousands of people.

Préval was "very receptive" to the Americans' plan, as a State Department cable about the meeting released by Wikileaks said. The Haitian government, in fact, had already started looking for land to relocate people in the near term, hoping to both decongest the city and spread out the squatter camps. But Préval also knew that this last part—land—wasn't going to be as easy as it sounded.

LAND IS A KEY TO HAITI. The country's history hinges on the struggle among powerful individual landowners, national leaders seeking centralized land control, and autonomous peasants defying them both. Following the overthrow of the French, there was debate about what to do with the valuable land they left behind. Haiti's first leaders tried to continue the plantation system through the use of forced or salaried labor. But the people refused to go back to being controlled by someone else and held on to dreams of their own land. It was "the only thing," historian Laurent Dubois has written, "that would provide them with real autonomy, dignity, and freedom."[8] Land provided sustenance and, perhaps as important, a share of the island's wealth. Owning their own land meant that no one else could own them.

Ultimately the plantations were divided among families with ties to the government. Peasants claimed whatever land they could, and over time organized themselves in clusters known as lakou. In the lakou, families shared food and responsibilities in cultivating the soil. In some, a newborn's umbilical cord was traditionally buried in the yard, under a fruit tree. That tree's fruit would then be used to buy essentials for the child until she was old enough to inherit part of the lakou for herself. The system promoted inner egalitarianism and resistance to outside control. It still operates in much of rural Haiti today.[9]

But the lakou system had little currency in Port-au-Prince. The state had no way to regulate land in the crowded city, where unscrupulous brokers sometimes sold parcels they didn't own or sold the same piece multiple times. Moreover, during the U.S. occupation, Marines simply seized land from peasants to give to clients such as the Haitian American Sugar Company.[10] When the occupation ended in the 1930s, the departing Americans gave much of the seized land to favored families, who used it to build their fortunes. Other families might have claimed title too, either because they'd squatted there or perhaps been granted legitimate title sometime after independence back in 1804. It was almost impossible to say who was right. No one even knew how much habitable land the country had—foreigners estimated by comparing to the area of the Dominican Republic, which was twice Haiti's size and far less mountainous. Perhaps because so many powerful landowners suspected they'd lose titles if the mess was truly straightened out, no one pushed for change.

At the time of the quake, the Haitian government agency tasked with overseeing land registration had an annual operating budget of just over $130,000, which did not come close to covering its expenses, and could account for less than 5 percent of the country's land.[11] That registry—2,500 bound, decaying, mostly handwritten logs, organized chronologically (instead of geographically)—was stored in the musty basement of the central tax office. It collapsed in the earthquake, swallowing the books in the rubble. Now it was really impossible to say who owned what, who had the responsibility to clear a parcel of rubble, and who had the right to rebuild.

The claimant landowners did have one ace in the hole, though. Since no one really knew whose land was whose, multiple families could demand compensation when the government got around to purchasing or expropriating land for resettlement. Every player set out to screw everyone else: Préval's commission tasked with finding land for relocation was going to try to exploit the confusion about ownership to avoid paying anyone, and the landowning families would try to exploit the confusion to get more money than they might otherwise be entitled to. Not even a month after the earthquake, Haiti's politicians and landowning families were back to business as usual.

WHILE THE RESPONDERS, OFFICIALS, AND LANDOWNERS DELIBERATED, the camps began governing themselves. The NGOs delivering assistance to the settlements asked for representatives to come forward to receive the bounty, considering this "community participation." But the new "camp committees" were rarely elected. The young men—and nearly all were young men—had come forward on their own, and no one knew how they would use their new power.

One day, almost a month after the earthquake, Evens and I visited a camp in the dry bed of Rivière Grise, close to the highway that connects Port-au-Prince and Santo Domingo. Under a busy overpass, children were flying homemade kites fashioned from plastic bags and sticks. We were greeted by Dieusin St. Vil, who introduced himself as the chairman of the camp, known as Marassa. St. Vil had a shaved head and a thick black crescent of a mustache, and he wore a very clean secondhand orange polo shirt from an Arizona golf resort. Like a good Caribbean bureaucrat, he had a stout pot belly, over which dangled a dark red whistle and what I thought at first was some sort of official identification. On closer inspection, I realized it was his worker's ID from a tailor shop.

Anyone who still considered the camps temporary needed only to visit St. Vil's operation to see that people were there to stay. St. Vil's committee had painted a number onto each makeshift tent, and the people put up cardboard street signs along the rows: Impasse Jerusalem, Rue La Paix, and one that translated as "Big Man, Stay Cool, Take-It-Easy Street." St. Vil called over a woman in a flowered dress and asked her to hand him her "ID." She turned over a green paper rectangle with the corners cut off—the sort that you'd get as a ticket in a tailor's shop. On one side was the number of her tent and on the other the camp's official stamp—a purplish blotch.

St. Vil told us that Marassa had received no aid since the earthquake—no food or water, no latrines. I tried to talk to one of the women in the camp, but he interrupted to talk about the importance of the committee's patrols. "We are living in a hole," he explained. "You never know when thieves might pop up."

We came back the next day but entered through the back, far from the committee's big tent. We wanted to see things without St. Vil's interference.

Evens and I wound around a corner and in the shade of a tarp house found a woman sitting on a low wooden chair with a bucket, a boiling pot, a cold pot, and a pile of green plantain skins at her dusty bare feet. She wore a hot-pink terry-cloth shirt and a tan skirt with big blue flowers that looked like a repurposed curtain.

"What are you cooking, *maman?*" Evens asked.

She pointed to the thick beige slices frying in brown oil under a homemade slotted spoon as big as my face. "I have some breadfruit, plantain. I have fried potato with *pikliz*"—a vinegary Haitian cole slaw, with cabbage, carrot, onion, and a crucial blast of scotch bonnet pepper. I asked where she'd gotten the ingredients. She laughed and wiped her brow with her shirt, nonchalantly exposing a breast. "You can't get vegetables nowadays, cherie. It's just the marinade."

A young man interrupted: "Don't cook here, Adrienne. If you cook here, it will look like people don't have problems." She laughed and waved him off. But now a larger crowd started to form. Someone went off in a huff down one of the rows, and before I knew it, St. Vil was rounding a corner. He shouted to the crowd: "I have not given anyone from outside the camp authorization to be here today! No one is to talk to blan without authorization of the committee."

Evens put up his hand. "*Monché,* anyone can talk to us who wants to."

St. Vil kept his back turned to us. "If anyone talks to the blan they will answer to me. All discussions with blan must go through the committee. These blan are here to tell the world that we do not need food."

There was serious stirring now and some agitated looks in my direction. Adrienne wasn't smiling anymore. When Evens tried to ask her another question and she moved to respond, St. Vil shouted at the top of his lungs, so that half the camp could hear: "THE BLAN ARE BLOCKING THE AID TO THE CAMP!"

The words crackled through the air. People emerged to see the foreigners who were keeping food from their children. Evens stepped forward. "We are not blocking aid," he said. "We are here to tell the truth: That there is food, but there is not enough to live on. If we tell people that there is no food, then they will think that we are exaggerating and they will not listen."

This argument went on for a while. St. Vil cursed Evens' mother. But soon some of the young men were yelling back at the committee chief. "They are here to tell the truth!" one yelled. "They need information!" Several young men came over and, putting their arms around me, led me and Evens away. "Don't worry," one said. "You go and work how you want to. *Trankil.*"

Now people started complaining about the committee—how they saved the best food for themselves and forced other squatters off the best spots to build their own tents. Some men brought us to see a gray-haired woman, nearly ninety years old, who'd had her tarp taken away so many times that she'd resorted to living in the hollowed-out shell of a taptap. She slept on the sloping, splintery wooden floor. Some days, she said, her grandchildren brought her rice. The day before, a neighbor had brought her some fortified high-energy biscuits in the World Food Programme's shiny foil-stamped packs, but each provided only 450 calories.[12] Malnutrition was taking its toll. Walking alone a few days earlier, she had fainted and cut her arm. Foreigners found her and took her to an NGO clinic. The doctors put a bandage on her arm and sent her back to the camp.

As we were leaving, a truck rolled in, surrounded by UN peace-keepers. Dominicans in orange T-shirts got out, and they and the soldiers started handing out Styrofoam cartons of hot food. The first in line were members of St. Vil's committee. I thought about asking St. Vil if this was really the first food delivered to the camp, but his glare said I'd caught him in his exaggeration. He kept glaring as I left.

On the one-year anniversary of the earthquake, St. Vil would show up in another news story, by the *Washington Post*. "We have just enough to survive," he explained to the reporter. "But not enough to live."[13]

THE RELIEF EFFORT HAD SUCCESSES. The U.S. Air Force Special Operations Team landed 140 flights a day at an airport that normally averaged seven, while U.S. military engineers successfully led the effort to repair the port. Despite the early, misguided focus on bottled water, by February, thanks to increased fuel shipments, the Port-au-Prince municipal water authority was producing nearly 50 percent more treated water per day than it had before the quake. The influx of free food also kept prices lower than they might otherwise have been. Responders carried out a widespread vaccination campaign against measles, tetanus, and diphtheria. Thousands of life-saving emergency surgeries, amputations, and other interventions took place, probably the crowning achievement of the response.

Other efforts came up surprisingly short. Though thousands had been trapped in the rubble, one of the largest urban search-and-rescue deployments in history saved no more than 211 people, and most estimates are lower than that.[14] The six U.S. teams, deployed at a cost of $49 million, reached 47 people. It is possible that the rescuers arrived too late and were too limited in their reach. Disaster experts say up to 95 percent of rescues take place in the first 24 hours and are carried out by neighbors and passers-by. Indeed, the vast majority of survival stories I heard involved Haitians saving Haitians, often with bare hands. With better tools and a degree of readiness, they could have saved many more.[15]

Responders also limited the reach of their early efforts by committing to a command-and-control model led by General Keen's Joint Task Force–Haiti and a civilian analog, the Humanitarian Assistance Coordination Center. Military and civilian responders cooperated at an unprecedented level—the Pentagon even widely shared surveillance from its normally classified drone. But the nature of a top-down, highly centralized model, as opposed to a broader-based approach involving more Haitians, meant that parts of the capital such as Pétionville received tremendous amounts of attention while outlying areas such as Carrefour were mostly ignored. And while there were exceptions, typically the foreign authorities did not consult or collaborate with the people they were trying to help.

This is not unusual in disasters. "The unfounded belief that people in disasters will panic or become unusually dependent on authorities for help may be one reason why disaster planners and emergency authorities often rely on a 'command-and-control' model as the basis of their response," the disaster management expert Erik Auf der Heide has written. "This model presumes that strong, central, paramilitary-like leadership can overcome the problems posed by a dysfunctional public suffering from the effects of a disaster. . . . Authorities may develop elaborate plans outlining how they will direct disaster response, only to find that members of the public, unaware of these plans, have taken actions on their own."[16]

Even the American troops on the ground struggled to see the value of their mission. "I just realized another weekend has passed in Haiti," one soldier wrote home to his family:

> It seems like every [day] is the exact same. . . . The last battalion, who I'm supposed to leave with, just got word yesterday that they will not be leaving . . . for an undetermined amount of time. . . . From people that are from here, they're saying it's about back to

how it was before. There's nothing for a light infantry battalion left to do here, and I hope they realize this up top pretty soon. . . . We have 2,500 people back at Bragg, and all the sudden they want to keep people here because it looks good for the United States? What a joke. We aren't doing anything here now. So I don't know when I'll be home.[17]

Operation Unified Response—the U.S. military's name for the immediate-relief phase—would last about six months. In that time, the responders would distribute 2.6 million bottles of water, more than 4.9 million meals, and 17 million pounds of bulk food to about 3 million people. They would support the distribution of plastic tarps to 1.1 million people, clear 80 blocks of rubble, assess the safety of 40,000 buildings, dig trenches to deter floods in nine camps, and treat 9,758 patients. When the mission was over, one of the most-cited proofs of its success was that no riots had taken place.

IN LATE FEBRUARY, BILLY CHERY MARRIED his girlfriend and moved off the land next to the church to a spot closer to where she had lived. At twenty-nine, he thought it was time to set out on his own. He started looking for a job with the NGOs. It wasn't going to be easy. At Logbase, the General Hospital, and all over town, aid groups were posting signs that said: *No jobs. Pas d'emploi. Pa gen travay.* Still, Billy felt he had to try. "We couldn't stay under the care of aid," he explained. "They won't be around forever."

The cluster system kept going. After a month, in a letter leaked to *Foreign Policy* magazine, UN humanitarian chief John Holmes blasted the system's "lack of capacity" and failure to "establish a concise overview of needs and develop coherent response plans."[18] Alarmed organizers began debating how to improve their work.

One of the few Haitians who could attend the clusters was Leslie Voltaire, a Cornell-educated architect and Préval advisor, who had credentials and spoke English. "There were too many meetings for the small quantity of Haitian technicians that could participate," the slight technocrat recalled. "You end up not doing anything but participating in meetings. And also for the president, lots of visits to the president. Lots of countries coming. And the guy cannot do his work. And the ministers have to be there. And the policemen has to be there. Just because you have to be grateful because they are helping you. But you're not working."

One day at Logbase, I walked past some aid workers' deluxe tents and went into a trailer bathroom. On the blue stall door, someone had written:

HAITI: HELL ON EARTH. WHAT DO WE DO NOW??

An anonymous critic helpfully replied, in smaller letters: "The Answer is not in Logbase or in your email."

I was also living in a very nice tent. When I came back from Louisville at the beginning of the month, AP had moved from the Villa Creole to a hotel next door called the Ritz. It wasn't what the name implies, but it could have been worse. The latest rotation of visiting staff had set up a bureau in one of the larger rooms and were sleeping in rooms that ranged from glorified closets to efficiencies with kitchens. Evens and I said no thanks and set up tents out back. Annette and Elias, the maid and handyman from the old house, came to work too. They were sleeping with their families on the street, weighing the move to a camp. AP got them proper tents, like Evens' and mine.

On February 21, I got up the courage to go back indoors and took one of the small rooms at the back of the Ritz. I climbed onto the bed wearing my clothes and shoes in case evacuation was required. It was. At 4:36 A.M., I heard the telltale rattle. I leapt to my feet, but the shaking stopped. About an hour later, there was an alert from the U.S. Geological Survey: It had been a 4.6. The next night I was back in my tent, in time to be rocked with a head-batting 4.8. I smiled and went back to sleep.

Four nights later, shortly after 1:34 A.M. on February 27, the U.S. Geological Survey sent another alert. But this time it wasn't for us. A magnitude–8.8 earthquake had struck off the coast of Chile. The temblor was massive—it released five hundred times more energy than Haiti's—but originated more than two-and-a-half times deeper and sixty miles from the closest city, in a country far better prepared for earthquakes. There was, however, wide-spread damage and a tsunami warning. When the sun rose, much of the press corps that had remained in Haiti started making its way to the airport.

CHAPTER SIX

BON DOLA

IN THE YEARS BEFORE THE EARTHQUAKE, FOREIGNERS OFTEN TALKED about two ways to "fix Haiti." In the first, the Western powers would build a new country piece by piece: roads, neighborhoods, agriculture, industry, police, legislature, and so on. This vision was nicknamed "the Marshall Plan," after the multibillion-dollar U.S. effort to rebuild Western Europe after World War II.

The second was an even sicker joke: Drop a nuclear bomb and start over.

You could tell how long foreigners had been in-country by their reactions. Newcomers brightened at the first proposal and recoiled at the second. Those who'd worked in Haiti for years would break into laughter at the suggestion that anyone would commit resources or time to a Marshall Plan in Haiti. But at the mention of the bomb, longtimers would lower their voices and, a mad gleam in their eyes, detail their latest plan for evacuating the population as they personally entered the launch codes.

The scenarios were two sides of the same coin—the idea that only a transformative, external force could solve Haiti. It was born of the helplessness aid workers felt as they confronted seemingly straightforward issues, only to find that dozens of interrelated problems made solving them alone impossible.

Take deforestation. After French colonists cleared island forest for plantations, Haitians sold off precious mahogany to finance foreign debt while slashing remaining trees for farms, lumber, and cooking fuel. Fertile soil turned to desert, rivers previously held back by forest cover overflowed, and cities went to ruin. In the 1980s, forest cover fell below 10 percent. USAID, understanding the link between forest and income, spent $22.8 million raising saplings that peasants could plant, cut down, and sell. But the program, implemented while foreign food and trade policies were gutting farms, underestimated how severe the need for income had gotten. While a few million saplings were handed out each year, peasants were chopping down as many as 40 million grown trees annually.[1] Efforts to wean buyers from charcoal to recycled-garbage briquettes failed, in part because Haitians weren't thrilled about cooking on garbage. When thousands died in 2004 floods exacerbated by deforestation, USAID wisely decided to try addressing income, forestry, and flood threats all at once. But officials spent most of the funds on an admittedly excellent report, then saved money by implementing less ambitious pilot flood-control and tree-planting projects in areas where few people lived. In 2008, the same river flooded again. By 2010, some estimates put forest cover below 2 percent.[2]

There was another vision of aid, and it required neither epic investment nor mushroom clouds, nor even experts with all the answers. A growing contingent of academics and disillusioned aid workers said the problem had to do with whom the aid was going to. Although it's a surprise to many, foreign aid isn't just handed over to foreign countries. Instead, it tends to go to domestic NGOs and contractors, ostensibly to avoid local incompetence and corruption. A check billed as U.S. aid to Haiti is far more likely to make the half-mile walk from Treasury to the headquarters of Chemonics International—a for-profit development agency founded by a U.S. rice exporter to Haiti (censured in 2003 by the Securities and Exchange Commission for bribing Haitian officials), then bought by a former USAID official.[3] Chemonics might use the funds for overhead; transportation; housing; the hiring of cars, drivers, guards, and possibly a cook; and, finally, the project. Its report would go to USAID, Haitian opinions taken into account briefly, if at all. Since most of the money earmarked as aid was thus spent in the donor's country, the donor could set and judge its own priorities and take full credit for the program on the ground.

Reformers argued that going around governments made fragile states weaker. Local officials looked miserly beside foreigners
handing out free stuff, while foreign firms hired away talented
nationals. The private aid groups were no different—for the most
part, they just ran programs themselves. When funding ran out
or the source of funding bailed, a foreign-run program often left
nothing behind. Nobody knew whether giving money directly to
foreign governments and building up local infrastructure and resources would work better. But they knew that the current system
was not working at all.

Their arguments rapidly gained consensus. In 2005, more than
one hundred countries including the United States signed an aid-
reform declaration in Paris to work through "country systems and
procedures to the maximum extent possible." Reviews of direct
budget support programs in Africa—aid given directly to host governments—found that the direct funding of Zambia's state health
system had reduced child and maternal mortality. Mali, Tunisia,
and Zambia saw education gains "in terms of total enrollment, increased participation of girls, and access for students from poor
areas," although test scores did not improve. Aid, it turned out, addressed problems best when it matched a host country's priorities,
and often local governments could coordinate programs better
than squabbling donors. Most importantly perhaps, no evidence
had been found that giving money straight to governments increased corruption. In fact, because it strengthened government's
oversight roles, in some cases it helped bolster transparency.[4]

But Haiti's principal donor just didn't give aid that way. In
2009, USAID paid more than $6.9 billion to its top 20 vendors,
mostly U.S. firms that spent thousands lobbying for more. These
organizations, known as "Beltway bandits," had allies among lawmakers suspicious of sending free stuff to faraway lands, at least
without constituents making something in the bargain. As top officials including Hillary Clinton and Rajiv Shah, the head of USAID,
came around to reformist positions, there were halting attempts at
change. But the Congressional Research Service concluded that in
2009, just 1.7 percent of U.S. foreign assistance—$580 million—
flowed as direct budget support.[5] When President Préval asked

the U.S. permanent representative to the UN, Susan Rice, for budget support after the 2008 floods, Rice responded, according to a leaked cable, "The [U.S. government] is reluctant to engage in direct budget support. Any change in this policy would take time for the new Administration to work through."[6]

Then on January 12, 2010, the sick jokes came true. The fault line near Léogâne erupted with twenty-five times the force of the atomic blast that wiped out Hiroshima. Days later, Dominique Strauss-Kahn, then the head of the International Monetary Fund, wrote an op-ed titled "Why We Need a Marshall Plan for Haiti." The idea that whole swaths of the tangled Haitian capital might be cleared away for development was no longer a laugh line, the concept that transformative sums of money might be spent no longer a heartbreaking taunt. The question was: Could aid be handled differently from before? Would reconstruction be done to Haiti or by Haiti?

The weeks after the earthquake were not encouraging. Little of the $1.1 billion in U.S. postquake emergency assistance left the United States. Half went to U.S. government agencies preparing to aid the response, the rest to UN agencies, contractors, and NGOs.[7] The Haitian state got no support from France, Canada, Norway, Brazil, or the European Commission either. But that was emergency spending immediately after the earthquake, when the earthquake killed an estimated 17 percent of civil service employees and destroyed almost all ministry buildings.[8] There was now a chance to formulate a longer view.

A string of meetings about financing reconstruction began just weeks after the earthquake. Asked by donors to assess its needs, the Haitian government pegged reconstruction at $11.5 billion over the coming decade, starting with $3.8 billion for the first eighteen months. It also asked for $350 million in direct budget support. UN representatives, NGOs, and Haitian students were dispatched to carry out focus groups with Haitian peasants and the urban poor. Members of Haiti's business elite headed to a beach resort north of Port-au-Prince to discuss private-sector proposals.

The results would come together on March 31, 2010, at a one-day international donors' conference at UN headquarters in New York. Its organizers titled it "Towards a New Future for Haiti."

AS THE DONORS' CONFERENCE APPROACHED, its organizers went to Haiti to draw attention to what they considered priorities for the reconstruction. UN Secretary-General Ban Ki-moon arrived on March 14.

The days were getting longer now, dry tropical winter giving way to steamy spring heat. Farmers beyond the mountains awaited the daily rains to nourish their corn, potatoes, and manioc. But the weather looked more ominous in the city. It was impossible to say exactly how many people were sleeping under open skies, but the most widely used estimates wagered over a million, about a tenth of the country's population. Overseas journalists and policy makers, realizing that the camps were not going anywhere, began reporting on their hazards, portraying camps as uniformly unsanitary, crime-ridden hotbeds of simmering unrest at risk for further calamity—microcosms, in other words, of a widely held view of Haiti.

The highlight of the secretary-general's trip was a visit to one of these camps. He picked the most famous of all, three-quarters of the way up the hill from downtown Port-au-Prince, on the golf course of the Pétionville Club. The iron-gated clubhouse was still a forward operating base of the U.S. Army 82nd Airborne, and young paratroopers peered with curiosity as the South Korean diplomat entered with a phalanx of security guards, journalists, and handlers. Waiting out front was a more familiar face, smiling between a blue T-shirt and blue trucker hat. Its bearer was becoming a force even more powerful than the soldiers.

Sean Penn had arrived in Haiti nine days after the quake spearheading a new NGO bankrolled by Diana Jenkins, a Bosnian-born philanthropist who lived near Penn in California. For a few days, the landing team of the Jenkins-Penn Haitian Relief Organization (J/P HRO), distributed water filters and medical aid here and there; then an army officer invited it inside the wire. Of everyone on the team, the soldiers were most excited about Penn's fellow actor–turned–aid worker Maria Bello, who a jazzed grunt pointed out to me had played a bartender in *Coyote Ugly*. Both actors lived in a tall, white, barnlike temporary structure, tucked safely behind the clubhouse, that protected them from the elements.

Ban walked with the actors down the hill, stopping to tour the aid tents above the camp. At a J/P HRO clinic, he highlighted the ongoing need for medical aid. At a UN and Haitian police stand, he emphasized the need to protect women and girls from sexual violence. Finally, Ban's staff led him to a ridge overlooking the golf course. "Cameras!" his head speechwriter called out, directing journalists toward a shot of the secretary-general before thousands of blue, white, orange, and silver tarpaulins. Once everyone was in place, Ban spoke. "I am concerned that the rainy season is approaching. What will happen to those people who are living here?" The secretary-general motioned woodenly toward the 45,000 people in the gully below. "We have to move these—displaced persons—to a safer place."

Once again, it was important to understand both the threat and its limits: On a normal day in Port-au-Prince, rain is dangerous. There's little drainage on the streets, causing roads to back up like bathtubs. And storms hit hard—there will be one drop, and then a thousand drops, and then suddenly a river falling from the sky. (It's an old joke in Haiti that street merchants will sit patiently through gunfire but run over one another if two drops hit their heads.) If the rain goes on long enough, some pedestrians will get swept away, and a house or two might get knocked into a ravine.

It was a major overstatement, however, to believe the rains would cause a "second round of death" in any way commensurate with the earthquake, as Bill Clinton would soon warn, or that the ground would become significantly more dangerous or diseased than it had been before the quake.[9] The rain can be bad, but it isn't usually *that* bad—the Caribbean doesn't have monsoons. The danger of floods and landslides would be somewhat greater when hurricane season got under way in the late summer and fall, but in March, there were still several months to mitigate the danger.

Nevertheless, after returning to New York, Ban would expand on his concerns in the *Washington Post,* writing that "the steeply sloping ground" of the Pétionville Club would soon "turn to mud, dangerous and diseased." He joined a drumbeat of warnings about the approaching of the rains. "Aid agencies are in a race against time," read a typical pre-rainy season press release by CARE.[10] Once again, it was as if the only way to get aid groups and donors to act was to create indiscriminate panic. And, again, media were not immune. When the first decent rain shower hit in February, my editors rushed me out mid-storm to—where else?—the Pétionville golf course. In full waders, rain jacket, and poncho with a waterproof notebook and headlamp, I looked as if I was entering the Mekong Delta in July. I squished into camp as the drizzle stopped, to the amused greetings of two men playing cards in the lamplight outside their tarp.

Now no mother would want to spend a night holding her crying baby in two feet of shit-filled water while the wind blew and thunder crashed over a leaky tarp, and no just world would stand by while she had to. Nearly every major NGO had signed on in 2000 to a minimum global standard for disaster response that, "people have sufficient covered living space providing thermal comfort, fresh air and protection from the climate ensuring their privacy, safety and health."[11] This was a lofty goal, as many Haitians had not enjoyed those conditions even before the earthquake—though it was also part of what Bill Clinton meant when he said that Haiti should "Build Back Better." But to meet it, responders would have done well to avoid the panic that had scuttled so much in the early going. After all, had those who'd rushed in after the earthquake not panicked over imagined threats of famine and widespread civil unrest, and had the clusters carefully considered strategies to take advantage of the spontaneous decentralization of 600,000 people who went to the countryside after the earthquake, the quake zone might not have ended up with huge camps in the first place.

Anyway, the secretary-general's plea at the golf course notwithstanding, no one was going to be relocated before the rains started in earnest. The Haitian government's attempts to find relocation space kept stalling because the wealthy families who controlled most of the land in and around the city refused to donate it. But it was equally unlikely that an official as diligent and cautious as Ban Ki-moon would have made such a statement without knowing that people would be relocated soon or at least where. It seemed he knew something we didn't.

I ran to ask him more, but after a few vague words, he was enveloped by cameras. Then I saw Sean Penn walking alone. I reached the actor just before a UN Population Fund spokesman came over to introduce a blushing colleague and then asked some questions of his own. "What's the plan for the rains?" the spokesman asked. To my surprise, the actor answered in detail.

"What is the plan or what should be the plan?" Penn replied, drawing an impatient breath. "What should be the plan is total relocation."

Penn started giving the extended answer the secretary-general hadn't, and his delivery was everything Ban's wasn't: demonstrative, vivid, intense. You could forgive all the swooning he had elicited: He was handsome, if weathered by forty-nine years on earth and seven weeks in Haiti, with tanned skin wrapped tight around hollow cheeks, blue-ink tattoos running over veiny, muscular arms, and a pair of aviator sunglasses dangling from his neckline. As Penn explained the details of camp life, he seemed to draw from his recent portrayal of Willie Stark, the charismatic but vindictive governor of Louisiana in Steven Zaillian's remake of *All the King's Men*—though where that doomed character seethed with 1930s southern populism, Penn in Haiti went for the argot of the modern NGO. "Another thing that I think has to be very clear is that a tarp is not a tent," he said, squinting in the midday light. "A tarp structure is not a tent. A tarp structure sits on dirt. This is toxic dirt. This is dirt which carries bacteria. This is dirt which could carry in high numbers of life-threatening bacteria, very shortly." Finally he nailed his point: "This is a camp that should be relocated, as many of them should be, flood zones and so on—and frankly in my view, we have to work to understand how to address the relative unliveability, currently, of this city, if only for children. You know, every good deed today is another cancer patient tomorrow, from what they are breathing on these streets."

The actor set out parameters for relocation with the confidence of a hardened field manager: outside Port-au-Prince (the old dream of decentralization). Not in a flood zone. "Large-scale urban camps with manufacturing, deeded lands for agriculture, the ability to build communities." It was an impassioned plea, unafraid to contradict U.S. policy—tarps were a measly solution—and impressively informed on squatters' needs, especially considering it came from a newly minted, recently arrived aid worker. But perhaps it wasn't so hypothetical after all? When the Population Fund spokesman asked if Penn was helping to choose the resettlement sites himself—an odd question for an aid worker, let alone a celebrity, when you think about it—Penn surprised me again by saying that he "had a meeting with President Préval the other day in Washington and he's extended the members of his government to us who can advise us on this. We're going to be shown some of these sites."

I was confused. Sean Penn had a meeting with Préval? In Washington? Granted, the actresses Nicole Kidman and Angelina Jolie were official UN ambassadors now, more visible and probably more widely influential than Ban himself. George Clooney would become a quasi-spymaster later that year, organizing a system of private satellites to monitor troop movements in Sudan. Penn, who had been involved in politics for years as an advocate, seemed to be taking the next step: contributing directly to policy making. Perhaps there had been more to Ban Ki-moon's choice of camp to visit than a one-off round of publicity.

THE NEEDS WERE JUST AS GREAT in less publicized parts of the city. The Cherys became homeless again when the owner of the land beside the church on Delmas 33 demanded that the squatters move immediately. No one knew whether he really owned the land—he didn't have a paper deed. But the Cherys decided he had been generous so far and certainly didn't have any rent to offer him. Yet where could they go now?

One day, while Twenty was walking down the airport road, he came to a field where a warehouse stood. In the bushy field, Twenty spotted a group of young men hacking with machetes, among them his friend Jonas, pointing and shouting orders.[12] Jonas walked with a limp and often walked around without a shirt, his thick potbelly hanging out.

Twenty snuck up behind Jonas and gave him a playful shove. Jonas turned around, pissed.

Twenty laughed. "What are you doing here?"

Jonas looked Twenty up and down as he dusted himself off. "Do you see an owner around here?" he asked. "It's our land now." Jonas and his friends, like many squatters after the quake, were counting on landowners being too distracted and the government too enfeebled to stop them from grabbing space for themselves and their friends and selling it to anyone else. But for Twenty, their friend, they'd give some plots for nothing. "Everyone's getting a piece of land here," Jonas invited. "Come get yours."

At first Twenty demurred, skeptical of getting caught up in a scheme. But eviction loomed at his family's camp, and he knew he wouldn't get a better offer than free. So, a few days later, Twenty came back to pick out two plots, one for his family and another for him and his girlfriend Kettelie. In the middle of the field, he saw what looked at first like another woody shrub. But as he walked closer, he could tell that it was a small ash tree with tender green leaves, standing alone. One of the men was walking toward it with a machete.

"No, man!" Twenty yelled, running over. "This is my tree! This is my space. No one is to touch it." The machete man shrugged and walked off. Pleased with his choice, Twenty marked his lot with a wooden fence and some chalky white rocks he dug up nearby.

The new camp was called Trazelie, and more shacks appeared in it every day. The police came once with a man who said he owned the warehouse, but word traveled faster than traffic, and the authorities arrived to find a dozen of Jonas's men waiting with rocks and machetes. The police shrugged and left, leaving the fuming landlord no choice but to follow. Rosemide's boyfriend, David, thought it was an ugly thing, people taking land that wasn't theirs. But even from the relative comfort of his still-standing tin-roofed house nearby, he also knew they had little choice. "Going into the river isn't a good idea," he explained by way of metaphor. "You're worse off in the river than out. But you still have to go into the river because you know you'll die if you stay on the other side."

A short woman named Lovelie built a low shack across the path from Twenty's and started selling soda, water, and food. Next door was a man named Chrispain, who never stopped talking about the fact that he'd lived for years in the Dominican Republic and had a son there who was a policeman. "I can go back to Santo Domingo anytime," he'd insist, which everyone took to mean that he couldn't.

Twenty bought gray tarps on the street and some nails and wood. He hammered the wood into a frame, then affixed the plastic-coated tarps by driving nails through old bottle caps. When he was done, his new house had three rooms: a bedroom, a small kitchen where he'd keep a cookstove, and some space in the back for taking bucket baths. He fenced off a porch with a frail gray railing of driftwood, which he decorated with splotches of yellow, black, and red paint. To the side he dug out space for a little garden where he could grow vegetables and herbs. Over the door he hung his welcome sign: the emblem of a pinkish man on a yellow background, full of holes, with an empty light socket for a nose, from a discarded copy of the game Operation. And when the tree grew, it would provide him shade.

When Jonas saw Twenty's house, he realized he'd made a mistake. His associates had managed to fetch as much as $300 a plot from willing buyers—that's bon dola, U.S. cash—and here he'd let Twenty build one of the nicest houses in Trazelie for free.

Jonas limped over, lips pursed, looking for a fight. He demanded Twenty pay for the land.

Twenty jumped to his feet. "How am I going to pay you, man?" he replied. "This land isn't yours." Jonas took a step forward, but Twenty rose over him and stuck his nose right in his face, the thin scar on Twenty's forehead hovering over Jonas's eyes. "Don't try to scam me. There are a lot of people you know who you can scam. Don't scam me here. I know the movement on this land. You understand what I'm saying?"

Jonas shrunk back. "OK, Twenty," he said. "Respect."

ON MARCH 19, TWELVE DAYS BEFORE the donors' conference, a hard rain fell on the Pétionville golf course. The water swept residents into swirling eddies. Latrines overflowed; tent schools and tarp homes collapsed. "They were crying. There was just fear down there," an aid worker told AP. "It was chaos." The storm seemed like a simulacrum of what the secretary-general had warned about just five days before. No one died, but anyone looking for justification to panic could chalk that up to luck. General Keen, still running Joint Task Force-Haiti, and by now a friend of Sean Penn, dispatched a U.S. Navy engineering battalion to the Pétionville Club with orders to mitigate flood risks until people could be moved.[13]

The pressure on Préval to close a land deal outside Port-au-Prince for relocation camps was now unbearable. He knew there was little anyone could do to prevent suffering from the rains—projects to prevent large-scale floods would take years under the best circumstances. Further, he knew the hope for flood-safe land outside the capital was mostly fantasy: Nearly everything could flood on the barren Cul-de-Sac plain. Even mountain high ground could get washed out from above. USAID's comprehensive 2007 flood report—the one prompted by the deforestation-provoked floods—called Port-au-Prince and its outlying areas "by far the most vulnerable of all of Haiti's watersheds."

But Préval also knew he couldn't afford the impression that earthquake survivors drowned as his government dithered, not while he lobbied for a bigger role in reconstruction. The president's relocation commission had failed to cut a deal with landowners for territory north of the capital, along the massive stretch of land one and a quarter times the size of Manhattan called Corail-Cesselesse. So, on March 22, he did the only other thing it was in his power as president to do: He expropriated the whole thing.

Corail was once dotted with sugarcane fields that supplied the Haitian American Sugar Company, and sisal that was braided into ropes for export to the United States during World War II. It was now a cactus-studded desert. The base of barren mountains was considered a moderate floodplain, although it probably was safer than lower-lying areas, such as the nearby slum of Cité Soleil. For years landowners and speculators had been buying up the territory—sometimes multiple buyers being sold the same spot. It wasn't clear whether these landowners, many of whom engaged private security forces, would respect the expropriation's authority, or how the government would enforce its claim of eminent domain. But the president had to act. There were only nine days before the donors' conference, and the two highest-profile visitors Préval had ever hosted were on their way.

BILL CLINTON AND GEORGE W. BUSH needed a camp to visit. Their handlers settled on a fenced-in postage stamp of tarpaulin shacks across from the National Palace. The press teams liked the visual of the camp. The security details liked the fence. But nobody could do anything about the smell. There were only about four hundred latrines across the plaza for tens of thousands of people.

The camp's residents put on their best shirts or cleaned the only ones they had. Hands and faces dripped from recent bucket baths. The adults had seen enough journalists to know a photo-op when they were part of one, but most still took the presidents' visit as a sign of respect. It was a welcome reassurance that they had not been forgotten as the soldiers and aid groups began to leave. "The presidents' visit might help the country if they see how we live," said Jimmy Joseph, who lost his business, apartment, and sister in the quake. "We are a country that can advance, but they have to see us as people."

Clinton and Bush had been tapped by President Obama to head up U.S. fundraising after the earthquake. It was Bush's first trip to Haiti, and as he and Clinton made their way into the camp amid a stampede of aides and photographers, he looked uncomfortable. Clinton, however, was ebullient. The man could not have been more genuinely thrilled to be in a tent camp. This was his third trip to Haiti since the earthquake and his seventh in twelve months. A slight pallor in his normally ruddy Scots-Irish cheeks was the only reminder that he'd ended up in the hospital with chest pains after his last visit a few weeks before.

Bill Clinton loved Haiti. He would tell anyone who would listen that he and Hillary had first visited as newlyweds in 1975.[14] It was a transformative vacation. The twenty-nine-year-old lawyer had been at a professional and personal crossroads, a year past his first, failed bid for Congress and resisting calls to run again. He would recall sitting with Hillary on a pew in the National Cathedral and watching Jean-Claude Duvalier drive across the Champ de Mars, just a few hundred yards from the park where he was hugging people now. It is not clear what exactly changed his mind, but it was after that trip he resolved to enter the race for Arkansas attorney general.[15] It proved to be his first major electoral victory, launching his political career.

In 1992, the junta that overthrew Jean-Bertrand Aristide was terrorizing the population, forcing thousands to flee the island on rafts. In his run for the White House, Clinton promised to help the Haitian refugees and oppose the military regime. As president, he

froze the U.S. bank accounts of the putschists and their supporters among the business elite. Haiti's economy went into a tailspin.
Then he ordered an invasion to reinstall President Aristide. The
operation was a success, but Aristide, as viewed from Washington,
was a disappointment. He was slow to condemn political violence
and confrontational in response to U.S. criticism. When Aristide
was reelected in 2000, Clinton withheld his congratulations. That
fall Bush successfully—if ironically, considering what was to come
in the Middle East—derided the Democrat's Haiti policy as a failed
misadventure in nation building. Then he withdrew support and
provided the plane to fly Aristide back into exile. Many at home
saw Haiti as a wing on Clinton's albatross.

Clinton, now a graying elder statesman, was banking his retirement, and legacy, on solving the crises of the underdeveloped
world. He had a particular fondness for places he had mucked up
as president: Rwanda, for one, and now Haiti, after Ban Ki-moon
asked Clinton to be his UN Special Envoy. The former president
was charged with encouraging investment and fundraising for reconstruction after the 2008 hurricanes, as he had done in Asia after the Indian Ocean tsunami a few years earlier. Clinton pledged
to rebuild the economy he'd gutted, to complete the restoration of
democracy he felt he had left unfinished, and to repay the nation
that had inspired him and Hillary so long ago.

When the earthquake struck, he doubled down. "I believed before this earthquake Haiti had the best chance in my lifetime to
escape its history," he told reporters in Obama's White House Rose
Garden. "I still believe that." What was so auspicious about the circumstances, I couldn't see. But then, he was the visionary.

On that steaming March day, Presidents Clinton, Bush, and
Préval stood shoulder to shoulder. When Aristide loyalists, sight-
ing Bush, erupted into chants of "No Préval!" (they had earlier
been chanting "No Bush!" but demurred at insulting a visiting dig-
nitary to his face), the Connecticut Texan leapt back as his guards
rushed to collect him. An aide told Clinton it was time to move on,
but there was no way he'd let this moment pass. The forty-second
president surged into the crowd, cheering Haitians grabbing his
big white hands and pulling the ex-president, laughing like a kid on

his birthday, six shacks deep into the camp. Bush's people threw up their hands and walked their president to an SUV.

For the rest of the tour, Clinton was at the center. He had thoughts on everything, and everyone wanted to hear them. On food, Clinton reiterated the startling comments he'd made to the U.S. Senate Foreign Relations Committee a few days before, taking personal responsibility for free-trade policies that flooded Haiti with cheap U.S. rice—from Arkansas, no less—that undercut local farms and destroyed the nation's ability to feed itself. (He had strengthened policies that began before him, but the apology was a powerful gesture.[16]) Clinton also now boasted that investors from South Korea were interested in opening new garment factories in Haiti if Congress would only pass a pending piece of legislation to allow more clothing sewn in Haiti to enter the United States duty free.[17] He finally praised Préval's expropriation of land north of the capital and said people should be moved out quickly before the rains worsened.

Bush faded into the background. I tried talking to him at a few points along the way, but he only shook his head. At the last spot on the itinerary, a workshop to build temporary homes, Clinton stood in a pocket of fresh-smelling wooden panels, gabbing with CNN. Trying to get closer, I almost ran headlong into the other president.

"AP man!" Bush exclaimed, recognizing my press pass. He looked up at my ball cap and thought up one of his signature rhymes. "AP man. AP man—is a Yankee fan."

"I—true," I stammered.

The former Texas Rangers owner smiled, having found a topic for discussion. "Y'all had a pretty good year last year," he observed.

It took me a moment to realize he was referring to the 2009 World Series. Baseball wasn't on my mind much those days. As I tried to form a response, Bush slapped me on the shoulder and walked away. It was the last I saw of him.

ON WEDNESDAY, MARCH 31, representatives of 150 countries and organizations filed into the Trusteeship Council chamber at the UN headquarters in New York carrying pledges for Haiti's reconstruction. The session's four leaders sat at a high ashwood dais. Ban Ki-moon and René Préval, the latter in a wide-lapeled suit the color of charcoal, were in the middle. Each was bracketed by a Clinton. To the far left, in a yellow shawl, Hillary reviewed her notes. On the right, talking, giving thumbs up, and bouncing in his chair was her husband.

The delegates' pledges were supposed to respond to a fifty-five-page proposal titled *Action Plan for National Recovery and Development of Haiti*. In the fashion of preferences for "country-led" development, the document was universally referred to as the Haitian government's official reconstruction plan. But it was widely known that it also had significant "foreign consultation." To my eye, the influence showed. The plan featured more emphasis on private enterprise than I would have expected from Préval the agronomist; he and the country's major business leaders regarded each other with enmity. And while some of the language matched his zeal for decentralization, it included little about implementation. In fact, most of the proposals were so general, it seemed donors would be forgiven for doing whatever they wanted. The section on housing was only about three hundred words and mostly talked in general terms about moving "100,000 inhabitants of Port-au-Prince" to relocation sites, presumably Corail-Cesselesse. If the government or donors had a plan for building new houses, or engineering those in the capital to be storm and earthquake resistant, it was not mentioned.

After an introduction by the secretary-general, Hillary Clinton took the microphone. Some delegates shifted in their seats. European and Latin American officials had grumbled that the United States was dominating the conference, with the Clintons in particular controlling the agenda. This concern was backhanded on the conference's FAQ:

Q: Why are the United States and the United Nations the co-hosts of the Conference?

A: The United States has been the largest donor to Haiti, and the United Nations has a long-established valuable role in Haiti and provides a forum to mobilize a truly global response. It is natural that both would co-host.

(Omitted but implied: "So there.")

In demeanor, Secretary Clinton was the salt to her husband's pepper, urging support for Haiti with an unqualified threat. There were two possible futures for the island republic, she portended. Haiti could become "an engine for progress and prosperity" whose benefits would be felt throughout the hemisphere. "But," she continued, "there is another path that Haiti could take, a path that demands far less of Haiti and far less of us. If the effort to rebuild is slow or insufficient, if it is marked by conflict, lack of coordination, or lack of transparency, then the challenges that have plagued Haiti for years could erupt with regional and global consequences." She gave a hard glare to the crowd that said: Your choice.

But, stern as it was, her speech would have given hope to the most discouraged supporter of direct support for local governments. After lecturing Préval on the need to "take responsibility" for his country's reconstruction and guiding a "strong, accountable, and transparent recovery," the secretary of state turned to the donors:

> And we in the global community, we must also do things differently. It will be tempting to fall back on old habits, to work around the government rather than to work with them as partners, or to fund a scattered array of well-meaning projects rather than making the deeper, long-term investments that Haiti needs now. We cannot retreat to failed strategies. I know we've heard these imperatives before: the need to coordinate our aid, hold ourselves accountable, share our knowledge, track results. But now, we cannot just declare our intentions. We have to follow through and put them into practice.[18]

She then made the day's first pledge: $1.15 billion for Haiti's long-term recovery and reconstruction.

I was struck by her words. The day before, her second in command, Cheryl Mills—who was overseeing the overall U.S. response in Haiti—had said that direct budget support was not going to get past congressional objections. One reason for the apparent shift may have been sitting behind Bill. Paul Farmer, a cofounder of the medical NGO Partners in Health, had been a strong supporter of Haitian governments since Aristide and was now UN Deputy Special Envoy. It was strange that he had joined forces with the former president, whom he'd once lambasted as continuing malign Haiti policies under the guise of reform, but perhaps he was now managing to exert influence.[19] The question was: Would the United States, which, according to Bill Clinton and Farmer's office directed zero-point-zero percent of its emergency relief money to the Haitian government, now change its tune with the $1.15 billion pledge? It wouldn't be easy. To convince Congress, as well as dissenters within its own ranks, the State Department would have to overcome the biggest public concern of all.

CORRUPTION WAS THE DONORS' CONFERENCE'S shadow theme, the toxic undercurrent of its bubbling optimism. The delegates, in their diplomatic politesse, usually referred to the scourge by the antonyms *transparency* and *accountability*, but the meaning was plain: The Haitian government would steal their money if given the chance.

In much of the world's perception, Haiti is a cesspool of corruption. A deep impression was made on many Americans in 1986, when CBS's Ed Bradley presented a *60 Minutes* piece on Jean-Claude "Baby Doc" Duvalier's departure. In its signature moment, an interviewee told Bradley that the dictator's first lady had refrigerated a room at the National Palace to show off furs she purchased with state funds on a multimillion-dollar Paris spree. Twenty-four years later, this was the image in many Americans' minds. Days after the earthquake, the influential aid monitor Charity Navigator warned, "Do Not Give to the Haitian Government: Haiti is known to be a corrupt country." Fox News commentator Christian Whiton identified "the chief culprit of current or past suffering in Haiti: intense corruption." Neither gave direct examples.

There is corruption in Haiti, in both public and private life. Extra money makes paperwork go faster. The broker who sold me my car off-lot wanted a "tip" for having given me a good price. Water delivery trucks wanted extra to show up the day you called. The government's anti-corruption division—yes, there was one—reported that the Haitian public considered the traffic police and customs bureau their most corrupt institutions, with those agencies' most common indulgence the pot-de-vin, or bribe. A staggering 70 percent of government officials told the surveyors that business owners paid bribes to get out of paying taxes.[20] In 2004, the Chamber of Commerce and Industry, a consortium of the business elite, estimated that customs fraud cost the Haitian economy $200 million a year. (It was not clear if they were describing their own practices or accusing competitors.)[21] In return, those businessmen were routinely accused of collusion and intimidation to push out competitors and artificially raise the prices of goods. A 2010 report commissioned by USAID quoted an unnamed "major importer," saying, "If this were the U.S., we would go to jail."[22]

The challenge is knowing what conclusion to draw from all this. Those who accuse Haiti of corruption often use the term in indefensibly broad ways. A diner paying a waiter for a better table, a traffic cop shaking down a driver for $1, importers colluding on prices, and an official routing humanitarian aid into a private account can all be called "corrupt," but finding an instance of one says little about the likelihood of the others. Moreover, practices condemned as corruption in one context are accepted in another. U.S. congressmen routinely sponsor bills that benefit companies that lobby them and then leave office to make millions working as lobbyists or for the companies themselves. After three months as U.S. Relief Coordinator for the Haiti earthquake, Lewis Lucke returned to the private sector, consulting for a partnership of U.S. and Haitian companies on securing reconstruction contracts. The partnership's portfolio included building the "T-shelters" that Lucke, as a U.S. official, had helped convince Préval to endorse. Lucke's promised services as a consultant included "strategic introductions to key stakeholders" and "facilitat[ing] interactions and coordination" with international agencies, including the Haitian government and USAID. While he was on retainer, members of the group landed $20 million in contracts. Lucke denies any conflict of interest.[23] Such dealings are so much a part of Washington culture that few even blink. Those who complain that the revolving door is an example of corruption risk being admonished that they just don't understand.

One difference I've observed between American and Haitian officials is directness. A Haitian bureaucrat might say flat-out that he is asking for a bribe, instead of assuming a favor will eventually be returned. And there's no point in promising a big donation to his upcoming campaign, given the low odds that an election will actually go off on time. But the difference is usually described in terms of pervasiveness. In stories about Haiti, English-language journalists frequently cited Transparency International's annual Corruption Perceptions Index, which in 2009 placed Haiti tied for 168th out of 180 nations. But few realized that Transparency International's rankings don't actually measure corruption. The Berlin-based watchdog has been upfront: "Corruption generally comprises illegal activities, which mainly come to light only through scandals, investigations or prosecutions. It is thus difficult to assess absolute levels of corruption in countries or territories on the basis of hard empirical data."[24]

As the index's name made clear, it instead measured perception, using a compilation of other organizations' surveys. Some surveys reflected a kind of experience, such as one that asked respondents to report how frequently they had observed bribery. Others asked outside experts to estimate how often public officials who broke the law in certain countries were prosecuted. Some researchers have criticized TI's surveys for lumping disparate forms of corruption. (In 2005, a pair of researchers described the CPI's conflation of grand embezzlement with petty bribery as "averaging apples and oranges."[25]) But a bigger problem with surveying perception is that perception isn't scientific at all. In 2009, Harvard researcher Dilyan Donchev and Gergely Ujhelyi of the University of Houston separated survey questions asking for perception from those asking for direct experience. They found using regression analysis that countries which have a Protestant tradition, high economic production, and "British legal origins" tend to have a lower perception of corruption, regardless of actual experience, and thus a better rating on the CPI.[26]

As it happened, 19 of the index's top 20 ranking countries in 2009 were European, a former British colony (including New Zealand, the United States, Canada, and Barbados), or in East Asia. The bottom 20 consisted mainly of African states along with a mix of Middle Eastern and Central Asian nations, plus Venezuela, Myanmar—and Haiti. Were Europeans less corrupt than those from other regions? Or did the experts who conducted the surveys just think so? The answer may come down to perception. Transparency International acknowledges the concern: It promoted its own 1997 survey by saying it was "less biased against developing countries than in previous years."

So, was Haiti too corrupt for direct budget support, whether a check to the treasury or to an individual ministry? The answer wasn't clear. Take the traffic cops and customs bureau. A typical salary for employees of both was less than $400 a month, in a city where surveys said families needed between about $530 and $749 a month get by at anything above abject poverty.[27] The remedy, it would seem, was not to halt financial support for the government, but to increase it, so that government could pay higher salaries and step up training and monitoring. Likewise, responsibility for the practices of the business elite could fall on the state only if the state had the resources to monitor its practices and enforce laws. Refusing to support the Haitian government because businesses found ways to avoid paying it taxes simply punished the country further while making the problem worse. I was reminded of this situation later in 2010, when U.S. Senator Patrick Leahy, the Democratic chairman of the Judiciary Committee, blocked money for justice reform in Haiti until there was a "thorough, credible and transparent investigation" of killings in a prison by Haitian police.[28] In other words, he seemed to be arguing that the United States would not pay for justice reform in Haiti until the Haitian justice system reformed itself.[29]

This confusion helped explain the fiasco that resulted when, in the run-up to the donors' conference, Préval had gone to Washington to plead for direct support from his most important benefactor. At every stop, the president explained the need to build strong, well-funded institutions. At every stop, he was turned down. As the top Republican on the House Foreign Affairs Committee, Ileana Ros-Lehtinen, put it acidly to the *Miami Herald*, "We are a caring and generous nation, but not at the expense of our economic future."[30] The low point of the trip was a visit to the *Washington Post*. In a stinging editorial after a sit-down with Préval, the newspaper wrote, "Unsurprisingly, given Haiti's history of wasted and purloined foreign aid, he is being asked about the perils of corruption and what measures the Haitian govern-ment might devise to minimize misuse and theft of the billions of dollars in recovery assistance flowing into the country and the billions more expected. Surprisingly, he seems utterly unprepared to discuss the matter." The editorial board cited Haiti's Transpar-ency International rating and a quote from an expert that disaster zones were ripe for corruption.

While "no one accuses Mr. Préval of the abuses associated with so many of his predecessors," the editorial continued, "his insis-tence that Haiti's government has nothing to do with corruption since aid money is funneled from international donors to nongov-ernmental organizations rings hollow." The paper judged his visit "a public relations debacle."[31]

Why would a man who had spoken brazenly in the past about corruption in his own National Palace have no response at such a crucial moment? It was a level of obstinacy impressive even for Préval. Yet as Préval looked out at the table of incredulous Ameri-cans, he had to have been thinking: But it's *true*. Ninety-nine-point-one percent of humanitarian funding after the quake had gone to NGOs and the Red Cross movement, contractors, or UN agencies, or had stayed with the foreign governments themselves. As Préval's prime minister, Jean-Max Bellerive, would tell the BBC later that year: "In a lot of instances, we as a government do not receive the money. The money is going through NGOs or the insti-tutions, but we are the ones accused of corruption, for the money that we don't receive."[32]

Préval also might have been thinking about one of the biggest corruption cases unfolding around Haiti at the time. In Decem-ber 2009, the U.S. Department of Justice had charged that Hai-ti's state-run telephone company, Teleco, had taken bribes from U.S. telecom companies in exchange for lower calling rates, a case the members of the *Post* board likely knew about. Five U.S. tele-phone executives would be convicted in the scam, along with at least two Haitian officials. The largest company implicated, though none of its staff was convicted, was U.S. telecom giant IDT, whose CEO James Courter was a longtime congressman and a national finance co-chair for John McCain in his 2008 presidential bid. The FCC fined IDT $1.3 million for failing to properly file its Teleco contract, and Courter resigned from McCain's campaign. IDT had also been a top donor to the campaigns of at least two members of the House Foreign Affairs Committee.[33] The case was often cited as an example of Haiti's systemic rot. It was generally not used to demonstrate that the U.S. telecom industry, Congress, or the whole of the United States was corrupt.

The donors at the conference did not have to make the case that Préval's government would be corrupt. They just squirmed their way around the issue as they announced their pledges. Norway's thirty-two-year-old representative lectured the Haitian president: "The main responsibility for Haiti's future rests with the Haitian people and their leaders. We therefore look forward to working with the Haitian Government—for better governance." She pledged 600 million kroner, roughly $100 million, of which 15 percent was earmarked for a trust fund to be managed in Haiti's stead and the rest left out of official Haitian hands entirely. Some groups pointed to cases that were not examples of corruption per se: Oxfam's pre-donors' conference report referred to "charges at the hospital to get a sterile syringe or cotton ball"—a longstanding, on-the-books policy caused by chronic underfunding that was not even in effect at the time. The Haitian group affiliated with Transparency International pointed to quake survivors reselling donated food—neither illegal nor illogical for people who needed money more than free rice—and, later, others using connections to obtain choice locations for their stalls in open-air markets.

The irony was that, by keeping the money under their own control, the donors reinforced the perception of systemic Haitian corruption. Just like the people in Congresswoman Ros-Lehtinen's district, many—if not most—Haitians were also under the misapprehension that aid money went to the Haitian government. If money were pledged but not delivered, they assumed their leaders had stolen it. And it was a rule of donors' conferences that pledges were not typically delivered.

In April 2009, donors had gathered for another conference—for reconstruction from the hurricanes that had ravaged Haiti months before. Attendees pledged $479 million. But only a third of that amount was delivered. There were lots of reasons for this. Donors were dealing with the economic downturn brought on by turmoil—some would say corruption—in the U.S. financial system. Also, attendees often over-promise and under-deliver. Exuberant pledges get announced by foreign ministries such as the State Department, but they almost always have to be taken back to legislatures less interested in diplomatic heroics than, as Ros-Lehtinen indicated, keeping money close to home. At both donors' conferences—the posthurricane one in 2009 and the postquake one in March 2010—the Obama administration simply drew up what it thought would be a reasonable pledge and announced it, having no guarantee that Congress would deliver.

Additionally, a lot of sleight of hand goes into pledging. One beloved donor tactic is to pledge money already allocated for an existing project. Another is to count debt forgiveness as part of pledged funds. In 2009, Haiti owed $1.9 billion in debt, most of that inherited from the Duvaliers. Haiti could not pay, and donors had already been in the process of forgiving much of the debt when the earthquake struck. At the UN conference, the U.S. pledge of $1.15 billion included $212 million in debt forgiveness, making the actual pledge $940 million. Telling the Haitian government it was now free to use $212 million it didn't have was a creative stroke of accounting, to say the least. Bill Clinton's UN Office of the Special Envoy put that figure aside as it calculated how much money was promised at the donors' conference.

Finally, and most prosaically, once the enthusiasm abates, the donors move on to other things. What seemed vital when a pledge was made often pales beside other priorities months later and promises are forgotten.

But in the ruckus of the street, these nuances get lost. People across the quake zone hear pledges rolling in and expect that money to show up. If it doesn't, it becomes too easy to believe a *vòlè*—a thief—has stolen it. The government tends to be the first accused. And the next time a pollster comes around asking about corruption, you can guess what the answer will be.

PRÉVAL'S GOVERNMENT KNEW THAT NO DONOR would give money unless non-Haitians oversaw it. Many would choose to continue spending money "bilaterally"—controlling it directly, as they had in the past. But the Haitian government agreed to two compromise options, considered innovations from previous methods of aid. Donors could now choose to disburse some of their donations into a World Bank-managed fund that promised to coordinate projects—though donors would still virtually control where the money went by telling the World Bank its preference. In what was billed as the biggest experiment, some of the money in that fund would be managed by a board, empowered by an emergency law to be approved by Haiti's parliament to operate for eighteen months as a surrogate branch of the Haitian government.

But the commission would not be Haitian, exactly. The Action Plan called for a board consisting of eleven Haitians and twelve representatives of the multilateral banks and governments that pledged at least $100 million.[34] This entity, the Interim Haiti Recovery Commission, would be co-chaired by Haitian Prime Minister Jean-Max Bellerive and an "eminent foreign figure involved in the reconstruction" to be named at the conference.

There was only one person to whom those words could refer. As he was introduced, Bill Clinton nodded thoughtfully and accepted the honor.

CHAPTER SEVEN

THE GOVERNOR

THE FIRST PROTESTANT MISSIONARIES ARRIVED IN HAITI WITHIN A FEW
years of independence in 1804, alarmed equally by its twin heri-
tages of African spirit worship and the Roman Catholicism be-
queathed by the French. By the dawn of the nation's third century,
the mission trip became the template for how many Americans
experienced Haiti firsthand, lending a familiar arc to their reports:
First, shock at the deprivation; then uplift by the spirit of the
people; finally, after the construction of a breeze-block school or
a delivery of Bibles, exultation in a new closeness and humanity
through faith. In remote areas, missions operated hospitals, or-
phanages, and schools. Thousands of missionaries went into the
countryside as self-led volunteers. Many emphasized that one of
their primary goals was to teach Haitians self-reliance.

Ironically, the Haitians not only tended to harbor a faith more
fervent and deeply tested than that of the missionaries, but also
self-reliance beyond anything the visitors were likely to imagine.
They were, after all, still alive in a country that spent 180 times
less on healthcare per person than the United States, offered 83
percent fewer people adequate sanitation, and offered almost none
of the basic highway, plumbing, or building infrastructure of the
United States. They didn't need survival techniques, introduction
to the New Testament, or even a new breeze-block school. But as
in many interactions involving the wealthy North and the struggling island, community leaders didn't object, taking what they
could get in the hope that the relationships would eventually yield

more. What distinguished the missionaries from other foreigners was their zeal, and the assuredness that they could bring hope and salvation to a blighted land through faith and good works.

I thought about this sometimes while trailing a certain Southern Baptist–raised Arkansan through Haiti. Bill Clinton's message wasn't exactly the Word of the Lord, but he expressed it with equal fervor. His trumpeting of Haiti's beaches and markets bore echoes of a Sunday sermon. ("Sometimes we focus so much on the problems," he once remarked, "we forget to acknowledge the small miracles."[1]) He also shared the missionaries' conviction that only an outside force could save Haiti, writing in his 2005 memoir, "Haiti will never develop into a stable democracy without more help from the United States." Clinton thumped his own scripture too, especially his axiom that Haiti, before and after the earthquake, had the "best chance in my lifetime" to advance.[2] Clinton was not being blithe—he had studied the country in depth. After decades of tumult, Haiti under Préval was enjoying relative peace and political freedom. It also had a president who, when he'd been elected at least, had been popular with the poor, yet seemed answerable to foreigners.

Clinton also brought an incredible attention to detail. At a hospital in the dried-out flood zone of Gonaïves in 2009, a survivor of a motorcycle accident named Jean Adam showed the ex-president a deep serosanguineous wound and a nearly empty silver tube of sulfadiazine, an antibiotic ointment. After talking to Adam's doctors for all of five minutes, Clinton asked me to join him at the bedside, then motioned toward the man's wound like a doctor on rounds. "His leg was so shredded they couldn't put stitches in." He pointed to a cut-away bandage. "So what they had to do was keep the leg wrapped and it will ooze both blood and fluids. That's why you have the dual color—you see? It's not bright red. But you can't stop either the blood or the fluids as long as it's an open wound. And the sulfadiazine gives it a chance to stay sterile and then congeal. And so he needs to have this medicine. Because otherwise, if he runs out of the medicine, it won't heal, and sooner or later it could get infected. And it would be tragic to have a system pay for an amputation that wouldn't pay for a tube of medicine."

The "system" Clinton was referring to was humanitarian aid. Since the floods of 2008, the hospital had been getting free medicine from an NGO, Pharmacists Without Borders, but the money for the program had run out. The hospital had neither a permanent building nor a reliable budget. Before leaving Adam's side, Clinton pledged to find the antibiotic he needed, then tackle the bigger issue of the hospital's medicine supply. It was a perfect Clinton moment: a high-stakes problem with a human face, which he could help solve by pairing the right donor with the right need.

At first, many couldn't understand why Clinton was so boost-erish. In a story I filed in 2009, an editor cut out Clinton's opti-mism, changed references to his seeking investment to seeking "aid" and inserted a warning about Haiti "sliding back into chaos." But once Clinton's message got through, it was a hit. Journalists were thrilled to have a positive story, and Clinton's heady mix of detailed pragmatism and unflappable optimism made some won-der if he might be Haiti's long-awaited savior himself.

The people Clinton was coming to help were not entirely sure what to make of the commotion. On his first trip back to Haiti in early 2009, hundreds cheered his arrival. Many were Aristide sup-porters who thought Clinton might deliver their man from exile, as he had in 1994. But after Ban Ki-moon officially named Clin-ton his UN Special Envoy for Haiti in June 2009, the enthusiasm cooled. Donors had not come through with promised funds. The hospital where Clinton had fretted over Jean Adam's leg wound still lacked a permanent building and reliable supplies in 2012. People had heard promises before. They wanted change.

It wasn't even clear to most Haitians what a Special Envoy was supposed to do. Haiti already had a president, and the UN peace-keeping mission already had a chief. A wry joke spread that Clin-ton was coming to lead a new colonial regime. The Haitian press dubbed him *Le Gouverneur*.

The business elite's reactions were mixed. Those whose busi-nesses were gutted and bank accounts frozen under his trade em-bargo in the 1990s had no love for the Arkansan. ("The man is a snake," the owner of a string of car dealerships once seethed.) But the savvy noted his talk about boosting foreign investment and recognized an opportunity.

Préval never seemed sure whether Clinton was his ally or com-petition. While publicly amenable to the Special Envoy's proposals, he seemed to undercut the American at every turn. At a 2009 investment fair in Pétionville, Préval sulked while Clinton gushed over the potential for growth through foreign investment. Then the Haitian president took the podium and launched into a low-intensity diatribe about the uselessness of investment in a country that remained a trans-shipment point for South American cocaine. At the hospital in Gonaïves, while doctors and staff climbed over each other to have their pictures taken with the famous American, Préval huffed to a nurse in Kreyòl: "I'm not the president today." Like a community leader confronted with a misguided missionary, Préval kept saying and doing what was needed to keep Clinton coming back. But the lack of results in the first months of their partnership spoke for itself.

"I think Clinton misread the situation in Haiti," recalled Leslie Voltaire, who served as Préval's liaison with Clinton. "He thought the Haitians were easygoing. [But] he saw that the Haitians have circular thoughts. When they say 'yes,' it's not a yes. It's maybe yes. It's not a no."

Still, the Special Envoy persevered. He had a vision and a plan.

CLINTON'S GOSPEL WAS NINETEEN PAGES LONG. It had five sections. And one of the sections was divided into five subsections, and one of those subsections had two sub-subsections.

The report had been authored in 2009 by Paul Collier, a professor of economics at Oxford, former director of the World Bank's Development Research Group, and author of *The Bottom Billion*, an influential book that posits poverty can be alleviated through mutually beneficial trade deals, corruption crackdowns, and occasional military interventions. In 2008, Ban Ki-moon had asked him to serve as his special advisor on Haiti, though Collier primarily studied African countries and had never been to Haiti before. Collier visited the Caribbean nation for five days, then wrote the report: "Haiti: From Natural Catastrophe to Economic Security."[3]

The report's first sections discussed the tropical storms and hurricanes that had struck Haiti in 2008, the ongoing food crisis, and overpopulation. Collier warned that these were shocks that could spread unrest and waste years of aid. "For the maintenance of social order military security must rapidly be superseded by economic security," he wrote. The most important thing was jobs, Collier said. Jobs "give dignity and structure to the lives of young people." Jobs were the key to security and growth.

Collier laid out the types of jobs he foresaw in Section 4, the one with all the sub-sections. First, he advised that some jobs could come from storm reconstruction, such as the rebuilding of washed-out roads. Then he got to the point. Sub-subsection 4.2.2 was four times longer than the one before it. In fact it was longer than any other part of the report, making up a quarter of the text. It was titled "Export Zones," and it began this way: "The global garments industry is huge and the Haitian economy is tiny."

The report went on:

> To an outsider it is striking how modest are the impediments to competitiveness relative to the huge opportunities offered by the fundamentals. The garments industry has the scope to provide *several hundred thousand jobs* to Haitians and to do so over a period of just a few years.

Haiti already had about thirty garment factories, holdovers from the Duvalier era when the dictator and U.S. government sought to turn Haiti into the "Taiwan of the Caribbean." Political turmoil and the 1990s Clinton embargo had all but gutted the industry. But if Haiti could rebuild its garment sector, Collier wrote, the country would enter a "virtuous circle of increasing competitiveness." He noted that the U.S. Congress had expanded a preferential trade law called the Haitian Hemispheric Opportunity through Partnership Encouragement Act, or HOPE II, allowing up to 140 million square meters of knit or woven clothes assembled in Haiti to enter the U.S. market duty free every year until 2018.

Of course, Haiti's laws needed a few tweaks, Collier wrote. Labor regulations restricting night shifts and customs enforcement by the state would have to be loosened. But the outlook was good so long as one key requirement was met: wages remained low. "In garments the largest single component of costs is labour," the professor explained. "Due to its poverty and relatively unregulated labour market, Haiti has labour costs that are fully competitive with China, which is the global benchmark."

When Collier wrote his report, the minimum wage in Haiti was $1.75 a day.

The importance of the Collier Report to those planning Haiti's future could not be overstated. It was the blueprint and the word Bill Clinton spread as Special Envoy. At his first press conference as Special Envoy in June 2009, the former president told reporters that he had asked Préval's then-prime minister, Michèle Pierre-Louis, to respond to the Collier Report with a plan of her government's own. That plan placed slightly less emphasis on garments and more on construction and agriculture, but overall it was a close copy and a sign that the Haitians were ready to go along.

The garment industry's chief benefit is that it scales up quickly, anywhere. You don't need a lot of equipment or training. But this modularity is also the problem. It's too easy for the factory owners to pick up and go wherever wages are cheaper. Haiti's $1.75 minimum wage—which Collier called a "propitious" fundamental of the strategy—put a worker squarely between the World Bank's definitions of moderate poverty (living on $2 a day) and extreme poverty ($1.25). "As manufacturing skills advance and the value-added of products produced increases, wages also rise," the consulting firm Nathan Associates, which studies the sector, has found.[4] The consultants saw this as a bad thing: the garment industry would employ Haitians until their increasing ability to produce caused wages to rise, at which point the garment factories would move elsewhere. And what would that leave the Haitians? Collier did not consider this in his report.

The U.S. Congressional Research Service noted pressure from Haitian workers and lawmakers to increase wages as a "key challenge to Haitian apparel competitiveness."[5] In his report, Collier had pointed to the success story of Bangladesh, where, according to the New York Times, the apparel industry would soon employ 3.6 million people. But in 2010, when the government in Dhaka raised the minimum wage from 78 cents a day to $1.41, many factory owners refused to pay.[6] Workers rioted. At least four people were killed and dozens arrested; in 2012, a protest organizer was found murdered by the side of a road.[7]

Defenders of low garment-factory wages say their hands are tied: For a "Captain America Infant Toddler Boys Short-Sleeve

Tee" to sell for $8 at Target—and, they might add, for importers and factory owners to enjoy generous margins—garment-worker wages must remain at poverty levels.[8] The U.S. National Retail Federation and National Council of Textile Organizations, whose members include Gap Inc. and Hanesbrands Inc., and supply Target and other major retailers, lobbied for the passage of a 2010 law that made it even easier for Haitian garment exports to enter the United States. If workers complain, the owners can move shop to where others will work for less. And there is always somewhere.

For Collier, the Clintons, and Ban Ki-moon, "getting a job" meant becoming part of what they saw as the productive global economy. In agriculture, their attention centered on export initiatives such as the development of mango groves to supply North America and Europe, where consumers could look forward to cheap, delicious fruit, and perhaps the feeling of having helped an impoverished farmer. But the implications for Haiti were mixed. By producing mainly for foreign markets, farmers would by necessity focus away from the real problem with agriculture in Haiti—not producing enough food to feed Haitians—and, worse, would live and die at the whim of foreign consumers.

The one thing most observers could agree on was that even imperfect, unsustainable jobs were better than nothing. Haiti's prequake unemployment rate was pegged between 40 and 70 percent. In a 2009 piece mostly supportive of the garment factory push (headlined, "In Haiti, a Low-Wage Job Is Better Than None"), a visiting NPR reporter described a street scene in Port-au-Prince:

> Life without a job is an all-day, everyday scramble to turn something—anything—into money or barter. Men and boys dodge the crawling traffic, wiping down moving cars in the hope of making a few coins. People line the streets to hawk mangos and fried plantains, plastic water bottles refilled with juice, phone cards, hand-me-down baby clothes—anything that can be sold or traded with people as poor as themselves.[9]

But if the reporter had dug deeper, he might have come to feel that this was a strange way of assessing that scene. He emphasized chaos—dodging, scrambling, hawking, hoping—but sales of juice, fruit, clothing, phone cards, baby clothes, and even car washes aren't random acts. Most of the people he saw did this every day and were the ends of long supply chains. They depended on importers, middlemen, remittances from relatives, and credit from loan sharks. A typical juice seller might wake up early, negotiate a price with a supplier (who obtained stock from a distributor in the Dominican Republic), refrigerate his inventory with ice, and start looking for customers. In fact, if you put a uniform on him and stuck his juice box inside a building with a sign, you could even call what he was doing a "job." In Kreyòl, this type of work was generally known as *cherche lavi*—"seeking life" or "making a living." Economists call it the informal sector. And nearly everyone in Haiti, even people with what Paul Collier would call a job, participated in it. It wasn't jobs that Haiti lacked; it was stable, sustainable incomes—something the garment plan would do little to provide.

This disconnect had been noted as far back as the 1970s and 1980s, when a University of Texas at Dallas professor of political economy named Simon Fass carried out an in-depth study of Haitian employment. Fass spent years living in Port-au-Prince getting to know dozens of families and several more years analyzing his data. He found that despite official unemployment statistics higher than 70 percent, just about everyone was working. By changing his employment criteria from holding a formal job to "people making a living providing a good or service" and accounting for those who were sick or raising newborn children, the unemployment figure in his estimate dropped to between 4 and 20 percent. Unemployment "held no obvious meaning for workers who by force of circumstance had to work all the time and who had to be productive all the time," he wrote. "*A more pertinent issue was earnings*" [emphasis mine].[10]

My experience was similar. What most Haitians meant when they talked about a job was reliable and sufficient income, and— daring to dream—the security that if they got sick and couldn't function for a while, they could at least someday come back to work. Yet the garment industry provided little or none of that. In a 2011 survey of twenty-seven Haitian garment factories by the International Labor Organization, not one was in compliance in the categories of Social Security and Other Benefits, Employment

Contracts, Welfare Facilities, Safety and Health, Health Services and First Aid, Regular Hours, or Overtime. More than half did not provide hand-washing facilities or soap. Only eight had clearly marked emergency exits and escape routes. Nine kept the exits locked. The majority paid workers less than the law required. When Collier praised Haiti's "unregulated" labor market, he may have been referring to the fact that just one garment factory that submitted to the ILO check had an operating union.

After the earthquake, I visited a cavernous warehouse housing a factory owned by South Korea's DKDR, where hundreds of workers made suits for Jos. A. Bank. A stylish young woman named Jordanie Pinquie Rebeca, who sewed the sleeves on suit jackets, told me that her day's pay allowed for a cupful of rice, transport to and from work, with a little extra to help her quake-injured boyfriend and her son, whom she'd sent to live with relatives in the countryside. She was sleeping on the street while occasionally paying down the loan she had taken out for rent on her destroyed house. The suit she worked on would later sell for $500 in the Jos. A. Bank catalog with a label that said "imported." When you sat down and looked at it, her job was not that different from the "everyday scramble" the NPR reporter had witnessed. Working at the factory was another form of cherche lavi.[11]

When Fass considered why other statisticians saw unemployment differently, he posited that their metrics reflected disdainful attitudes toward the poor and the interests of particular NGOs and agencies. The New York University economist William Easterly has proposed that there are two major camps of development theorists: Planners and Searchers. "A Planner thinks he already knows the answers," Easterly wrote in his book *The White Man's Burden*. "A Searcher admits he doesn't know the answers in advance; he believes that poverty is a complicated tangle of political, social, historical, institutional and technological factors." To a Planner like Collier, garment factories made for a natural solution, with the side benefit of being good for business in the United States. A searcher might have wondered how jobs that pay too little to save money, offer no security, and only in rare cases present a chance for training or advancement would be different from selling juice on the street, much less lead to an economic boom.

This split ran through the Haitian government as well: The Collier Report incensed parliamentarians, whose jobs depended on support from poor constituents, just as the U.S. Congress' entrenched nationalism often put the brakes on State Department diplomacy. Soon after Clinton's appointment as Special Envoy, Haitian lawmaker Steven Benoit introduced a measure to raise the minimum wage from $1.79 a day to $5. Benoit noted that his proposed wage—62 cents an hour, assuming an eight-hour day—was not luxurious, but he also knew it went further than factory owners wanted. But if employers didn't want to pay, he said, they shouldn't be allowed to do business in Haiti. The measure sailed through both chambers. Then Préval, strangely, tabled it. Protesters took to the streets, and for weeks in May and June 2009, parts of the capital were awash in rocks, tear gas, and rubber bullets.

"Everybody wants to raise wages," Clinton told me later that year, "but the way it has to be evaluated is what the impact on employment will be."[12] The businessmen who owned the garment factories warned the wage increase would devastate their sector. As two thousand people raged in front of parliament, ripping down the flags of UN member nations that flew over an adjacent plaza, parliament passed the increase again.

Préval was stuck. The last time garment factories were prescribed as Haiti's saving grace, under Baby Doc, it did little to help the economy and arguably contributed to its decline, the factories' legacy a workers' village that became the slum of Cité Soleil. But it turned out the president was under pressure. The U.S. ambassador had just advised the State Department to seek "a more visible and active engagement by Préval" on the wage issue to prevent the political environment from "spiraling out of control."[13] So in an extraconstitutional act that passed without reproach from the State Department or United Nations, Préval simply rewrote the bill and sent it back to parliament to consider a third time. The unilateral compromise would raise wages for most workers, such as gas station attendants, to $5, but "outsourced" workers—garment stitchers—would get just $3 a day. The full increase for all workers would be postponed for three years, when Préval would be safely out of office.

The protesters begrudgingly accepted the compromise. Benoit became a hero (and won a Senate seat in a landslide in the next election). In the end, most owners just found other ways to cut costs. The South Korean firm running Jordanie Pinquie Rebeca's factory slashed production-based incentives: Where producing six hundred pieces a day once yielded a bonus of $2.47, it now garnered $1.23.

Shortly after raising the minimum wage, the Haitian Senate threw Michèle Pierre-Louis out of the prime minister's office, in part alleging she had turned control of the economy over to foreigners.[14] On November 11, 2009, Préval replaced her with his minister of planning and external cooperation, a Swiss-educated technocrat named Jean-Max Bellerive, who pledged to back the Collier Report.[15] The quake struck six weeks later.

As the earthquake response moved from relief to reconstruction, the Collier Report returned to the headlines as the linchpin of the long-term plan. Some journalists thought the strategy was new. Some activists thought the international leaders were cynically taking advantage of a desperate situation. But I think the Clintons, Ban Ki-moon, and Paul Collier were sincere. They believed that putting Haitians to work for foreign corporations was the best way to grow a moribund economy. Even if it meant paying people too little to feed their families for a while, they had faith that eventually this would be the path from poverty. As the earthquake would for most missionaries, it only confirmed to them how right they'd been all along.

THE MOOD WAS DOUR IN THE TRUSTEESHIP COUNCIL on March 31, 2010, as Ban Ki-moon introduced the Special Envoy, weighed down by Hillary Clinton's warnings of unrest and disease if the donors failed. Elegant in a suit lined with thin pinstripes, Bill Clinton tried to lighten things up. He made the shortcomings of the 2009 conference into a joke at his expense, telling the delegates that his job as Special Envoy had been to "harass all the donors to see that they honored their commitments" but that "I was a failure at that." Silence. Then he turned to a favorite line: When it came to U.S. relations with Venezuela and Cuba, Haiti was "the only thing we all agree on." Finally, a few diplomats chuckled.

Clinton was the emcee for this portion of the proceedings, moderating and responding to a slate of speakers invited by the conference organizers. The first up was Michèle Montas, a former Haitian journalist who until a few months before had been the spokeswoman for Ban Ki-moon. Montas would present the results of focus groups in Haiti, in which 1,750 people from the urban and rural poor had given advice to donors. In English, the project was called a Voice for the Voiceless, but in Kreyòl, it was Youn Vwa Pou Pèp La—A Voice for the People. Initially the focus group results were not going to be presented at the conference, but Paul Farmer had managed to persuade the organizers to carve out seven minutes. Presented secondhand, they were the only views of regular Haitians heard that day.[16]

The testimonials were striking. Nearly all the focus groups shared an overriding desire: that the nation as a whole benefit from reconstruction and that this reconstruction reinforce self-sufficiency and sovereignty. One participant said, "We saw the National Palace destroyed. I would like to see Haitian engineers rebuild it, not foreign engineers, so we can look proudly in the future and say that Haitians built the National Palace." Said another, "For us to be adults, we must be able to feed ourselves. If they really want to help us, they need to invest in agriculture." Many hoped reconstruction would break down divisions in society: "The children of the rich go to school and develop a profession. The children of the poor sometimes get to go to school but never go to college." The participants expressed deep skepticism about the ability of their current government, but their proposed remedy was to train civil servants and improve state infrastructure, not hand reconstruction to an outside body. The interviewees, especially women and young people, wanted to participate directly, stressing "their desire to be consulted in setting priorities, selecting projects, and assessing tangible and measurable outcomes."

"There is hope," Montas noted, "for profound change."

Clinton said that he was "delighted that the citizenry of Haiti want Haiti to be self-sufficient in food," but didn't ponder the comments in more detail. There were no proposals discussed at the conference for the direct participation of ordinary Haitians.

Bill Clinton talks to the author about Haiti's prequake healthcare crisis at a hospital in Gonaïves. July 7, 2009 (photo by Marco Dormino/MINUSTAH)

Evens Sanon, AP "fixer" extraordinaire, at a postquake camp built on a golf course in Pétionville. Clinton talks to an aid worker from Sean Penn's NGO in the background. October 6, 2010 (author's photo)

In a rare photo from the night of the earthquake, a young woman stares into the wreckage of a six-story apartment building where her entire family is trapped. January 12, 2010 (author's photo)

Haitian President René Préval looks into the camera while Evens lights his cigarette. February 10, 2010 (photo by Javier Galeano/AP)

Workers sew Jos. A. Bank suits inside a Port-au-Prince garment factory, for export to the United States, one month after the earthquake. February 19, 2010 (author's photo)

The earthquake-shattered main room at AP House in Pétionville. Author's desk is in the foreground right. Evens' desk is under the rubble. March 23, 2010 (author's photo)

A United Nations soldier from Brazil and a Haitian boy keep an eye on the Champ de Mars. April 8, 2010 (author's photo)

Days after his stunning return after a twenty-five-year exile, former Haitian dictator Jean-Claude "Baby Doc" Duvalier is escorted out of the Karibe Hotel for a hearing with a judge. January 18, 2011 (author's photo)

Carnival singer turned presidential candidate Michel "Sweet Micky" Martelly grinds for the crowd at a campaign rally in Croix-des-Bouquets. September 11, 2010 (author's photo)

A Vodou pilgrim is blessed with a plume of rum during a ceremony at the annual pilgrimage to the Saut d'Eau waterfall. July 16, 2010 (photo by Claire Payton)

Claire Payton and colleague Stanley Michaud (brother of Valerie Michaud) introduce themselves to an earthquake survivor at a cholera clinic in Cité Soleil slum, recording oral histories for the Haiti Memory Project. November 10, 2010 (author's photo)

United Nations military police clandestinely take groundwater samples at the rural UN base suspected of causing the deadliest cholera epidemic in recent history. At the time, back in Port-au-Prince, UN officials were publicly discounting all suspicion that the base was the source of the bacteria. October 27, 2010 (author's photo)

Residents of Camp Trazelie, Port-au-Prince, Haiti. Summer 2010 (photo by Kervins Cimeus)

Thousands of protesters flood the Port-au-Prince street Route de Delmas demanding the reinstatement of Michel "Sweet Micky" Martelly in the presidential race, two days after he is eliminated by the Provisional Electoral Council. December 9, 2010 (photo by Claire Payton)

Street art, depicting the cholera epidemic's devastating toll, by Haitian artist Jerry Rosembert. December 17, 2010 (author's photo)

A young woman sits beside a flatted building on Port-au-Prince's Route de Delmas more than eight months after the earthquake. The ruins are decked with political graffiti and posters for the upcoming presidential election. September 30, 2010 (author's photo)

"Now I'd like to call on the representatives of the diaspora," the former president continued. "I'd ask you to keep your presentations to four or five minutes so we can stay on time here."

Squeezed into this restriction was the day's most passionate speech. Marie St. Fleur, a Haitian-American member of the Massachusetts statehouse, echoed the call for all levels of Haitian society to be included in decisions on rebuilding. She demanded that NGOs define and be held accountable for results or lack thereof; that the aid groups "support and not supplant the role of the state." She added, "Haiti's sovereignty is best protected when we invest in building the capacity of the state to take care of its people."

St. Fleur's speech was built around the phrase "building Haiti differently." I don't know if she intended it, but I heard a subtle tweak of Bill Clinton's slogan, "Build Back Better." Clinton's goal was noble. It wasn't enough to merely re-create a country with a prequake life expectancy 11 to 17 years shorter than its neighbors in Cuba, Jamaica, and the Dominican Republic.[17] But like Easterly's Searchers, St. Fleur wasn't convinced that any plan hatched at a donors' conference would necessarily make things *better*. After decades of failed policies imposed from without, it was just time to do things *differently*: strengthen the Haitian state and, working with its entire people, from peasants to businessmen, find new solutions.

Bill Clinton praised St. Fleur's oratory but, again, did not elaborate on the remarks. He seemed focused on the next group of presenters, whom he brought forward somewhat more enthusiastically: "I want to introduce, now, representatives of the private sector, and I thank them very much for the enormous amount of time they have given to me and to our staff in working together. Reginald Boulos and Brad Horwitz . . . are the representatives."

IN HAITI, "BOULOS" WAS SYNONYMOUS WITH "RICH." Haitians uttered it the way Americans said "Rockefeller" or "Trump." Like many of Haiti's most powerful families, the Bouloses had hailed generations before from what is now Lebanon, a wave of mainly French-speaking Christians who fled the disintegration of the Ottoman Empire. The Boulos clan owned Haiti's largest supermarket chain, the second-largest car dealership, the newspaper *Le Matin*, and a prominent radio station. "Reggie," a former physician who spoke fluent English, had long been a favorite source of counsel for the U.S. Embassy. He was equally reviled by Aristide's supporters in Haiti's slums, for having been a prominent member of the coalition that demanded the populist's departure in 2004.

After the earthquake, Boulos had been a vocal proponent that rebuilding should begin with the private sector—always careful to point out that it included millions of informal entrepreneurs, though presumably investment would start at the top. "This is what the earthquake is today—an opportunity, a huge opportunity," Boulos had told the *Washington Post* a month after the quake. "I think we need to give the message that we are open for business. This is really a land of opportunities."[18] His role at the conference was to present this vision, and the donors would have been wise to listen. If the Collier Report was the philosophy, Boulos' speech was the process by which it would be implemented.

Stout in a blue suit, peering at the donors through gold-rimmed glasses, the bald magnate laid out the need for "economic growth poles" anchored by garment factories producing for export to the United States in the north and south of the country, as well as outside Port-au-Prince. He called on donors to finance roads, power plants, and improved ports and airports servicing the industrial parks—infrastructure that would also be used by a renewed tourism industry and large-scale agriculture. Inverting the call for involvement by the masses, Boulos envisioned "a responsible elite laying out and implementing a vision of development that benefits all Haitians."

Clinton gave a thumbs up to the next speaker: Brad Horwitz, a U.S. telecom executive. It might have seemed strange to have an American speaking on behalf of the Haitian private sector, but Horwitz's Trilogy International Partners, headquartered outside Seattle, owned Voilà, the second-largest cell phone network in the country, known for ubiquitous lime-green billboards featuring its spokesman, the Haitian-American rap star Wyclef Jean, mugging for the camera.

At the time, Trilogy was in the midst of its biggest lobbying campaign on record, spending $15,000 a quarter to encourage the State and Commerce departments to support its Haiti operations.

I'd seen an example of such public-private cooperation the night before, when I ran into President Clinton with a group of Coca-Cola Company representatives in the hallway of the UN Secretariat. They had just finalized a deal to source mangos from 25,000 Haitian farmers: USAID agreed to supply $1 million, the Inter-American Development Bank $3 million, and the Coca-Cola Company $3.5 million in start-up costs. Profits from the resulting "Odwalla Haiti Hope Mango Lime-Aid" would be sunk back into a mango-growing partnership that also included the Clinton-Bush Haiti Fund. But while the program would benefit mango exporters—if the drink proved popular—it would only increase production of one of the few crops Haiti already had too much of, doing little to augment the domestic food supply. And it wasn't always small farmers who would benefit—much of Haiti's mango production was on land owned by its most powerful families. It wasn't clear what kind of public-private partnership his company's lobbying had in mind. But Horwitz appeared to have yielded symbolic results. A month before the earthquake, the State Department presented Trilogy with the State Department's award for corporate excellence.[19]

At the donors' conference, it fell to the American to present the business critique of Haiti's government. The private sector, he explained, wanted tax breaks, a cut of aid, and for the government to privatize state-run infrastructure. At the climax of his speech, the long-haired businessman turned to Préval and repeated what was becoming a slogan: "We need Haiti open for business."

The blank expression on Préval's face gave no sign that his foot-dragging and skepticism over foreign investment were lifting. If the conferees wanted a Haiti that was "open for business," they probably would need a new government too.

THE DIVIDE BETWEEN THE PÈP LA (OR "VOICELESS") and diaspora presentations and those of the businessmen reflected one of the thorniest issues underlying reconstruction: sovereignty. Who was going to run Haiti's rebuilding, and who was going to run the rebuilt Haiti? Would it be Haitians and, if so, which ones?

This was no small issue. Young men in twenty-first-century Port-au-Prince talk about eighteenth-century revolutionary heroes the way Illinois high schoolers debate NBA superstars. This sense of self, however, is under regular assault. Since the UN peacekeeping operation, MINUSTAH, arrived in 2004, Haiti has been overrun with foreign troops seemingly able to act at will. Its capital's hills house foreigners of unimaginable wealth, and its elite carries foreign passports and sends its children abroad for school.

That the Haitian government was weak, and had been weakened further by the earthquake, was not in dispute. So some in the quake zone were open to foreign control over at least the near-term recovery. Others were bitterly opposed. The debate raged on the backs of taptaps, the radio, and at sessions of a soon-to-be-disbanded Parliament. An Oxfam poll taken in early March 2010 showed a fairly even split among Haitians, with some 31 percent supporting Haitian government control, especially in concert with local authorities and civil society, and 39 percent favoring foreign oversight. Twenty-one percent said they hadn't made up their minds, more than enough to swing the decision either way.[20]

But the debate never got a hearing. The matter was not put to a vote in Haiti, and donors had finalized their pledges long before Michèle Montas and Marie St. Fleur spoke. That Haiti was coming to foreign governments for money, the implicit argument seemed to go, gave those governments the right to dictate terms. "Prickly assertions of sovereignty are an inadequate response to legitimate concerns," Paul Collier would write in 2011, arguing that only an entity independent of the Haitian government could be entrusted with reconstruction.[21]

That entity was the Interim Haiti Recovery Commission, the voting body co-chaired by Bill Clinton and Haitian Prime Minister Jean-Max Bellerive that would vote on allocating some of the reconstruction money. Collier viewed this as a happy medium between Haitian leaders he called "venal" and NGOs he saw as eager to protect "unaccountable power." The Oxford professor called the IHRC a "potentially far-reaching innovation . . . that could serve as the prototype for aid in fragile states."[22]

In fact, the IHRC was based on another entity, formed five years before, in Indonesia after the December 2004 tsunami. As in Haiti, the international community had pledged billions of dollars of support and sent critical, life-saving aid. In the province of Aceh, arguably the worst-hit area, NGOs were criticized for stymieing the relief effort by refusing to work with local officials or one an-other.[23] But donors refused to fund the government directly, citing concerns about corruption.

To break the impasse, the Indonesian government set up the Aceh Rehabilitation and Reconstruction Agency, or Badan Reha-bilitasi dan Rekonstruksi (BRR).[24] The government gave the BRR a four-year mandate to oversee reconstruction in Aceh and selected Kuntoro Mangkusubroto, a respected professor and former gov-ernment official, as chairman. To convince donors it was safe to give money, the new agency set up transparency mechanisms such as an online financial tracking system.[25]

The measures worked. "International agencies will not coor-dinate effectively among themselves, either because they are not equipped to do so or because they view other agencies as competi-tors for favored projects, labor, or supplies," the BRR explained in a 2009 document advising other countries how to deal with di-sasters. "However, international agencies will take direction from a sovereign government or a coordinating agency officially sanc-tioned by it."[26] By the time its mandate had concluded, the agency estimated it had built more houses than had been destroyed by the waves, laid more miles of road than had been lost, trained thou-sands more teachers than had been killed, and reclaimed nearly all the farmland that had been damaged. "Despite the presence of nearly 500 participating actors on the ground, results were achieved in a remarkably short time," said the Brookings Institu-tion.[27] The *Jakarta Post* was more succinct. It called Kuntoro "the hand of God."[28]

At the time, Bill Clinton was the UN Special Envoy for Tsu-nami Relief, tasked with raising money, developing partnerships between the public and the private sector, and guiding the general reconstruction under the slogan "Build Back Better." Witnessing Kuntoro's success, Clinton praised the BRR as a model that should be employed from New Orleans to postquake Pakistan.[29] It was not surprising that, five years later, he wanted a BRR-type agency to coordinate reconstruction in Haiti. But Washington, its allies, and even Haitian officials such as Prime Minister Bellerive did not con-sider Haiti ready to manage its own reconstruction. So instead of jumping straight into a Haitian-led version of the BRR, the major donors pushed for a joint commission between Haitians and for-eigners, with Clinton and Bellerive dividing the responsibilities of chairman.

Haiti had advantages over Aceh. It was less than half the size of the Indonesian province and far more peaceful: When the tsu-nami struck, Aceh was in the midst of a three-decades-long civil war between Muslim separatists and the government. But the dis-advantages were starker. The BRR was a branch of a strong central government that appointed its members and could fund the com-mission's work—a manifestly Indonesian institution focused on a national affair. The IHRC was associated with, well, the Haitian government. Non-Haitians would maintain parity, if not a major-ity, at its meetings. And where the Indonesian commission had been granted four years to carry out its work, the IHRC would have just 18 months.

In Indonesia, three major figures had played important roles: Kuntoro, as head of the BRR; Eric Morris, a specially appointed UN liaison; and Bill Clinton, the UN Special Envoy for Tsunami Relief. While Prime Minister Bellerive would hold a title equal to Clinton's on the IHRC, there was no mistaking who held clout. In other words, in addition to running the Clinton Foundation and the Clinton-Bush Haiti Fund, along with a political and speaking schedule that took him all over the world, Clinton would be play-ing the roles of Kuntoro, Morris, and himself—ensuring pledges were delivered, deciding how they would be spent, and lobbying for more. Something was bound to get lost in the shuffle.

AT THE END OF THE DONORS' CONFERENCE, journalists were invited into the chamber to hear closing remarks and ask questions. Ban Ki-moon met the moment with high drama: "Today, the interna-tional community has come together dramatically in solidarity with Haiti and its people. President Préval's 'rendezvous with his-tory' has come to pass. By their actions this day, the friends of Haiti have acted far beyond the expectation."

The official totals were indeed impressive. Ultimately, after all the commitments were tallied and debt relief was excluded, fifty-five nations and organizations had pledged $8.4 billion over ten years.[30] For 2010 and 2011 alone, $4.6 billion was pledged—more than the Action Plan had requested for the period, although the overall total was just shy of the full decade-long request. The United States came in with the largest one-year pledge; its $940 million was to be delivered by the end of the fiscal year in September. Venezuela offered the largest total pledge with $1.16 billion in new funds, parceled out over the coming decade.[31] The European Community, International Monetary Fund, and Canada were also leading pledgers. Some unexpected sources joined in: Nigeria came through with a $5 million pledge; Thailand, $2.5 million. Benin, ancestral home of many of the sacred rites of Vodou, pledged $300,000. Montenegro offered $10,000.

When the floor was opened for questions, a reporter for the Spanish agency EFE asked how the money pledged would be guarded against corruption. Ban Ki-moon assured him without specifics that the Haitian government would be accountable to its people. A follow-up later turned this exchange on its head: How would the secretary-general, the correspondent for Haiti's Scoop FM wanted to know, ensure that the *donors* would deliver their pledges on time? He was assured in equally broad terms that Bill Clinton's Office of the Special Envoy would make sure the donors remained engaged.

But the key moment came during the second question, from Andrew Quinn of Reuters. He tried a classic press conference gambit, asking as many questions as possible before someone made him stop. His first was: Had the Haitian government's request for $350 million in direct budget support been met? But before anyone could answer, he pivoted to Hillary Clinton and asked a second question, about the negotiations over Iran's nuclear program. Quinn, his colleagues now openly laughing, then turned and posed a third question, again about Iran, to Brazilian foreign minister Celso Amorim.

With mild annoyance in her voice, Clinton read some boilerplate about commitments to Haiti, avoiding the question on budget support, which would not be answered that day. Then she turned to the nuclear negotiations with Iran. Then Celso Amorim took the mic to discuss the nuclear issue. Clinton jumped in to respond. Then French foreign minister Bernard Kouchner, unbidden, started to argue about Iran as well.

As this was going on, René Préval turned his head back and forth, watching as the assembled ministers talked about things more important than his wrecked country. If ever he needed a reminder of where his people ranked on the scale of world affairs, even at what was supposed to be its day of solidarity at the United Nations, here it was. Finally he coughed and leaned toward the microphone. "Do I need to develop a nuclear program for Haiti so that we come back to talking about Haiti?" the Haitian president asked.

The argument skidded to a halt. Everyone on the dais started laughing, and then everyone in the room. Préval laughed too.

APRIL FELL LIKE A HANGOVER. Ears tickled across town with rumors of the riches promised in New York, which through games of broken telephone crystallized into the reasonably accurate figure of *six milliards de dollars*. But all this sounded like a far-off dream. For now there was smaller money to hustle, food to find, and looming rain clouds. When a tanker carrying fuel from Venezuela was delayed in Antigua for two days, Haiti found itself in a full-blown gas shortage, with fights at the pumps, and Evens driving off like a madman at word that a gas station across town had opened.

Now out of my tent and under a roof at the Hotel Ritz, I soon had a breakthrough in my living situation: a house for a reasonable enough price, off a hillside in Pétionville, which we nicknamed "the narcopalace" for its Scarface-like decorating style. AP sprang for a seismic inspection; the engineer, from Japan, glanced at a column and said, thoughtfully, "Well, I'd let my wife live here. Not my kids." My mood was not helped when, in one of his stranger moments, President Préval set off a panic by warning without scientific cause that another major earthquake was imminent.

Soon after there was an equally shocking announcement: After two months of delays, the first relocation of displaced people to safer ground was about to begin. The first group would come from the Pétionville Club golf course, just as Ban Ki-moon and Sean Penn had said they should.

CHAPTER EIGHT

"WHEN I GET OLDER"

TWENTY CHERYS'S RAP CREW WAS CALLED I. L. CLICK—AS IN *CLIQUE,* the generic name for rap groups that seemed to crop up on every Port-au-Prince block. *Hip Hop Kreyòl* was the music of the earthquake generation, the heartbeat of an increasingly urban and very young country, where high birth rates and low life expectancy meant 70 percent of the population was under 30. Music has always occupied a central role in Haiti, in the drum-pounding spirit-calls of Vodou ceremonies, and the soulful lyrics of the guitar *troubadours;* in times of repression, protest music was often the only way for people to speak out against untouchable regimes. Haitian hip-hop and rap drew inspiration from them all, though the clearest influence came from up north, in the styles of Dr. Dre, Jay-Z, 50 Cent, and the Haitian hero Wyclef Jean.

Many Haitian cliques specialized in homages to gangsta life laced with references to imported rice and the UN Stabilization Mission in Haiti, MINUSTAH. But that wasn't Twenty's style. Whenever he could gather some crumpled wads of cash, Twenty fixed his braids and met his crew at a little concrete studio where he laid down tracks about parties, girls, and the way the world should be. "Every stroke of the pen is what allows me to remain positive," Twenty would say. "Even if my music is saying 'Wow! Fuck these things! The system's no good!' It's like: I'm going to change it."

After the quake, the young guys in I. L. Click didn't have much of an appetite for rapping about current events—politics was too depressing, and in the camps there was little to do except worry, play soccer, and drink. But sometimes Twenty would sing a verse he'd written before the quake about President Préval, the jokers in parliament, and the people who really ran the country. It was called "I Think It's Time," and the first verses were sung to a tune that looped like a music-box waltz:

N te vote w atan
n pat panse wonte n t ap pran
kounyeya li lè li tan
Ayisyen pou n gade devan
Yon peyi k ap fè back nèg yo menm se plezi y ap pran
Si tout bon n se granmoun an nou sispann mache sou lòd blan

There was a time we voted for you
We didn't think we would be embarrassing ourselves
Now it's about time
Haitians, for us to look forward
A country going backward, and these guys [politicians] are living the
    high life
If we're truly grown-ups, let's stop marching under orders of the
    blan

IT'S NOT THAT POLITICIANS IN HAITI are more venal, petty, or brutal than elsewhere; it's just that, too often, that's all there is to them. While impoverished people struggle and starve, officials abuse their scraps of power to grind governance to a halt. The 1987 constitution, in an effort to prevent Duvalier-style dictatorship, had granted parliament the power to fire the prime minister and cabinet with a simple majority vote in either house. Presidents reserved the right to approve all nine members of the Provisional Electoral Council, known by its French initials CEP, which set up the elections that legislators needed to renew their terms.[1] Predictably, with no funding to do much else, the executive and legislative branches have used these cudgels with impunity. From 2007 to 2009, parliament twice fired Préval's prime ministers and cabinets. The CEP then postponed elections, with parliament emptying as lawmakers' terms expired. It's no wonder that the only consistent power in the nation, as young men like Twenty saw it, was in the hands of blue-helmeted UN soldiers and foreign diplomats in fancy cars—the country marching sou lòd blan.

Haiti had been bracing for two elections in 2010—a legislative race in February and a presidential contest set for November—and everyone had been expecting trouble. All through 2009, the political opposition had been threatening to disrupt the elections, accusing Préval of trying to fix the vote. In some ways, he was. Haiti had gone through seventeen transfers of power in the twenty-three years since Jean-Claude Duvalier's flight, many of those coups d'état. As Préval told me repeatedly, one of his main goals in office was to create lasting political stability and end the gridlock between the executive branch and parliament.

Unlike many past Haitian leaders, Préval's idea of stability wasn't to stay in power forever. He was barred by the constitution from running again in the fall, and, reportedly, he was happy about it; at 67, he was eager to retire with his new bride, a glamorous and sharp-witted former economic advisor 19 years his junior. But Préval was also reportedly bent on ensuring a successor who would not follow the Haitian tradition of arresting or expelling his predecessor. Préval's father, a minister of agriculture, had been forced to flee to the Belgian Congo after the 1957 election of Jean-Claude's father, François Duvalier. Préval's own previous transition from power, in 2000, was smooth because he handed power to a then-ally, Jean-Bertrand Aristide. Préval decided that the way to ensure both a smooth, exile-free retirement and political stability in the country would be to found a new political party, the most powerful in Haiti—a political machine.

Though never substantively accused of raiding state coffers or political repression, Préval wasn't above suspicion of electoral chicanery. After the first round of his 2006 election, the agronomist had the most votes but was short of the first-round majority that would have declared him an outright winner. Supporters of Aristide, who hoped the candidate would bring back the ex-president from exile, set barricades blazing across the capital, and clashed with UN peacekeepers until Préval was declared the winner. On the day of a 2009 Senate election, the electoral council declared an inexplicable public transportation ban that severely depressed voter turnout, favoring incumbents in Préval's then-party, who won in a landslide.

Préval had founded his machine just before the earthquake. In a few months of 2009, the Unity Party snapped up near majorities in both houses of parliament, including its leadership and numerous government ministers. Taking no chances, the CEP also kicked at least fifteen rival platforms off the February parliamentary ballot, including those of former Préval allies who had declined or hadn't been asked to join Unity. The opposition, unsurprisingly, cried foul. A slapdash coalition of rivals, from disgruntled Aristide loyalists who resented Préval for leaving their leader in exile to allies of the factory owners and importers who would forever see Préval as an income-redistributing leftist, threatened to unleash riots. "The game is rigged," one opposition leader fumed to me at the Hotel Montana in December 2009. "The only way to confront Préval's plan is to mobilize the population." A month later that hotel, and the political crisis, were buried by the earthquake—but not forgotten.

The first shivers of a returning political crisis were felt in spring 2010. The February parliamentary election, scheduled for six weeks after the quake, had been canceled without debate, leaving the terms of the entire lower house and a third of the Senate to expire in May. In the weeks before, the population had begun realizing that an entire branch of government was about to dissolve; with the headquarters of the nation's highest court smashed by the quake, that left the presidency as the lone functioning branch of constitutional government—a dangerous concentration of power. Then, in April, the dissolving Senate authorized the Interim Haiti Recovery Commission, which meant that a foreign-dominated board would be the executive's only potential counterpoint. The opposition blamed Préval for allowing this to happen, and with reason: Twelve of the 13 "yes" votes for the IHRC's razor-thin passage came from Unity members. Opponents charged that the president or his party must have gotten something in exchange for turning so much power over to Bill Clinton and the IHRC. Many thought they got their answer on May 4, when Préval issued an executive order saying he would extend his term by three months (from February to May 2011) if the fall presidential election was postponed, and neither the UN nor the U.S. Embassy objected.[2]

Préval didn't want to remain in office. He was not a fan of crowds, avoided big speeches, and often traveled around town without a motorcade. It was not unusual to run into him eating in Pétionville, with a minimum of security. If he had an ulterior motive in extending his term, it might have been that preparations for Unity's steamroller victory had been delayed. But it was easy for the opposition to persuade voters, already incensed by the slow pace of recovery, that the president was taking a step toward dictatorship. On May 10, as the senators gathered to ratify the proposed extension of Préval's term, more than two thousand protesters marched through central Port-au-Prince, banging drums and carrying signs and rocks. "[Préval] is profiting from this disaster in order to stay in power!" an unemployed sociologist told me.[3] Defying shotgun blasts from apparent counterprotesters, the marchers pelted UN peacekeepers with rocks. Haitian police responded with tear gas as a U.S. Army Black Hawk helicopter circled overhead.

Undaunted, Préval's allies pushed the term extension through. Préval maintained his usual, infuriating silence. Then on May 18, during his annual Flag Day speech, he seemed to reverse course. Over heckles of "He must go!" he affirmed that he would step down in February after all.

The aid response's greatest concern after the quake was social unrest. But the episode was a reminder that the threat came not from some instinctive panic, but the age-old machinations of political struggle. Even if some of the anti-Préval protesters had been remunerated for their services, as protesters in Haiti often are, that thousands still reeling from the earthquake found the challenge to a constitutional provision compelling enough to leave their tarps and battle police in the streets was telling. The president's gambit also revealed that, though he was not running, the most vulnerable piece of his Unity Party strategy was Préval himself. The longer the postquake recovery stalled, the more trouble he would have convincing people to trust anyone associated with him.

BECAUSE SO FEW HAITIANS HAD ACCESS TO HEALTHCARE before the earthquake, the free clinics set up by NGOs and militaries after the quake had indeed felt like something of a miracle. But by May 2010, four months after the earthquake, it was becoming less clear what the remaining aid groups should be doing. The needs were still enormous, but increasingly had nothing to do with the earthquake. Paul Farmer, who had been working in Haiti since the 1980s, aptly described the disaster as an acute-on-chronic event: an emergency made more severe by poor governance, degraded infrastructure, and vulnerability to shocks. Many of the medical professionals who'd come to help vowed that they would remain in Haiti "as long as necessary." But they were now finding out that "as long as necessary" could well mean forever.

One talented newcomer was Megan Coffee, a thirty-three-year-old infectious diseases fellow from New Jersey by way of Berkeley. She had arrived a few weeks after the quake, while NGOs were still tripping over one another to treat the lingering injured brought to the General Hospital's rubble-strewn yard. A friend in Haiti had begged her to come; Coffee's Oxford Ph.D. in mathematical modeling and Harvard medical degree would give her invaluable insight into the spread of disease amid the mass postquake displacement. But the young doctor quickly realized that what was really needed was a quartermaster to set up supply chains. An acute shortage of blood—which requires good refrigeration, constant electricity, and volunteers with faith that their donations will be properly handled—cost scores of lives. "People were dying for the stupidest things," Coffee would recall one hot day at the hospital two years after the quake, her cheeks glossy from the relentless sun. The first casualty on Coffee's watch was a young man with tuberculosis. Even with the help of a dedicated Haitian-American soldier from the 82nd Airborne, they couldn't get him oxygen in time.

Years of systemic rot and bureaucratic malfeasance had left the General Hospital with a reputation as a place where people went to die. Rats ran through operating rooms exposed to the elements. The hospital's nurses had not been paid since before the earthquake. The foreigners quickly registered their lack of experience with expensive Western medicines, but often failed to appreciate their skills, such as managing as many as 70 patients at a time.

Coffee set out to work where she felt most comfortable: the quarantine tent. A Haitian nurse joined her, noting that scores of new tuberculosis cases were being diagnosed—some new since the quake, others previously unnoticed—and recruited other nurses to help. The ward filled up fast. As word of the brilliant young doctor spread, aid groups started dropping off patients they didn't know how to handle, some no longer breathing when they arrived. Stable patients helped Coffee and the nurses ration oxygen to those who needed it most. Once, with a patient in respiratory distress, Coffee was confronted with a man controlling access to the oxygen supply. She offered some diapers for his child, and he let her use the machine. The American learned the importance of greasing the wheels in an underfunded system. "It's like having sugar on hand for your neighbors," she explained.

The free care wasn't good for everyone though. Many of the General Hospital's doctors had private practices on the side. Undercut by aid, many of them went out of business, losing the sideline that made their public work possible. A few years before the quake, Dr. Reynold Savain, a Haitian radiologist, had opened a modern, private hospital in downtown Port-au-Prince with twenty-one beds, digital X-ray machines, ultrasounds, and one of the only two computed tomography scanners in the country. After the earthquake, it had thrown open its doors and treated what Savain estimated to be 12,600 patients, including thousands of surgeries. Préval promised to reimburse the hospital's costs but never followed through, and the hospital was forced to close. Savain blamed his unintentional foreign competitors, whom he said gave the government cover to let his hospital wither on the vine. "One day," Savain told me for an AP story that May, "they are going to leave this country and we are going to have big problems."[4]

The gap between foreigners' efforts and the depth of need plaguing Haitian healthcare was brutally illustrated in early May. A twenty-two-year-old named John Smith Bonhomme was on an after-school errand to pick up ice when a truck swiped him on a busy road, ripping open his legs. A passing man in a pick-up truck rushed him to the University of Miami/Medishare field hospital beside the airport, where doctors debated amputating both his legs to save his life. Evens and I happened to be there, working on a story about the improvements to general healthcare brought on by the quake response. We waited with Bonhomme's family near the towering white tent while surgeons worked furiously inside. "We hope the blan doctors can give him life, because they told us he is probably going to die," his grandmother whispered.

After a while, the chief medical officer on duty, a shoulder-slapping American named Vince Boyd, came out with good news: The doctors had stopped the bleeding, had closed the wounds, and were warding off infection.

As the family sighed and hugged, relieved, Evens and I walked over to get some dinner from a hamburger stand an enterprising Haitian had set up on site. As we got ready to go, Evens spotted Dr. Boyd rushing back into the big tent. I followed, just in time to see him confer with a nurse, who shook her head sadly. I asked what had happened. Boyd's face turned red and tears welled in his eyes. Bonhomme was dying. "It's *so stupid!*" Boyd cried. "Everybody was going balls out! Everyone was working like crazy! We had the manpower. But we didn't have the blood."

THIS IS WHAT WE KNOW about the biggest public health scare in the nine months after the earthquake: On the morning of May 3, a fifteen-year-old boy named Oriel showed up at the NGO clinic above the Pétionville Club golf course with a scratchy throat and fever.[5] Noting a gray hue at the back of his throat, the doctors made a startling diagnosis: diphtheria, a dreaded airborne bacterium that attacks the lungs and throat. Few of the blan doctors would have ever seen the disease: Thanks to widespread use of the diphtheria-pertussis-tetanus vaccine, it has all but been eradicated in the developed world.[6] But the aid workers knew that in Haiti, where just half the population had received a full three-dose course of the vaccine, it remained endemic. There had been 605 diagnosed cases in Haiti over the previous five years.

The boy's symptoms had been going on for six days. He needed a hospital, fast. At any time, the infection could close his threat, suffocating him to death. The doctors' first choice, the Medishare tent hospital, had caught fire after being struck by lightning a few hours before. So they went to the General Hospital. But the NGO on duty there, International Medical Corps (IMC), was reluctant to introduce a highly contagious infection into a damaged facility housing patients with tuberculosis and AIDS.

That's when the director of the NGO that ran the clinic in Pétionville stepped in. By now, Sean Penn had become a major figure in the reconstruction. He was a constant presence at cluster meetings and Pétionville bars, working as hard as anyone in the zone. Even veterans who had dismissed him as an arriviste praised his NGO, the Jenkins-Penn Haitian Relief Organization, whose experienced aid workers, given a Haiti-only focus and independence of USAID strictures, had shown agility in dealing with the problems of the quake zone. On a more personal level, it also turned out the skills that made leading men were also useful in the humanitarian world. Amid the bureaucratic blustering of the cluster meetings, a confident speaker who could command the attention of a rotating cast of strangers, and the media, would win the most consistent platform for his ideas.

Oriel may have reminded Penn of his own teenage son, who months before been hospitalized after a serious skateboarding accident. When the General Hospital seemed to close its doors, the actor loaded the boy into a pick-up truck and stormed off in search of another facility—perhaps not realizing that there wasn't one with the equipment needed to save the boy if he stopped breathing.

But the NGOs at the General Hospital hadn't categorically refused. Those hesitant to take the patient were overruled. Others argued that so long as Oriel was isolated, the risk would be manageable. It seems the communication breakdown got worse from there. The standard treatment would be to administer a dose of diphtheria antitoxin (DAT), which in Haiti was housed only at a warehouse operated by the health ministry and World Health Organization. Doctors at the hospital said that Oriel had to be admitted before the warehouse would release the antitoxin. Penn said, two years later, that he had to ensure he could get the antitoxin before Oriel would be allowed in the hospital. After a confusing couple of hours, Oriel finally arrived at the General Hospital's green gates—reportedly just after 5 P.M. The warehouse had just closed.

Penn played his advantage. With a few phone calls, by his account, he soon had the American Red Cross, WHO, USAID, U.S. Centers for Disease Control and Prevention (CDC), Haitian officials, and the command of the U.S. military's Joint Task Force-Haiti scrambling to procure medication for a fifteen-year-old boy.

It seemed that Penn could marshal more resources than even the president, much less any other camp manager, could imagine. Some responders appeared eager to please a movie star. Others may have feared that he could break them: Penn was "like his own walking accountability mechanism," said Timothy Schwartz, an anthropologist of Haiti who befriended the actor after the earthquake. "Everybody shapes up . . . and if you don't do it, he's going to scream at you and denounce you to the world. And it works."

Even in the United States, DAT takes a while to procure: The CDC, which usually quarantines it at major airports, promises to deliver it only "within hours."[7] In Haiti, despite infinitely more difficult circumstances, Penn and a CDC representative were able to reopen the warehouse and get the serum. Furious over the hours of delay, Penn lashed out at the hospital and then went back to camp. "We had a hard night, we drank some rum, and we went to sleep," he recalled.

But Oriel's story had a heartbreaking end. As his days-old condition deteriorated, the doctors put him on a respirator. At some point overnight, perhaps during a shift change between IMC and the overnight doctors from Partners in Health, Oriel was left alone. When doctors returned, the breathing tube was dangling, and Oriel was in a coma. The boy had probably awoken, panicked, and ripped the life-sustaining tube out. The doctors revived him, but the lack of oxygen to his brain likely dealt an irreversible blow. Two days later, he was dead—another "stupid" death in Haiti.

But this case would be remembered. The next night, an enraged Sean Penn appeared on *Anderson Cooper 360* in an olive-drab collared shirt, his unwashed hair slicked back. Voice shaking as he jabbed his finger into his palm, the actor-turned-activist-turned-aid worker unleashed a righteous fury at aid workers inured to tragedy and a Haitian healthcare system that, for all its improvements since the quake, was still horribly inadequate. Then he issued a warning: "It's just the very beginning," the actor nearly shouted at Cooper. "This is a disaster, and a bigger one than the earthquake, waiting to happen." Unless the NGOs were pushed to "get off their butts," Penn railed, "people are going to die en masse."

CNN ran the interview with the title "Epidemic Threatens Haiti."

The interview set off alarms. Aid workers scrambled to ensure there was enough DAT on hand for the few dozen cases expected in Haiti each year. (There was.) Haitian medical authorities ordered still more. Aid groups planned an education campaign for camp managers and communities about the disease. I called Anshu Banerjee, the leader of the health cluster. He told me Oriel's death was a tragic but isolated case. The CDC had said since the quake that diphtheria cases were possible but a large-scale outbreak unlikely. Moreover, UNICEF had an ongoing campaign to vaccinate 888,000 people in the camps against diphtheria and other diseases. But in large part because of the attention Penn drummed up, the health cluster continued to focus on diphtheria for weeks.

Penn's outrage was understandable. Had the NGOs coordinated or had there been a healthcare system Oriel's parents could have turned to days before, the boy might have lived. But no diphtheria epidemic broke out, nor did medical experts expect one. The megaphone that enabled Penn to procure extraordinary help for the boy also made his unscientific pronouncements more reckless, adding another dose of panic to an already panic-driven response.

Days later, Penn was called to Washington to testify before the U.S. Senate Foreign Relations Committee about the diphtheria case and priorities for healthcare in the Haiti response—a responsibility bestowed on few aid workers and far fewer Haitian officials. A few weeks later, *Vanity Fair* would further sanctify him with a profile, cementing his image as a "camp boss . . . with a Glock pistol and a golden Rolodex."[8] The mythology that would rise thereafter—that he had "traded his Malibu home" for a muddy tent in a refugee camp, as opposed to joining the hard-working yet still rarified Blan Bubble—would overshadow discussion of the commendable work of his NGO. Penn's importance to the response and the media coverage that we provided fed off each other. As the philosopher Jay Newman has written, "celebrity and authority have a way of enhancing one another, especially in the eyes of a journalist."[9]

ORDINARY HAITIANS TRIED TO MAKE SENSE of the new normal in the same halting, improvised way as everyone else. One mosquito-swarmed day on the cusp of summer, a Haitian man with a creased and jagged face presented himself to a recently arrived foreigner.

"My name is Brother Chrispain Mondésir," he explained. "Before I die, God will reveal to me how it will happen. I am not afraid of anything."

The blan, a 25-year-old history Ph.D. student from New York University, her hair in a ponytail to allay the heat, nodded respectfully. Knowing that archives related to the Haitian Revolution rarely included voices of ordinary men and women, Claire Payton had come to Haiti with a digital recorder to help prevent that absence for future historians of the earthquake. She called her effort the *Haiti Memory Project*.[10] We met through a mutual friend, and I found her idealism both stirring and charming—probably a sign I'd been in Haiti too long.

Mondésir turned out to be a good observer—sometimes a photographer, sometimes a preacher, always a storyteller. He'd lived a few lives of his own. One had been in the Dominican Republic, where, like many Haitians, he'd gone to find work and start a family. He returned to Haiti, for reasons he always left unclear, with a sort of split personality. When he spoke in the rhythmic *capitaleño* Spanish of Santo Domingo, he called himself Armando. In the Kreyòl he spoke to his neighbors in Camp Trazelie, he was always Chrispain.

Claire asked Chrispain what caused the earthquake. "Some people believed that U.S. had fired a missile underground," he answered. But he shared a more common view: "It is God's word being fulfilled! It was written in the Bible that there would be many earthquakes throughout the world. . . . God let this earthquake happen because people are defiant to God; they don't want to receive His word."

Through her translator, Payton asked Mondésir what he thought about life in Trazelie.

It was a bigger question than he had expected, it seemed. He closed his crow-footed eyes and thought hard. "Life in the camps . . . ," he repeated. His answer meandered. Sometimes he spoke in the third person, perhaps viewing his camp neighbors through Armando's eyes. He kept circling back to the same themes—a tarp roof was better than concrete, because one never knew when an earthquake would strike, even if it was too hot under a tarp and the sun burned his flesh (unlike his next-door

neighbor, Twenty Chery, he had no prospect of shade from a growing ash tree); that at least rent was free. Payton had heard these
notions in interviews throughout the quake zone, but the answer
seemed to press harder on Mondésir's soul. The graver the subject,
the more he broke into incongruous laughter.

The aid groups often gave out day-labor jobs—building temporary facilities, assisting with distributions, unloading trucks—but
Mondésir thought they were just taking advantage of cheap labor.
"Five dollars a day!" he exclaimed. "For me $5 is worthless. I may
get up in the morning, if I want to buy food somewhere, I may
spend $2 to $3. Then I have to drink something. At noon, I have to
eat again. I must spend $5 to $6. If I am going to have supper, that
will cost in total $18 per day." He shook his head. "Someone would
agree to work for $5 per day for Caritas [an NGO] because he is
facing a hard time! He resigns himself to accept it. But this little
salary cannot do much for a Haitian."

Payton asked, "What do you think about the presence of the
foreigners in the country?"

The translator, a petite college student named Valérie Michaud, knew that many Haitians expressed this thought with more
vinegar. As Evens often did, she translated in a way that better
matched the local conversation: "What do you think about the
fact that, after the earthquake, many foreigners came in the country? . . . There are many rumors saying that they are invaders, that
they overrun the country. What do you think about that?"

Mondésir became indignant. "Do you know what's happened?"
he shouted. "The earthquake destroyed *everything*. It *emptied* us.
We don't have anything left. The president was not wise enough to
prepare for this tragedy. He can't even rebuild the country. Therefore, it is very important to find help from others, particularly the
Americans. The Americans can control the country, I don't have
any problem with that. [Haitian] authorities rob the country. They
used the money of the country to fill their account overseas." He
said other countries' leaders were more capable. "They are aware of
what God says in the Bible. They know that earthquake is happening everywhere in the world. They know that they are next. Therefore, they prepare to face it. [Préval] was supposed to do the same
thing."

When I listened to the interview later, I recognized the familiar pattern. The underfunded, incapable government was first to be blamed for problems that it was only one part of—donors too slow to deliver funds, NGOs stuck in emergency mode, a lack of experience and organization among the people themselves. Some, as Twenty sang and Michaud expressed, thought the foreigners called too many shots. Mondésir just hoped everyone could pitch in and help. He was even still willing to give the government a shot—as he put it, the earthquake "helped us to understand that we have to love each other." Even months after the demonstration against Préval's term extension in May, Haiti was not on the verge of a political crisis. There was still time to prevent one.

BY MID-JUNE, THE CITY WAS EXHAUSTED. When the World Cup in South Africa rolled around, it was as if God had ordained the distraction. The whole country was riveted. If baseball was the true religion on the Spanish-speaking side of Hispaniola, in Haiti, the passion ran nearly as deep for *foutbòl*. The league or country didn't matter—crowds were going to form around every fuzzy street-side TV. People wanted to root for the Haitian national team, of course, but they seldom had much to root about. So they transferred their affections to the indomitable champions of Brazil. No love ran as true. Whenever the *Selecão Brasileira* took the field, life in Haiti's capital slowed to a crawl. You could track the goals by the shouts rising from every bidonville.

As the Brazilians arrived across the world in Johannesburg, the year's hardship seemed to fade away. The flag-seller off Route de Delmas who hawked U.S. stars and stripes while Marines roamed the city switched back to Brazil's green and gold. Suddenly, that was the color of every barrette in girls' braids, too. Work and antigovernment protests were canceled, malt liquor and beer put on ice, favors for generators and color TVs called in. A palpable buzz could be felt as Brazil's first match, against unknowns from North Korea, approached. A *ra-ra* drum band stepped up practices behind my house. After a few days, the horn players, each of whose valveless metal tubes could play only two or three notes, had taught themselves the cup's unofficial anthem "Wavin' Flag" by the Somali-Canadian artist K'naan. I'd sing along with the chorus:

"When I get older, I will be stronger, they'll call me freedom, just like a wavin' flag."

I watched the game at home with Evens. Claire watched it at Camp Trazelie, across the street from where she was living. She'd become a regular, interviewing a woman named Lillian, who had lost four children in the quake, and Chrispain, and his neighbor, the rapper Twenty Chery. She'd met potbellied Jonas, who'd emerged as a leader of the committee running the upper part of the camp, reserving for himself a fancy ShelterBox tent with a pouch for an ostentatious display of condoms. She'd also gotten to know two of the young teens in the camp, Richard and Kervins, who loved to borrow her digital camera and take hundreds of shots of themselves making imaginary gang signs. The people invited her to watch the big game with them, under the large blue tarp on the main drag that served as a church. Walking into Trazelie from Maïs Gâté, she ran into the man who coached the camp's kids in soccer walking with a big smile on his face and a borrowed TV on his head. Everyone had thrown in a few gourdes to gas the generator.

For much of the match, Kim Jong-Il's side threatened to ruin Haiti's good time. It took until the tenth minute of the second half for Brazil wingback Maicon to find a hard pass from the midfielder while the North Korea keeper was out of position. Claire would enshrine the scene on her blog: "Goal!!! Joy exploded in the tent, beads of sweat flying everywhere, with children dancing and men punching the air. The whole tent vibrated. . . . Women held their babies up in the air, dancing. . . . Out in the street cars and taptaps honked vigorously, people hollering at one another with pride."

The honking and shouting reached all the way up to Pétion-ville. As Brazil held on for a 2–1 finish, the hillside neighborhoods exhaled and then erupted in full-throated joy. It was only the first game of the first round. But the people of Port-au-Prince were going to squeeze out every moment of celebration that they could.

CHAPTER NINE

SUGAR LAND

IT STARTED WITH A TIP: *FIND OUT WHO OWNS THE LAND UNDER CAMP Corail, and you'll know why reconstruction is stalled.* Corail-Cesselesse was the 18,500 acres that Préval had expropriated on the eve of Bill Clinton and George W. Bush's March visit, where officials planned to relocate fifty thousand people whose tarp shelters were deemed most at risk from spring landslides and floods. Out past the last of the banana plants, where the capital's northern slums give way to cactus and rock, the vast plain half the size of Port-au-Prince had become a blank canvas for dreaming architects and the escaping poor alike.

"Camp Corail" referred to about a hundred acres in the middle of Corail-Cesselesse, where the first of 7,500 displaced people had been moved in early April. General Keen, in a last act of mission fulfillment before giving up command of Joint Task Force-Haiti, had provided Navy engineers to prepare the land and buses to move out residents. UN peacekeepers operated the heavy machinery, and NGOs built cinder-block latrines and tents. Sean Penn ensured the people relocated would come from the Pétionville Club, fulfilling his promise from March.

But why would Camp Corail, of all places, explain the continued lack of reconstruction since the quake? It was the bright spot of the effort so far, the one big thing that had worked. True, nine miles from the edge of the city, the camp seemed a bit remote, and when the relocation was announced a few aid groups had complained that they hadn't had time to get ready. But those were quibbles.

Préval, confident he had shown leadership to foreign donors eager to see displaced people relocated to safety, went out to greet the new residents with an equally exuberant Sean Penn. The four-star General Douglas Fraser, Keen's boss, stopped by on a Black Hawk helicopter to see the progress for himself.

Stepping off the bus into the desert, the new residents got a wheelbarrow of food, toiletries, and other supplies and a guided tour of the latrines, showers, and police tent. They also got wrist bands, as if Camp Corail were a desert resort. It kind of was. The roomy white tunnel tents were set up on spacious plots, with space for rocky gardens, firebreaks, and walking paths—a kind of accommodation unthinkable for most quake survivors. Each new arrival was futher promised that within three months he would get a sturdy provisional "T-shelter." A cell phone company even set up a concert stage, where the popular roots band R.A.M. came to play its fusion of funk, jazz, and Haitian drums while teenagers danced and kids batted inflated condoms from the on-site health clinic.

Other quake survivors were following these first lucky recipients to the official camp, squatting on the land nearby, perhaps hoping some of the aid might spill out.

The tip had all the makings of a Haitian rabbit hole, the kind of story you can go down forever, bouncing off dead ends. But it had one promising element. The tipster had used a magic word: *land*. When you dug down, so to speak, land was at the center of a lot of postquake paralysis. In order to clear and dump rubble, set up T-shelters, or start construction projects, you had to know who owned the land you were clearing, building, or dumping on. But aid groups and donor governments didn't know where to start. The office tasked with overseeing land registration—the one that only before the quake had clear title for 5 percent of Haiti's territory—was now destroyed. Aid workers also soon learned that Haitian land disputes have often ended with an under-the-table payment or a headless body in a field. With no pressure to contend with a hazardous problem—which most of their bosses and donors were unaware existed—the responders were content to ignore the issue entirely, even though they knew that leaving it unaddressed meant reconstruction would never get off the ground.

Land was a great mystery for my reporting as well. Earlier in the spring, rumors had spread about secret deals for territory on the periphery of the capital, strange construction trailers showing up in the middle of rutty cow pastures, and peasants being pushed off their property by police in the middle of the night. But I couldn't pin anything down. Some sources who'd whispered those rumors said they'd end up dead if we printed their names.

So I started poking around. First thing I found was that, whoever owned the land at Corail, a lot of people wished they did. For a generation, the betting money on where the ever-expanding capital would spread next had been on that massive stretch of former sugar and sisal plantation. A few miles from Haiti's biggest ports and past the bloody lip of its northernmost slums, it had been earmarked for urban dreams—a new international airport, a big cigarette factory, public housing—from the Duvaliers through Aristide. Those with the money and guile had snatched up rights to the territory or found notaries to say they had so they could cash in when the projects began. But none ever came to fruition. Now, whoever had the land under the official camp would finally be in line for compensation—under the terms of Préval's expropriation, the government would reimburse the owner, from a $7 million fund expected to balloon once the donor-conference billions streamed in. One official told me that 300 families had come forward claiming territory on Corail-Cesselesse.

Evens and I had one lead: Gérard-Emile "Aby" Brun. The tipster had said the savvy, well-connected businessman owned the parcel on which the aid groups and military had built Camp Corail. If true, this would have been no small revelation: As head of Préval's relocation commission, Brun had been tasked with finding the land. If Brun was double-dealing with reconstruction money, that could be the sort of clear corruption story every journalist was looking for. Many who claimed territory at Corail-Cesselesse told me they had gotten calls from Brun's commission. One landowner told me that some families had also heard from U.S. officials pushing them to make a deal. Everyone had dollar signs in their eyes. When Evens and I made an early visit to Corail, the owners of the few real houses on the plain, mostly empty concrete husks painted pink and yellow, had offered to rent them for more than AP was paying for the narcopalace in Pétionville.

But even if Brun did own the land, why would so many powerful players have gone along with him? It was open territory, true, maybe good enough for an airport, but years away from being ready for mass settlement. In fact, while billed as a safe haven from the floodable Pétionville Club golf course, people who knew Corail said it flooded all the time, when rain came washing down the barren mountains. Something didn't add up.

"WHERE WOULD THEY KEEP A DEED like that, for Corail?" I asked Evens.

"The IRS, most likely." He meant the tax office, the Direction Generale des Impôts (DGI). (As many Haitians did when talking to blan, Evens tended to overtranslate. It was how I'd spent two years thinking that Jean, a Reuters cameraman, was named Gene.)

It turned out that some of the land registry, or *cadastre,* had been fished out of the rubble and moved to the DGI's new digs. After an hour and a half dehydrating in traffic, we got to the temporary office in a wooden house downtown. Evens tried his usual shortcuts—flirting with the secretaries ("Cherie, where can we see the cadastre?") and palm-slapping old friends in positions of midlevel authority ("*Mon frè,* how's the family? Hey, do you know . . ."). We were remanded to a tiny waiting room to wait for the director-general.

I think I spent a quarter of my life waiting for directors-general in Haiti. Without Evens' wheel-greasing talents, I would have probably spent twice as long. The sit-and-wait is of critical importance in a government office on Hispaniola because no bureaucrat wants to look available, especially if he is. It must be made clear to the visitors that he has things to do, hands to shake, and perhaps an important conference call. Then lunch.

"That's a nice wood roof," Evens said, staring at the lightweight, cabin-like beams. "That's what I want for the house I'm building."

My stomach growled. I took out a granola bar.

After another interminable stretch, we were let into the official's cramped office, a step down from what had probably been a needlessly cavernous space in the destroyed old building. "*Bon,*" said the official, looking cool in his guayabera. Bon usually means "good," but in a conversation like this, it means *Thank you for coming. I will politely refuse you now.* "The problem is that the cadastre has not been excavated from the rubble."

"But some of it has," Evens said.

"Bon." The official smiled, then changed the topic, saying he needed us to request the information in writing. A letter that couldn't be dropped off with the director himself, of course, but with the first of three sets of hands through which it would have to pass before reaching him. The meeting dragged for a few more stupid minutes, and then Evens and I left for a two-hour drive back up to Pétionville.

THE FASTEST WAY TO FIGURE OUT who owned the land under Corail would be to figure out who got paid first by the government. But no one had gotten paid, in part, because the money from the donors' conference still hadn't shown up. What may have seemed like a golden opportunity now looked more dubious to whoever owned that territory: no compensation, and by now too many survivors on-site for the owners to expect anyone to remove them.

When Bill Clinton came back for the first meeting of the Interim Haiti Recovery Commission on June 17, two and a half months after the donors' conference, only Brazil had delivered anything to the World Bank–managed reconstruction fund the IHRC was to oversee. The next day, Norway and Australia pitched in, raising the grand total to $100 million, a mere sliver of the $4.6 billion pledged for 2010–2011. Thirty million dollars of that was allocated to the Haitian government, but not directly; the IHRC had to approve use. Compensating landowners for land that had already begun to be settled was unlikely to be among the first priorities among so many urgent needs.

Préval was no fan of big landowners. He'd grown up in rice country. His father, the former agriculture minister, had watched in horror as the tyrannical François Duvalier rewrote the *code rural* to enrich his allies and secret police, pushing the poor off their land. In 1997, during his first term, Préval had tried to impose the first broad post-Duvalier land reform. Gathering peasants and reporters in his native Artibonite Valley, Préval declared, "Land is power!" and handed sixteen hundred families titles seized from Duvalier cronies or owned by the state.[1] Some reports say more than five thousand families ultimately benefited. Wealthy families feared that an aggressive land redistribution of the kind that was getting underway in Zimbabwe was planned. When Aristide was overthrown in 2004, gangs, reportedly backed by major landowners, took back almost everything Préval had handed out.

When Préval signed the order to expropriate Corail, many major landowners believed he was attempting another redistribution by fiat. "Left-wing . . . populist demagogue," scoffed one, adding that he would be more than happy to let the government steal his land and then take it back when Préval was thrown out of office.

Clinton told me he would be willing to step in and arbitrate. "I don't know if I'll be the real estate lawyer," he told me for an AP story. "I'm not above doing that. I've been known to make a deal or two in my life." But as weeks turned into months, the expropriated land remained uncompensated.

BITS OF SAND AND GRAVEL RICOCHETED off the windshield as the Beast II raced beyond the edge of Port-au-Prince. It was the last day of May. A treeless plain stretching to the foothills of the Morne à Cabrit came into view. Nearby lay the silent mass graves of Titanyen, full of countless thousands of earthquake dead and the victims of past regimes. A couple of lonely gas stations and the cracked roadway were the only reminders that a wrecked city was just a dozen miles behind us. We cleared a bend, and suddenly a wide vista of sagebrush and barren mountains was framed by an indigo sky. A band of rain wandered far off in the distance. If John Ford had shot a movie in the Caribbean, he would have chosen this as the spot. But this was starting to seem more like *Chinatown*.

Outside the official camp boundaries, an invasion had taken place. The first time Evens and I had visited, in April, a few thousand squatters had pitched makeshift tents on a hill facing the camp, calling the settlement Camp Obama to win attention of aid groups and the media. A month later, there were tens of thousands of tarps and bed-sheet tents across hundreds of acres, in new sub-settlements nicknamed Canaan and Jerusalem. As we entered the camp, we saw that newer squatters had begun claiming the flat land between the mountains and the road, the rough-hewn poles of their tents sticking up like toothpicks. There, on the unadulterated terrain, you could see how uneven the ground had been before the U.S. naval engineers and UN construction crews graded it to make the official camp. Down the mountains ran the scars of floods past, where rain had streamed together and come crashing across the plain. The squatter settlements were clearly in a vulnerable spot, and you had to wonder how safe even the official camp's land would be in a major storm.

Evens drove past Camp Corail, its white Quonset hut–like tents ruffling in the wind, and turned onto an unmarked trail. We rumbled up the goat path for a few minutes until we happened on a family sitting on rocks. The thick-built matriarch reposed on the ground, wearing a white T-shirt that read, in English, "BEAUTI-FUL." A younger man was tying wires among poles meant to delineate the family's purloined quarter-acre of land. He told me the family had come here on what it understood as orders from Préval. "This land belongs to the state," he told me. "The state says: If the land is not fenced in, it is ours."

There was nothing in the decree that conferred the expropriated land on any poor person who claimed it, but Préval had allowed people to form that impression. He certainly wasn't taking to the radio to disabuse people of the notion; in fact, he might have suspected that his springtime warning of an impending second earthquake would drive even more to chance it under the open skies. Was Préval taking advantage of the quake to try his land distribution scheme again? Not only landowners thought so. Squatters did too. Some even carried copies of the decree cut out of the newspaper.

What about the landowners? Evens asked. Had they given the family any trouble?

The young man smirked. "Granmoun pa jwe," he answered. Grown-ups don't play around.

He led us down the road to a circle of houses made of the same rough-hewn wood as the squatters' poles. Some had tarp walls. One ingenious architect had made a roof out of prickly pear cactuses. An older man named Sadrak was brought forth. He was emaciated, around sixty or so, exactly how old no one, including he, could say.

"They come with machetes," Sadrak said, listing slightly, either from drink or something else. "Some of them have guns." He scowled, his eyes rolling off somewhere. Who comes? Police? Gangsters, he answered. But one man had come in a police truck. "He called them over to me, and the police asked what I was doing on the land. I told them I wasn't doing anything. I was just sitting there." Sadrak laughed. "That policeman, he hit me in the chest with the butt of his rifle. Right there, oh my friend!" He pointed to the thick of his bony sternum. "I couldn't sleep for three days."

I was confused. "Who was 'he'?" I asked Evens. "A landowner? Someone who works for the landowners?" Evens translated. Everyone nodded. "The gangs work for the *grands-hommes*," one man expounded, using the colonial word for plantation masters. It seemed everyone had had a run-in with these men. Shacks torn down. People kicked. A mother of four had been thrown out of her tent by men with machetes. She was nine months pregnant. For days, she hid in an abandoned stone house, where she gave birth alone on the floor. Yet the squatters, caught in the middle between Préval's designs and landowners' retaliations, were convinced they had more to gain from staying on the boomtown land than from going back to the city's rubble. "I think all kinds of things are going to come here—schools, hospitals, stores," one said.

Evens nodded knowingly. "Granmoun pa jwe."

I DIDN'T WANT TO CONFRONT BRUN until I had more solid information, but weeks of searching turned up only more confusion: The land didn't seem to belong to Brun per se but rather to the company of which he was president and chief executive, Nabatec S.A. The firm, a consortium of some of Haiti's most powerful families, developed property: shopping centers, neighborhoods, and, especially, industrial parks—which, in Haiti, tended to mean garment factories. But would a company of Nabatec's size and influence—its unreported revenues were assumed to be among the highest in Haiti—really risk getting accused of corruption over a few million dollars in reconstruction money?

My AP editors thought this investigation was getting to be a waste of time. They asked me to focus on surefire stories, as the newspapers that carried our articles had as much use for everyday disaster news as they did arcana of Haitian land title—which was to say, not much at all. Demand for Haiti news stories had sharply declined by the late spring of 2010, but our staffing levels plummeted even faster. Since wire editors expect each bureau to score big investigative scoops, write a steady flow of features, and never get beaten on breaking news no matter what is going on, Evens and I were working seven days a week.

But I couldn't let Corail go. Whenever I had free time, I would call a landowner or a contact, or try to catch a meeting with an official who might know something about Préval's motives—or Brun's. On May 26, I was tending to the fires AP had deemed most important, so I asked if Evens would try the tax office once more on his own. I was reviewing the notes I'd made about Nabatec when he burst through the door, flustered, a few hours later.

"Man, they busted my window," he said.

"Who?"

"I don't know. I was in the tax office. Came out. Smashed."

I walked with him to the driveway. The rear window on the driver's side was broken, shards strewn over the back seat. Nothing was taken. It had happened on a thoroughfare not known for safety, so maybe it had nothing to do with the story. Or maybe someone had sent a message. I asked Evens what he thought. He shrugged.

INVESTIGATIONS OFTEN COME DOWN TO FIGURING OUT whom you need to talk to, how to reach them, and what to ask. For a while it seemed like the best person to talk to would be Aby Brun. But though few foreign reporters spent time chasing mid-level Haitian consultants, he avoided me like a starlet fending off a paparazzo. Once, about a month after the quake, I'd caught him coming out of the president's temporary office at the airport police station and tried to ask how the land negotiations were going. He used his car door like a shield to push me back and told me that, until he had $40 million—significantly more than the $7 million that I was later told was in the compensation fund—to secure land rights to all the prospective properties the government was looking at, he had nothing to discuss. After that he never returned my calls.

I realized I needed someone who knew both Brun and Préval. So two days after Evens lost his rear window, I went for a beer with Leslie Voltaire, a confidant of both. As Bill Clinton shifted from his role as Special Envoy into the job of IHRC co-chair, Voltaire had moved from being Clinton's liaison to a position closer to his architect's heart: designing a master plan for reconstruction.

We sat down at a table at the Kinam Hotel in Pétionville, a gingerbread building with an open courtyard. The Place Saint-Pierre internally displaced persons camp, which had some of the city's worst sanitation, was across the street. When the wind shifted, the smell wafted into the room. Voltaire was short, with a small, half-bald head. Because of his almond-shaped eyes, light brown skin, and thin mustache, many Haitians jokingly called him "Chinese." His hands moving like a conductor's, Voltaire divided, sliced, and wiped the stained white tablecloth, showing his plan for decongesting the capital: parkland here, flood control there, four new centers of commerce and services here, here, here, and here. He stopped occasionally to sip his beer. Downtown would be rebuilt and light rail installed. He imagined an architecture contest to redesign the destroyed ministries.

But the key to curing the overcrowding that had made the earthquake so fatal, he said, was to move some of the population north of the city. "Port-au-Prince is there," Voltaire said, pointing to a spot on the table. He moved his hand up the invisible map to the rough location of Corail-Cesselesse. "The second Port-au-Prince will be there."

I asked why that area was so promising.

He said it as casually as if it were public news. "I think the real incentive for those people is the industrial park that the Koreans will put up."

Voltaire said that Brun was negotiating a deal for his company's land while talking to a South Korean garment manufacturer called Sae-A Trading Co., Ltd., which had assembly plants all over the world, including Guatemala, Nicaragua, and Vietnam.

Suddenly it made sense. Of course Brun wanted the government to put the camp out there. A few million in compensation would be chicken feed if he could promise Sae-A a ready-made workers' community on-site. Brun knew Préval would be eager to move resources to the northern land too, Voltaire said. The president had eyed it as a target for resettlement for years. Meanwhile Préval must have known that Brun would be so eager for the real payoff, the investment, that he'd have been willing to overlook the compensation, at least at first, confident something larger would eventually come through. The rest of the earthquake survivors were caught in the middle.

Voltaire could tell this wasn't sitting right with me. "It's difficult for an outsider to understand," he admitted. Yes, it was, I replied. Voltaire knew as well as I did that donors were just waiting for an example of corruption like this to argue against giving the government money.

The architect leaned in toward me. "I told Aby also, because Aby is my friend, 'You are going to be in trouble.' He said, 'Yes, but what I can I do?' I said, 'You can quit from the commission of reconstruction.'"

AS I DROVE HOME, I THOUGHT ABOUT how well Brun's plan would have gone over in Washington too. Congress had been steadily expanding tariff-free access for garments made in Haiti since 2006, and after the earthquake—following a lobbying effort by Walmart, Hanesbrands, Target, Gap, and others—a bill sailed through both houses to expand access again.[2] USAID had even just announced the opening of garment-worker training center in Port-au-Prince.

This was part of a larger U.S. vision of the world. For decades policy had focused on integrating markets. Free trade agreements created trade surpluses for the United States while guaranteeing that the U.S. economy's health would be a global concern.[3] It also might have explained why Bill Clinton, when asked about the expropriation of land in March, imagined "100,000 jobs" being created by the relocation—it was the exact number of jobs the Collier Report had said could result from expanding the garment industry.

Meanwhile, Sae-A had a likely ally in the UN. Before becoming secretary-general, Ban Ki-moon had previously been South Korea's minister of foreign affairs and trade. The Asian country traced much of its success to garments; coming off the Korean War in the 1950s, its then-authoritarian rulers had channeled a population available for cheap labor into textiles and light manufacturing, then heavy industry and technology. Now the Koreans were the outsourcers, putting garment factories in poor countries around the world. Advocates said other countries could follow in their footsteps. But Haiti lacked many elements fundamental to South Korea's boom, including a strong central government, an effective national school system, and equitable land reform.[4] Haiti in 2010 looked more likely to follow its own model, demonstrated in the 1970s and 1980s under "Baby Doc" Duvalier, when low-wage assembly plants funneled profits out of the country, leaving little but slums and an untrained workforce behind. Yet the optimism that the model would work seemed unshakable.

Had all this been discussed when Ban Ki-moon visited the Pétionville camp in March? Even Sean Penn had mentioned the need for manufacturing jobs as a priority for relocation land when we spoke. When Penn met with Préval in March, had he found out this was why he would be sending people out to Corail? You had to wonder. But I knew that after what Voltaire told me, most people probably wouldn't care. Even if South Korean investors and U.S. retailers had stood to benefit from the move into the desert as well, the only thing most people would see was a Haitian trying to steal money.

AFTER MEETING WITH VOLTAIRE, Evens and I decided he should make another attempt at tracking down the land title—I wanted backup for his claims. He returned to the tax office a few days later. That afternoon, I got a phone call from a number I didn't recognize. It was Evens.

"Whose phone is this?" I said.

It was a friend's. "I got mugged. I parked down the street a little farther away so that shit wouldn't happen to my car. I walk out of the DGI, this guy freezes me, takes out a pistol. Took my BlackBerry, my wallet, all my shit. Middle of the day. Everyone was watching." Thankfully, Evens was fine.

In the end, it turned out we didn't need to track down the title. Jean-Max Bellerive, the prime minister, called me one night and confirmed that Brun had been double-dealing. "He's not representing us in any meeting anymore," Bellerive assured me. (Amusingly, the prime minister's office had to take Brun's word for it; even his staff couldn't track down the deed to prove Nabatec owned the land.) Had Brun found out that I had gotten wind of his role and volunteered to resign? Had someone tipped off Bellerive? The more I learned about this story, the less I understood.

Brun would defend his role in January 2011, telling the Huffington Post that he did not choose Camp Corail's location, though he acknowledged participating in the meetings where the decision was made. He characterized stepping down as a personal decision to avoid a conflict of interest. Brun added, however, that Nabatec was owed $20 million for the government's use of its property. "We have submitted a claim on that land," he said, "and we have not heard anything at all."[5]

BY MID-JUNE, THE BLOOM WAS OFF the rose at Camp Corail. The site, chosen for reasons that had nothing to do with sound relocation, combined the isolation of rural *andeyò* with the charm and farming potential of an Arizona parking lot. When it rained, water fell into tents. When Préval's government shut off food distribution as part of a larger, wise strategy to cut dependence on imports, the camp's twice-displaced residents, cut off from markets and their old businesses, had no way to get food. Some scraped together money to go back and forth to Delmas, a thirty-four-mile round trip, every day. At least four times, protesters broke out into table-tossing, rock-throwing protests that drove an experienced American Refugee Committee camp manager to quit. Only one other relocation camp, on swampland closer into the capital, was established. Plans to move tens of thousands more from the city were scrapped. They remained in flood-prone settlements back in the capital, with hurricane season around the corner.

The people of Camp Corail watched their new lives drag on, as the T-shelter construction was repeatedly delayed, and even the fanciful talk of jobs dried up like the soil. "Those factories aren't something we can talk about right now," said one camp resident when I asked about Nabatec's plan. "Right now we need help. We need money to buy water to drink. They got jobs for people back at Delmas 40 [the area near the Pétionville Club]. International organizations, they can help us for the first time now. The Haitian government did nothing for us."

Most aid groups and major donors continued avoiding the land problem. That fall the Organization of American States would draw up a plan to modernize and reorganize the land registry, but the project would require seven years and tens of millions of dollars. In the meantime, as always, it was easier for NGOs to go around the government and just keep handing out emergency tarps and blankets, insisting to the few outside Haiti aware of the problem that permanent solutions were beyond their control.

For Ban Ki-moon and Bill Clinton, Corail would have brought the Collier Report to life. The industrial park would have been the economic "growth pole" referred to in the private-sector's roadmap that Reginald Boulos introduced at the UN donors' conference in March. According to a 2011 report—compiled by the International Finance Corporation (IFC), an arm of the World Bank, after the plans became public—Nabatec had called for a 2,400-acre site with a 116-acre "apparel park," a 148-acre light industrial park, an "administrative center," and mixed-use development clustered around new neighborhoods.

But the IFC noted that land tenure problems, the failure to compensate Nabatec, and above all "the extensive informal settling that has taken place on the site" had crippled the project. The trickle of migration that Brun and Nabatec had wanted from Sean Penn's camp to provide the seeds of a workforce had turned into an avalanche of squatters, taking up the land needed to build the factories. Lured by free or cheap land and the increasingly mythical prospect of future development, the illegal squatter settlements spread across the hillsides, as much at risk for landslides and floods as any camp in the metropolitan area. Soon they grew into the largest of the IDP camps. The only upside was that the concentration had helped to create a small, informal economy. Carpenters, barbers, lotto sellers, market women, and cooked-food vendors turned the desert into something resembling a town, though without electricity or running water. As Corail becomes permanent, it threatens to overshadow even nearby Cité Soleil as the nation's largest slum.

In the end, the Corail industrial project was shelved. Sae-A, the Haitian government, and the U.S. State Department turned their attention to one of the other envisioned "growth poles," hundreds of miles north, on the coast between Cap-Haïtien and the Dominican border, where they would build a garment park on a piece of land called Caracol—farther from Haiti's central bureaucrats, displaced squatters, and other prying eyes.

For months, journalists had been scouring the quake zone for clear evidence of corruption, proof to justify the long-held image of Haiti's venality. Here it was: double-dealing officials, clandestine motives, quake survivors pushed around, machete gangs loosed on pregnant women. Yet when my story broke, there was hardly any reaction, either from readers, officials, or even my own editors. Was it too confusing? Was it because so many foreigners and investors had been involved? Or was it just that by the middle of July 2010, nobody cared?

MY EDITORS DECIDED TO RUN MY STORY about Corail on July 12, the six-month commemoration of the earthquake. That morning Evens and I headed downtown for the day's spot story, a memorial on the grounds of the broken National Palace. Driving across the Champ de Mars, we passed through the still-growing collection of tarps, shacks, and occasional tents. Half a year after the earthquake, just over 5,600 transitional shelters had been built out of the promised 125,000, none of them yet out at Corail. On the curb beside one of the tarp blocks, a boy, probably eight or nine, sat naked with his foot in a pool of water. "Blan!" he yelled to me as we drove on, the palace now in sight.

Just as it had half a year before when I'd seen it in the moonlight, the palace slumped, its plaster walls splintered and fractured, the domes listing, windows splayed like broken fingers. There were still broken chairs in the parking lot and broken statues in the garden. The palace peacock wandered obliviously. The ceremony would be held in a gazebo set up for press conferences, out of sight from the massive encampment just past the still-green palace lawn. I saw familiar faces: Sean Penn; the head of the UN mission; Anderson Cooper, back for the first time since early February and for some reason seated among dignitaries instead of standing in the media bullpen. Then Bill Clinton entered, followed by Préval, his wife, and Prime Minister Bellerive.

The interior minister, a graying official named Paul-Antoine Bien-Aimé, rose to begin the remembrance. To my surprise, he didn't call for a prayer, nor invite a priest to say a few words about the hundreds of thousands of lost lives. Instead, he offered thanks to the NGOs and foreign aid workers. Without them, he said, the toll of the quake would have been much greater. Then he pivoted into a defense of the government, saying that people did not understand how hard it, too, had worked. OK, I thought—now how about that moment of silence?

But there wasn't going to be a moment of silence. The interior minister kept going, his praise becoming gaudier and more self-serving, and, suddenly, what sounded like the opening to an awards ceremony turned into one. With snappy introductions and bursts of happy applause, Bien-Aimé called up people he identified as heroes of the response. Some, such as the head of the Haitian Red Cross, made sense. Some political triage seemed to be going on as well: Dr. Reynold Savain, who said Préval had screwed him out of his private hospital by not reimbursing its costs for post-quake triage, got a medal. I couldn't understand why a former commander of a paramilitary death squad that had tried to overthrow the government in 1989 appeared on the dais. But there he was.

Slack-jawed, the standing press corps watched as seemingly the entire audience got their names called for a medal and membership in the National Order of Honor and Merit, grade *Chevalier*—in other words, a knighting. Sean Penn: Medal. Edmond Mulet, head of the UN peacekeeping mission: Medal. Anderson Cooper—now I understood why he was seated where he was—medal, for reporting after the quake. The applause kept going and going. By the time it was over, twenty-two people were crowding the front of the gazebo. But the government wasn't done: There was one more medal, for the *gouverneur* himself, Bill Clinton.

The ceremony turned into a rally, with Préval lashing out at journalists who had criticized his government's response, at foreign donors who had said his government wasn't transparent enough to receive money, even at NGOs that he saw as being let off the hook by an angry population that blamed his government instead. "We do not know how much money the NGOs have received," he thundered. "That is none of our business!" Finally, in a bit of monumental spin, the Haitian leader attempted to explain away the dearth of reconstruction by clarifying that the previous six months had constituted an emergency phase. "This morning we are launching Operation Reconstruction," he declared. He promised the people of the camps that they would be getting out from under their tarps soon. Clinton then took over to promise that he would spend the next two months, "except for the time it takes me to marry my daughter off," convincing donors to make good on their donors' conference pledges.

As the ceremony broke up, photographers raced after Penn to get his picture holding his medal in front of a pile of rubble. I ran after Anderson Cooper, who explained that he had considered refusing his knighthood from the Haitian government—a pretty apparent conflict of interest—but "finally came to the opinion that it was recognition by the country for all journalists."

Outside the palace, in the survivor camp, no one Evens or I spoke to had any inkling of what had gone on inside. I talked to a man named Edouard James, quoted in my AP story that day. He told me that he had earned a college degree in diplomacy, but couldn't find a job anywhere. I asked him why, if people were so mad, we weren't seeing more protests. James' concern seemed to be that the government was too fragile to survive protests, and a government collapse wasn't a much sweeter alternative to living under a tarp. "Option A is bad. Option B is bad," he said. "We'll just wait and see."

That afternoon, around 4 P.M., a burst of wind, lightning, and driving rain hit Camp Corail. More than a quarter of the camp's deluxe white tents were ripped to shreds by the wind as pools of rising water on the unabsorbing ground forced screaming residents to flee. But there was nowhere safe to go. Six people were injured by tent poles and taken to a hospital. A few days later, Sean Penn, back at the Pétionville golf course, faced questions about Corail on the television program Democracy Now! "They are in a bad place," the chevalier admitted, motioning to the squatter camp behind him, "and a better bad place than this one."[6]

MIRACLE FALLS

By summer, the aftershocks had burned themselves out, and so had Evens and I. Whenever headquarters felt we'd missed a story, the what-the-fucks would flow downhill, bureau to subbureau, until they reached us, with me hurling the phone or swearing at Evens for no reason at all. Then he'd get forlorn and ask if he was about to lose his job, and I'd say, "No, no, it's not like that," and we'd go back to work, a fraction more bitter than before.

I was trying to get used to the narcopalace, learning the path from my room to the generator switch in the dark. I was getting better about not running out of the building every time there was a bump in the night, but the bad dreams and teeth-grinding were getting worse. Evens' big project was building a new house amid the cool pine trees farther up the mountain from Pétionville, atop bedrock that had proven more stable in the quake. He was building it in the Haitian style, which is to say very slowly: a layer of bricks when he could afford them, then a pause until he could scrounge up enough for a layer of cement, then another wait until he could buy more bricks— no mean feat given his losses when his stepfamily's house collapsed in the quake. Fortuitously, AP ran an emergency fund for just such a situation. I'd been lobbying hard for him to get reimbursed, and I helped him put together a detailed list of things he'd lost in the quake, down to the number of six-volt batteries (twelve) and the brand of the twenty-inch color TV (Westpoint).

Port-au-Prince offered all the warmth of a discarded eggshell. Pétionville was filled with aid workers and diplomats I didn't know. It had been easier to imagine that life had ended on January 12, as so many local preachers had promised after the quake, than face up to the fact that inconsiderately it had moved on.

Not every new arrival went to Pétionville. Claire Payton, the first-year doctoral student who had interviewed residents of Camp Trazelie for her oral history, wanted to live near them, too. She moved into a

Haitian family's concrete house with erratic electricity and no running water on an unpaved street off Delmas 33. Evens called her "the blan in the ghetto." But Claire didn't care. She learned to navigate the city and hung out in IDP camps after dark. Whenever I saw her, her face was a pointillist canvas of tiny black dots from riding through pollution on the back of a motorcycle, her legs and arms covered with angry, red mosquito bites.

Once I invited her to a poker game. Upon walking into our monstrous foyer, she politely stifled her laughter. Then she asked if she could take a shower. That night she slept on a pull-out upstairs. This became a pattern—she'd come over, use the shower and charge her electronics, and we'd talk. It turned out Claire had come to study Haiti by way of the French Revolution, then stumbled into oral history after the quake. She was quickly learning excellent Kreyòl. She also had these big, steel-blue eyes under long brown hair and a tiny gold ring in the left side of her button nose.

On the Fourth of July, she came over to make strawberry shortcake. She couldn't find any strawberries, and the cream she had bought that day at a high-end market near my house was already expired, so we ended up with mango-yogurt cakes instead. Another day, when there was a rumor of a general strike—which could mean barricades, rocks, and clashes with police—Claire asked if she could join us in touring the riot. I explained that Evens and I didn't take passengers. So she asked again. The strike turned out to be a bust. As we cruised around the barricadeless capital the next day, I could feel her disappointment emanating from the backseat.

In mid-July, Claire joined Evens, our photographer Ramon Espinosa, and me at the annual Vodou pilgrimage to Saut d'Eau, a waterfall where the spirit venerated in Haiti both as the Virgin Mary and Ezili Dantò, the goddess of love, once appeared to the faithful. Every year, thousands enter the falls to pray for wealth and love and wash away their sins, throwing their clothes over the lip of the waterfall until they cover the rocks below.

At the falls, we came upon a shirtless young man possessed by a spirit. He bobbed like a red-eyed puppet. A Vodou priest in a big straw hat passed him a wooden pipe, which another man lit with a candle. The possessed man breathed in the smoke with deep satisfaction and went limp.

"That's the good shit," Evens observed. Claire laughed. She asked the possessed man's name in Kreyòl.

"I am Bosou," he replied. Bosou is a three-horned lwa, or god, with the head of a bull, said to be hot-tempered and violent but intensely loyal to his followers.

"What are you doing here at Saut d'Eau?" I asked.

"I am here to celebrate my birthday," the man-god replied solemnly.

Recognizing a hard-to-get exclusive, I asked the mighty lwa what he might do to help his followers who had suffered in the quake.

He turned his head with a bovine dip. "Bosou can do," he said, "whatever you want him to do." He then pulled out pinches of baby powder, perfume, and rum, and sprinkled each of us.

Evens laughed. He put no stock in the stuff. At least, none he would admit to.

Claire told me she was going to go into the falls. "Be careful . . ." I started to say, but she'd already taken off her shoes and begun to make her way into the stream. She faced the high, cascading water, raised her arms, and soaked in the sun. I thought, watching her out there, that she had turned out to be the only person among the foreign arrivals brought by the quake to whom I could really talk. I could say something petty, dark, or plain weird, about the earthquake, and she only listened, waiting for more. It helped that she didn't work for an NGO or the government, that she wasn't a partisan flamethrower yelling at me about my stories, or a rival hack. But most of all, it didn't feel like she was taking someone's place in postquake Haiti. In fact, she wasn't like anyone I'd ever met.

A ra-ra band went by, their horns and drums at full blast as they marched straight into the waterfall. Belatedly, I realized that my camera had vanished with them. A few minutes later, Claire returned with a small setback of her own: a little saut of blood trickling from a toe.

When we got back to Port-au-Prince, we dropped her off in traffic on Delmas.

"So?" Ramon, the photographer, asked in Spanish.

"So what?"

"You know."

I looked in the rearview mirror and watched Claire's dark brown ponytail disappear in the crowd.

"Nah," I said. "She's too crazy. Even for me."

Ramon scowled. "No lo diga," *he replied.* "You never know."

Summer harbored another, less pleasant surprise. One morning I was at my desk, preparing the weekly spreadsheet of bureau expenses. I don't know why that particular role always seemed to fall to the writer—working in words doesn't actually imply expertise with numbers. But the company was meticulous about bookkeeping, and no one else around was going to do it.

The narcopalace's biggest regular expense was the diesel required to run the mighty 20,000-watt generator. It was procured by two brothers named Julian and Randy (not their real names), friends of Evens who were also drivers and translators. Three hundred dollars, with another hundred for the job, would get a plastic barrel that would usually hold up for a week or two. The company bookkeeping form asked the price per gallon, but Julian and Randy had never marked that on the receipts. Randy, the younger brother, happened to be at the house that day, so I asked him.

He stopped short. "I don't know."

Strange. I picked up the phone and called Pierre Richard Luxama, the bureau's television cameraman.

"It's 119 gourdes," he said.

Three dollars and five cents? We were paying way more than that. "No," I said. "Diesel."

"Diesel, diesel," Pierre said impatiently. "I told you. One hundred nineteen gourdes."

"That can't be right," I replied. "That barrel has forty gallons in it. If a gallon was 119 gourdes . . ."—I tapped on my calculator—"that's $122. We're paying—" I looked at Randy, who was standing next to me. "Randy, what are we paying?"

His face was quiet horror.

I told Pierre I would call him back. "Randy," I said, trying to sound calm. "How much is a gallon of diesel?"

"I'm going to go out and check that, all right?" he said, moving toward the door.

"What are you talking about?" I barked. "You go there every week. How much is a gallon of diesel?"

"I'll be right back." He rushed out the door.

My stomach dropped. This couldn't be right—Evens had brought in Julian and Randy. I'd known Julian for a long time, gone into protests with him when Evens was off or out of town. I trusted him. I trusted him almost as much as I trusted Evens.

I picked up the phone and dialed Evens.

"I don't know about that," he said when I explained the situation. "What are we paying?"

"We're paying $300 a barrel," I said. "It should be $122. What's going on?"

"I don't know. You talk to Julian?"

I paused. "Evens, if you know something—"

"Jon," he said. "This is the first I've heard. Why don't I talk to Julian and see what's going on?"

My gut clenched. I had to believe Evens. If I couldn't trust Evens, whom could I trust?

Evens called back and told me Randy was on his way to straighten things out. The guy showed up looking like a beaten dog. "Jon," he said. "I just wanted to tell you that—I'm very sorry."

I just stared.

"I'm sorry. It was stupid. I just hope—I wanted to tell you that. Because working with you has been great. I just hope I can do it still. Again."

I caught my anger. Things looked different from our perspectives. I had been to headquarters, with its football fields of computers and the big digital clocks flashing the time in Tokyo, Baghdad, and Mexico City. That was real to me. Down here, all those rules, those people watching, must have seemed like fiction. And the way all foreign media paid out must have seemed arbitrary. Why did driving to the gas station have to cost $100? Why did the same job cost three times more right after the earthquake than now? Why, when CNN came to town, did the price of a driver quadruple? Because prices were set by the funds available and fickle things like the demand for Haiti news overseas. Bumping up the price meant extra—for a better life, school for the kids, maybe investing in a business—in a place and time when everything was in short supply. Randy wasn't blowing the money on drugs. He had a family. Who could argue with him?

"Look," I said. "You're going to walk away right now, and then you'll pay us back, and that's it. It'll end there." I gritted my teeth. "But I've got to know one thing. You did this alone?"

"No one else," he told me. "It was my idea. I'm sorry."

My stomach was in knots for days. It didn't taste right for Randy to just show up and fall on the sword like that. I knew Julian was probably involved, because he did the deliveries as often as Randy. But that wasn't what worried me. Was there any way that he had something to do with this? I had zero evidence. I had little reason to even suspect it, except that he was their friend. The thing was, relationships were all you had in Haiti. And you had to take care of them. Yet what were they built on? You were assigned to work together, you went through shit, you had each other's backs. But these relationships didn't exist without money, and yet access to money was the thing that divided us most of all. Maybe Julian and Randy—for God's sake, I hoped only them—had seen me as an idiot blan with more money than sense. Or maybe they thought I wouldn't care, since it wasn't really my money, not realizing the company would have my ass, then my job.

It seems like a small thing in retrospect, but after that breach of trust, my skepticism grew—about everything. It was right around then that the company came through for Evens in a major way, reimbursing every cent we'd asked from the emergency fund. For an ugly moment I wondered if I'd gotten used again. I chased the thought out of my mind. But things were never quite as right after that.

At the end of the month, Claire ran into some quicksand of her own. One of her close Haitian friends felt menaced by someone Claire had interviewed for her project, but Claire, citing academic ethics, declined to offer that person's contact information to police. An ugly falling out took place, and friendships she had been cultivating disintegrated amid accusations of racism and betrayal. She was surprised and hurt, more hurt than I had been, I think because she was newer and younger and kinder than I was, and more vulnerable, too. Afterward she wrote:

> I have had the honor of some serious connections with people who live in refugee camps (and outside the camps), with people who never asked me for anything. But it's rare. For the most part, everyone is trying to move along in the world, make it to the next day, and to many people I met in Haiti, I am the suggestion or promise of a means to an end. . . . Being white in Haiti speaks certain things much louder than my voice. It speaks of disposable income, a life without hunger, the possibility of leaving that place.

Claire called me that evening and said something that I knew meant we had grown closer. I didn't know it meant she'd come that night to a concert at the Hotel Oloffson, where she'd tell me the whole saga, crying, as we sat on a concrete bank near the stage. Or that on the dance floor a little while later, a pint or two of rum between us, our hips moving to the funk-rock Vodou beat, we'd kiss. But I knew, in the first words she spoke when I picked up the phone, that no matter the particulars, there was something inside both of us that had just come together, deep and true. They were words you can truly understand only when you realize that to love Haiti is to come away bruised; that loving Haiti is to love something that may not even love itself, but that it's still love, after all.

"Jonathan?" Claire had said. "Fuck this place."

CHAPTER TEN

FACE TO FACE

SATURDAY NIGHT, MIDDLE OF JULY, AND PÉTIONVILLE WAS ROARING again. The emergency staff on two-week rotations at the UN and U.S. Embassy had given way to a new corps of semipermanent aid workers, and, like the Haitian middle and upper classes six months *après l'événement,* they were ready to get living again. It had been bumper to bumper all the way down Rue Louverture, a mosh pit at the door of Club Trotyl, and now on the dance floor it was bumper to bumper again. I probably wouldn't have braved the crowds in the sweat-drip heat after working all day, but this was a show not to miss. One of Haiti's great showmen, the swearingest, filthiest bad boy in all of Haitian *kompa* music, was back on the courtyard stage. A keyboardist and crooner who would put on a miniskirt, rip off his pants, and hump a drum set if it would rile the crowd, which it always did. Passing midnight, the house was packed, eyes dilated and voices murmuring in the dark. The band was on stage. But no sign of the man.

Then the guitar let loose, the bass broke into its telltale groove, and, to shouts and cheers, the bald head emerged. Sweet Micky, born Michel Martelly, took the stage in a shirt we all knew was not long for the night. Every man grabbed the closest woman, pulled her in, and started the low, hard grind called *ploge,* as in what a plug does to a socket. Kompa, that thumping love child of merengue, funk, and R&B, rocks on and on, with live songs lasting ten, twenty, thirty minutes without a break, segments flowing into each other—love song, call-out song, brag song, diss song, sex song—the crowd working itself sweatier and more frenzied with each one.

Micky might have perfected the style. In the 1990s, he took a genre long preferred by the Duvaliers and their military successors over politically edgier "roots" music and protest folk, because kompa's sole concern was having a good time, and turned it into something—well, if not deeper, then definitely *harder*. The only ideology Micky wanted to spread was the greatness of Micky. One of his all-time hits was called "I Don't Care." In the song, Micky taunts his listeners: "The band has a lot of problems!" Not fan problems. ("We have plenty of fans.") Not power problems. ("The country is ours, that's this country's problem.") Certainly not money problems! Micky lets loose a series of deep, head-tossing cackles, then growls: No, the problem is that everyone is *jealous of the band!* The musicians play on, as Micky repeats his slogan: "*If you don't like it, get out of here!*"

No one needed to get out of Club Trotyl that Saturday night. The club was pumping, ploge in the VIP lounge up the stairs, ploge down on the floor. But we were moving no more showily than Micky, his forty-nine-year-old bulging arms and belly straining out of his undershirt—hell, wife-beater. This was no place for delicacy with Micky on stage, cussing, calling out rival bands with every Kreyòl slur in the book, leering at the women, leering at the men.

Micky had been born in Port-au-Prince but spent many years in Miami, where he had been sent to a community college and dropped out. Once, a year and a half before the quake, I ran into him in an empty club near Trotyl. Unguarded with an American, he confessed something that had apparently been eating at him for a while. "Kompa is getting old, I think. It's for old people now, like me. The young people they listen to hip-hop. *Rrrrap.*" He rolled the r the way he did in his songs. "I'm going to have to find something new to do with myself."

Fortunately, he hadn't found that thing just yet, because in that moment we needed him on that floor, and maybe he needed us too. His music did what it was born to do, to make us all forget, to think only of the handsome man on stage, of the girls and boys rubbing against us, of the bass line moving forward and in a circle at the same time, the moon, the rum, and the thump da-da-da, thump da-da-da of the clave and the drums. Then the music stopped, and Micky started in with his patented Carnival banter, lewd jokes, and bashing on a rival, squeaky-clean band. Then he took things a step further, referring to the nightmare outside as if it was just another kompa taunt. I didn't catch what he said. Pooja Bhatia, a journalist and good friend, explained: "He said that we're all going to be dead in five years!" Then he added, "So take your pleasure while you can! Drink! Dance! Ladies, go out and have sex with guys! Have sex with me!"[1]

The crowd cheered, the music swirled, someone I didn't know was in my arms, and all the problems in this stupid world sailed out beyond the palm trees into the sweet-sick airy night. A man tried to climb onto the stage. Micky paused mid-lyric. "Excuse me, excuse me!" he shouted and walked toward him. He wagged a lanky finger at the invader and then, with a roundhouse punch, sent him flying back down the stairs. As the man landed with a thud, the band and the club shouted approval. Micky swaggered back to the front of the stage to finish his love song.

If you don't like it, roared the philosopher, *get out of here!*

WITH THE CITY STILL IN RUBBLE, mounds of shattered concrete and human remains eroding in the rain faster than they could be cleared, pop-star rants about apocalypses seemed saner than talk of an election actually taking place on November 28. The Provisional Electoral Council's headquarters was still a shambles, its logistics and records annex ruined to its foundation, key staffers dead inside. Polling places were wrecked. Countless voters had lost their registration cards in collapsed homes, and untold numbers of earthquake dead would have to be crossed off the rolls. Préval was still rolling his Unity Party strategy forward, its rival parties still disqualified. The party's leaders debated who to put forward as Préval's anointed successor—rumors said one of his old prime ministers or the first lady. Since the protests against Préval in May, his administration's enthusiasm for an on-time election had cooled even further.

The United States insisted that punctuality was a top priority. And Washington had a say: It was providing half the $29 million foreigners were paying for the election. "Congress and the international community have invested significant resources in the political, economic, and social development of Haiti, and have closely monitored the election process as a prelude to the next steps in Haiti's development," a Congressional Research Service report explained.[2] A successful election ten and a half months after Haiti's earthquake was, as far as Foggy Bottom was concerned, an essential demonstration that things were on the right track.

Sensing reluctance from Préval, in June, Washington laid down the law. Senator Richard Lugar, the ranking Republican on the Foreign Relations Committee, issued a series of election recommendations for the Haitian government, aimed at ending both Préval's obstructionism and shaming his rather obvious ploy to use the Provisional Electoral Council (CEP) to stack the election in the Unity Party's favor. Lugar demanded that Préval formally declare a November 28 Election Day, as scheduled, restructure the eight-member electoral council, and ensure the participation of excluded parties.[3]

Préval, stung, retaliated. "I'm not doing the CEP with international partners," he said coolly at a press conference called specifically to rebuke the American legislator. "I'm doing the CEP with national partners. The senator's proposition is inadmissible."

Lugar hit back, harder. "Having significantly delayed issuing the decree for presidential and parliamentary elections, President Rene Préval's actions do not suggest a departure from the self-destructive political behavior that has kept Haiti the poorest country in the Western Hemisphere," Lugar wrote in a follow-up report, employing a description of Haiti considered a deep insult in Haitian circles. "If reforms in this direction do not occur, American taxpayer investments in Haiti, beyond essential humanitarian aid, should be reassessed."[4]

This was no idle threat. The United States had yet to release a cent of the money it had promised at the donors' conference. An authorization bill that could push the funding through was being held up in the Senate.

Préval did not call another press conference but quietly affirmed November 28 as the election date, while saying nothing about restructuring the CEP or reinstating disqualified parties.

Lugar did not respond either. Washington continued to hold the money.

With the election pushing forward, a cavalcade of hopefuls began presenting themselves as candidates. As intractably wrecked as Haiti was, and as thankless and perilous a job as the presidency had long been, dozens wanted to seek the post even in that worst of all years. At a prequake welcome event for the new U.S. ambassador, a savvy young American political officer commented that there were likely presidential candidates among the Haitian bourgeoisie and power brokers present. "Who?" I asked. He extended his arm. "I'd say this half of the room—and that half." One of the more powerful landowners in Haiti put it to me this way: "Wanting to be president of this country is a disease for which there is no cure."

When we had met to talk about Corail-Cesselesse, I'd asked Leslie Voltaire if he was running. He shook his head. "Look, if you run and you're elected, you don't have power really, as a president. You do a lot of effort and then you have to share it with the prime minister, you have to share it with Bill Clinton and the international community, you have to share it with the parliamentarians and then you have nothing." Since the National Palace collapsed, you wouldn't even get to use it anymore, he added, laughing.

Confirming the landowner's maxim, just a few weeks later, Voltaire submitted his candidacy to the CEP. Although he would surely meet the six qualifications for the ballot—including five years' consecutive residency in Haiti, the ownership of a piece of property, and never having been "sentenced to death"—even Voltaire knew he didn't have much of a shot. I asked him who did.

"Wyclef Jean, I think," Voltaire replied. "If he runs, he wins."

WYCLEF JEAN WAS BORN IN CROIX-DES-BOUQUETS, a dusty suburb curled around the eastern edge of the capital, but his parents were able to move to Brooklyn when he was a boy. In high school, he, his cousin Prakazrel "Pras" Michel, and singer Lauryn Hill formed the Fugees—an act with a hip-hop, soul, and reggae blend that was as cool as cool got in the early 1990s. By the time Jean reached stardom, he spoke rudimentary Kreyòl and almost no French, and he had spent little time in his native country. But he wore his Haitian pride on his sleeve—sometimes in the form of a flag on his head—and was beloved on the island. After all, Jean was a symbol of two big dreams: getting out and striking rich.

In 2007, Préval, probably hoping some of Jean's popularity would rub off, made him an ambassador at large of the Haitian government. This was taken as cheeky celebrity news in the States, but the rap star was not a total political neophyte. His uncle, a political player who supported an expansion of the garment industry, was an Aristide opponent who had become Haiti's ambassador to the United States after the president was overthrown in 2004. The singer himself jabbed his finger at the blender weeks before Aristide's ouster, echoing his uncle's position in an MTV interview. That fall he released an album that featured a track titled "President." "I'd get elected on Friday," he sings, "assassinated on Saturday, buried on Sunday, then go back to work on Monday."

Diplomatic status in hand, Jean's tone got more political. (I quickly learned that the surest way to get him to stop for an interview was to address him as "Ambassador Jean.") He founded an NGO called Yelé-Haiti that distributed aid in the slums and dropped in for high-profile visits with more attention-getting stars, such as Matt Damon or Angelina Jolie. Then, in early 2009, Jean arrived with his highest-flying delegation yet: Bill Clinton and UN Secretary-General Ban Ki-moon. Although the rapper spent most of the trip slouching in his chair or clowning with crowds, his place beside two world leaders seemed like a kind of audition.

I asked him about his political ambitions every chance I got, knowing that "Wyclef for President" would be an instant global story. But he always laughed it off. When his press people hounded me for an interview six months after the quake, I thought I was about to get the scoop. But it turned out he just wanted to hype his new album and some youth movement he was calling Face to Face, or *Fas-a-Fas* in Kreyòl. When I asked the big question, he was coy. "I'm already the president of a record company," he said sheepishly. "And some people call me the president of Flatbush, Brooklyn."

I should have known that, as Leslie Voltaire demonstrated, the first prerequisite of running for office in Haiti might as well have been denying that you were going to do so. But I took Wyclef at his word. Who *would* want to be president now?

AS RENÉ PRÉVAL WAS LEARNING, there was no way to preside over Haiti without being held responsible for the dismal pace of reconstruction, however little power over that pace you had. Seven months after the quake—four after the donors' conference and two after the formation of the Interim Haiti Recovery Commission—less than 2 percent of the rubble had been cleared. A measly 13,000 temporary shelters had been built, of a promised 125,000, not to speak of permanent housing. One refrain was on the lips of ordinary Haitians and presidential aspirants alike: Where had the money gone? No survivors I met expected their country rebuilt in a year, or five, but there was good reason to be incensed that so little progress had taken place. Many among the millions overseas who had donated to the relief effort were asking too.

According to Bill Clinton's UN Office for the Special Envoy, the source of record on postquake aid to Haiti, donors had spent or promised roughly $16.3 billion for Haiti after the quake.[5] Knowing where that money went had implications for Haitian politics and the future of foreign aid in general. The supposition—shared from Port-au-Prince camps to North American living rooms—was that if the money wasn't making a difference on the ground, someone must have stolen it. In the quake zone, it was spelled out in anti-NGO graffiti and taunts about Préval. In the United States, online reader comments on my stories were filled with vitriol: "I was in 'prequake' Haiti in 1995. It was a @!$%#hole then, and it's still a @!$%#hole," opined one reader in the summer of 2010. "The government is corrupt, and the U.S. is stupid as hell to pump money into these corrupt governments, all over the world. The people who NEED the aid will NEVER see it."

But this view was based on some mistaken premises. The first was that $16.3 billion would necessarily have been a transformative sum. It paled in comparison not only to U.S. spending on the war and reconstruction of Iraq—$806 billion estimated through 2011—but simple stateside infrastructure projects. It had cost $20 billion just to maintain roads and trains for ten years in Maryland, a state nearly Haiti's size, with less than two-thirds the population and no major catastrophe from which to rebuild.[6] No doubt, at more than double Haiti's total yearly economic output, $16.3 billion could have had a major impact. But after two centuries of poverty, degradation, and exploitation, even $1,600 per Haitian man, woman, and child would have to have been extraordinarily well managed to have a profound effect—to ensure that, as Hillary Rodham Clinton had told delegates to the March donors' conference, Haiti would at last "fulfill [its] own God-given potentials . . . [and] become an engine for progress and prosperity."

Yet most of the money pledged by foreign governments had never been meant for Haitian consumption. As humanitarian relief spending continued to trickle through 2010, adding up in the end to $2.43 billion, in the end at least 93 percent would go right back to the UN or NGOs to pay for supplies and personnel, or never leave the donor states at all. Despite the emphasis donors placed on Haitian transparency, most of the money turned out to be very difficult to trace; 6 percent—$151 million—couldn't be accounted for at all. Just 1 percent—slightly more than $24 million—went to the Haitian government.[7] Had Préval or parliament stolen every cent of their share, and there's no indication they did, it would have made little difference.

Haiti's private sector fared even worse. Of the nearly $1 billion in U.S. government contracts for postquake Haiti, just twenty-two, worth less than $4.8 million, went to Haitian firms. By comparison, one manufacturer on a kibbutz near Tel Aviv received $7.9 million to supply the U.S. Navy with prefabricated metal buildings for the Haiti mission. What was contracted to Haiti mainly benefited the wealthy elite; nearly a third went to a port logistics firm owned and managed by Richard Coles, whose garment factories supply Kmart, Walmart, and others.[8]

Unusually for a disaster, a major chunk of U.S. government spending went through the Defense Department: $465 million through August 2010, mostly to the usual contractors or for standard deployment expenses. Operation of the nuclear supercarrier USS *Carl Vinson* alone cost an estimated $1 million a day for each of its eighteen days in Port-au-Prince harbor.[9] The Coast Guard, part of the Department of Homeland Security, spent $3.6 million on parts and repairs to its fleet of Sikorsky UH–60 Jayhawk helicopters. Other contracts were harder to trace, such as $16.7 million pushed through a logistics contractor called Contingency Response Services LLC. This may have been because one of its three partners, Kuwait-based Agility Public Warehousing KSC, had been blacklisted from government contracts since being indicted in 2009 for conspiracy to defraud the United States during the Iraq War.[10] An Agility spokesman denied that the company handled any of the U.S. government work in Haiti, although he declined to say whether Agility had been paid. The Pentagon declined to comment.

Responders also needed to sleep and eat. The United States spent at least $368,000 on hotel rooms and meals, and not in Haiti either: Rooms were booked at four luxury hotels on Santo Domingo's oceanfront esplanade, at a Tampa Bay resort, and at the five-star Mandarin Oriental in Washington. A State Department shuttle to ferry staff and evacuees between Haiti and the Dominican Republic cost $18,000—a steal compared with the $46,400 of Haiti money that State Department would pay for a new Toyota Prado SUV eight months after the quake. The State Department itself struggled to track down how $50,000 in Haiti funds were spent on elevator maintenance, in a country with about a dozen elevators in all. (It was likely spent at the U.S. Embassy.)

Why did the U.S. Navy burn through $194,000 in Haiti money on photo and video equipment at a Manhattan store? Why did it sign an $18,000 contract for a jungle gym from a Georgia company, especially since the "Gorilla Big Skye I" retailed for a third that online? What earthquake fallout prompted the Coast Guard to buy a $4,462 deep-fat fryer—years of Haitian income—in early 2011? Despite repeated enquiries, spokesmen declined to answer these questions. When the mission was over, the Coast Guard used a Haiti contract to buy medals and ribbons from a Virginia store. Price tag: $11,352.50.

Huge logistical operations cost money, especially when they involve nuclear-powered aircraft carriers and tens of thousands of personnel. But it's misleading to call such spending "money for Haiti," especially when it gives the impression that any Haitian could have misappropriated or even profited from it. If anything,

much of the money was a stimulus program for the donor countries themselves.

The Office of the Special Envoy estimated that more than $3
billion was donated to international NGOs for relief, mostly right
after the quake. The American Red Cross alone raised $486 mil-
lion, by far the largest component of the more than $1.14 billion
raised after the quake by all Red Cross and Red Crescent societies around the world. I suspect many donated to that organization because they imagined the U.S. branch of Red Cross as a kind
of global clearinghouse for donations—that's how I thought of it
when I gave $20 after the 2004 Indian Ocean tsunami. But the
American Red Cross is one chapter of a particular organization
that specializes in short-term emergency relief. "For the most part
we don't do development," spokeswoman Jana Sweeny would explain to me. This seems obvious when you think about it, yet I have
met scores of very intelligent people who wondered why their $20
sent to an agency that primarily provided food, tarps, and medical
aid didn't rebuild Haiti.

The American Red Cross could not spend $486 million, or close
to that, on postquake emergency relief. When the disaster struck,
the organization had three foreign staffers on the ground. Though
it quickly ramped up to 24, and increased the number of Haitian
Red Cross volunteers it subcontracted, there was a finite amount
of aid to be pushed through to a finite number of people in need.
(There are only so many times you can give someone a hygiene
kit.) By July 2010, the American Red Cross had signed contracts
to spend—not *spent,* but *signed contracts* to spend—less than a
third of that amount.[11] Its president, Gail McGovern, promised her
agency would keep working in Haiti "until every donated dollar has
been spent." But while the organization did try to do some development work ("When we're entrusted with such a massive amount
of money we're really forced into that position," the spokeswoman
would explain), that required pushing money out through other
NGOs, who then had to take their own cut for administration and
overhead.

This was typical. The thirty-eight aid groups that responded to
a survey by the U.S.-based watchdog Disaster Accountability Project
in January 2011 would report having raised $1.4 billion after the

quake while spending only $731 million by the one-year mark. One hundred fifty-eight aid groups declined to respond.

Some aid groups were up-front with donors. When Doctors Without Borders realized that the 30 million euros it had raised in the days after the quake were more than it could reasonably expect to spend in Haiti, it encouraged donors to contribute to its general fund so that the money could be used on emergencies elsewhere.

The greatest fallacy of all was that there had ever been $16.3 billion, or even half that, to spend on anything. The Office of the Special Envoy itself immediately discounted the $972 million in pledged debt relief from the total, since it was money Haiti never had in the first place. Another $3.9 billion had been pledged for 2012 and beyond, meaning it couldn't even be sniffed in late 2010. When you exclude those huge sums, along with $3 billion in NGO donations often used for overhead or left unspent, and the $2.43 billion of humanitarian aid spent almost entirely outside Haiti, you're left with $5.5 billion from the donors' conference. As of the presidential candidates' registration period in August 2010, 90 percent of *that* remained undelivered. Just five countries—Brazil, Colombia, Estonia, Norway, and Australia, along with multilateral organizations such as the World Bank—had paid the money they promised. All told, just $210 million had been given to the Haitian government, all with restrictive strings attached, and much of it awaiting the approval of the IHRC to allocate.

This condition would persist. As late as March 2012, less than half the long-term money pledged at the donors' conference for 2010 and 2011 would have been delivered, and the most egregious spendthrifts, perhaps predictably, were the biggest pledgers: Venezuela and the United States, each delivering less than a fifth of what it had promised.

Where did the money go? Most of it never arrived. But the donors didn't seem to want to talk about that. It was easier to have the Haitian government carry the blame, especially a president whose intransigence over the election was doing him no favors with Washington.

"There is another path that Haiti could take," Hillary Clinton had warned the UN donors' conference, "a path that demands far less of Haiti and far less of us. If the effort to rebuild is slow or insufficient, if it is marked by conflict, lack of coordination, or lack of transparency, then the challenges that have plagued Haiti for years could erupt, with regional and global consequences." As the preliminaries for the election arrived, those words were ringing truer than ever.

IN THE FIRST WEEK OF AUGUST 2010, Wyclef Jean's Twitter feed, usually occupied with fan shout-outs and music videos, got distinctly political. The rapper wrote and reposted about roads, food distributions, hospitals, and "Haiti's new revolution." One read: "#Haitians have no confidence in the prospects of free elections, portending turbulent times ahead." The message seemed clear. On August 3, thanks to Evens' expert sourcing, we broke the story that Wyclef Jean was running for president.

Two days later he went to register at the headquarters of the CEP on Route de Delmas. All morning the radio replayed Wyclef's interview from the day before in Miami, where in halting Kreyòl supplemented with English he had defended his inexperience. "For two hundred years people have been governing this country—I don't need that training. I need logic," he said. He also insisted that he wouldn't fail the five-year residence requirement because he was an ambassador. (If so, Préval might have been regretting having conferred that title—given his popularity and name recognition, Jean would be an instant front-runner.) The radio announcers reported that the Haitian American had also hired a Kreyòl tutor.

The electoral council would take until month's end to decide which of the dozens of applicants fit the constitutional criteria for inclusion on the ballot, though it would never have to account for its reasoning. But even if admitted to the ballot, few candidates who weren't music superstars, established political figures, or backed by the Unity Party stood a chance of winning. Most knew that registration was the climax of their campaigns.

The scene could have been a Carnival battle of the bands. On either side of the entrance along Route de Delmas were police barricades, holding back as many supporters in as the campaigns' backers could manage to bring out. Nearly all were young men, on motorcycles and milling in the midsummer heat, or bouncing to music pumped from speakers nearby. Whenever their appointed candidate arrived, fans yelled songs and slogans, blew horns, pushed against the barricades, and screamed *Viv!—LONG LIVE!*—whomever. If the police shoved back, even better.

In true star fashion, Wyclef Jean kept us waiting. There was a commotion on the street, and the gaggle of reporters looked up.

"Oh," someone said. "It's just Sweet Micky."

Although Jean was the only pop star our editors cared about, he was not the only Haitian celebrity vying for a spot in the race. Michel Martelly, the king of *kompa*, was making good on his promise to find something else to do. It wasn't clear if his candidacy was serious, a publicity stunt, or a copycat move. Wyclef and Micky were supposedly cousins. Micky might have even given Jean the idea to run: In the 1990s, he had released his own song about the presidency, "*Prezidan,*" in which he fantasized about becoming the first *kompa* president of Haiti. In an interview soon after, Micky had promised that, were he ever actually elected, he would dance naked atop National Palace. Ever since, "President of Kompa" had been his *nom de show.* For a decade already, people had been addressing him as "Mr. President."

Martelly emerged from the registration office, dapper, his unmistakable toffee-hued bald head perched above a medium-shiny gray suit. He spotted Trenton Daniel, a *Herald* reporter he knew from Miami, and walked over to greet us. I almost called him "Mr. President" out of habit, then caught myself.

"It's time to change the direction of our country," Martelly said vaguely when I asked why he was running. "We are going toward a disaster. We are going toward catastrophe. And somebody must step up and say enough is enough."

"Do you think your rival Wyclef has a shot at winning?" Daniel asked.

"I welcome him!" Martelly responded. "I won't say that I will *vote* for him because I don't know his plan. And I'm a candidate too." It sounded like he was trying to remind us.

The next question, from a Haitian writer named Wadner Pierre, probably made him wish he wasn't: "What is the first thing you'd do in power?"

Suddenly Sweet Micky lost his swagger. He stammered about a team, vision, steps. "The team might, might decide that—the other—that something else is the priority," he tried. Then he tried to save the set. "It's not about *me!* It's about achieving this *goal!* And we are going to work as a team. So I am not here to promise and promise. I'm here to deliver. And we are going to work as a team with the party with the people with the press—with the international. With everyone!" He paused. "Is that OK?"

We nodded.

SOON AFTER, WYCLEF JEAN APPEARED, thousands of eager young men awaiting him in white T-shirts reading *Fas a Fas,* the name of his new youth movement. After years of disillusionment, here was a hip-hop icon, a man whose songs reflected their dreams, saying he wanted to be their real live leader. With the tremendous size of Haiti's youth population, a real youth movement could prove decisive at the ballot box.

"No matter who else is running, I'm voting for Wyclef," a twenty-something waiter from Cap-Haïtien would tell me several days later.

"But he speaks Kreyòl like I do," I responded.

"Yes, but that is because he is an American."

"You want to vote for him because he's an American?"

"If he's American," the Capois said, smiling, "then when he is president, *everyone* will get a visa."

As sweat-dripping photographers, politicians, electoral officials, and Jean family members jostled for position in the registration room, a blue ballpoint pen was passed to Wyclef. He printed a full name, Jeannel Wyclef Jean, and signed under that "Nel Ust Wyclef J." Age: forty (three years older than he'd said before). Outside, the jazz and ra-ra bands partied, clouds of marijuana and rum vapors hung in the air. Jean's visage stared down presidentially from large photographs mounted on a Carnival truck. "Fas a Fas! Fas a Fas!" the crowd chanted. Finally, they broke into a song that stopped me cold—an old hymn usually sung for Aristide, whom Jean had called to step down in 2004. The crucial line was changed to "Our blood is the blood of Wyclef Jean!"

Wyclef went out to the crowd and body-surfed toward the truck. He then mounted and proclaimed in New York Kreyòl that he was indeed a real Haitian. Then he declared that he would win. "America has Barack Obama!" he shouted. "And Haiti has Wyclef Jean!" There was an eruption from the crowd. The singer climbed down for a tour of the city, ending at a satellite linkup at the Plaza Hotel. Although the news was everywhere by now, Jean went ahead with his official announcement—in English, on CNN.

"*Sak pa-se! Na bou-le!*" Wyclef said to open the interview.

Wolf Blitzer laughed via satellite. "I don't know what it means. Tell me what it means first."

"Sak—it means what's up, what's going on, how you feeling?" Wyclef replied.

A few hours later I sat down with the candidate. In the intervening time, CNN had sought out a news-balancing rebuttal to his candidacy—not from a Unity Party rep or political scientist, but from Sean Penn. "For those of us *in Haiti* he has been a nonpresence," the actor/aid worker told Blitzer, opining that Wyclef came to Haiti only to show off, not really help.

Now the actor was all Wyclef wanted to talk about. "Can somebody show exactly what Sean Penn said about me online? So I can straight up rebuttal on him?"

I read him back the basic notes. Grimacing, he said he was a "big fan" of Sean Penn but that the actor didn't know everything that happened in Haiti. It felt strange to be mediating a postquake political debate between an ex-Fugee and the guy from Mystic River. I wanted to hear the candidate talk about the issues.

Seated beside Jean was Pierre Eric Jean-Jacques, a gray-haired Haitian lawmaker who'd gotten rich wholesaling grain alcohol and now seemed to be Jean's main advisor. Occasionally Jean-Jacques would break into our conversation, whisper at the candidate for a minute or two, then sit back as the rapper repeated his words to me. "You know, Alexander the Great always had an old guy next to him," Wyclef explained sheepishly at one point.

Whether the ideas were his advisor's or his, they were mostly about investment—in mining concessions, Haitian agriculture, and the garment industry.

"Some of the things you're talking about sound like the Collier Report," I said. "Are you in favor of the program that Bill Clinton has been advocating?"

"Bill Clinton?" Jean replied. "I used to be at the White House saying 'throw your hands up in the air for Bill Clinton.' And he believes heavy in investment. Garment. And what's going to help get Haiti out of what Haiti's in right now is purely investment. And bringing jobs. We clear on that."

But was he endorsing the garment industry, specifically? I asked.

"One of the pillars," he responded, for some reason talking backward. "Investment in garment, is, I think, one of them."

IN A PERSONALITY-DRIVEN CAMPAIGN in a country mad about music, candidates connected with people through song. Something catchy could make the candidate seem more approachable and set apart an otherwise indistinguishable platform. Here music stars had advantages. Like celebrities entering any field, they could also skip the training, dues-paying, and often embarrassing trial-and-error required of other souls and proceed straight to competing for the highest levels of power.

One day, the staff for a minor contender named Yves Cristalin gave Twenty Chery and his clique a call. Cristalin was an old Aristide associate who didn't stand much of a chance, a good-enough choice for Twenty and his guys, who were mostly interested in an opportunity to perform and a little campaign cash.

Claire had begun slowly introducing me to her new friends at Trazelie—including the Cherys—and we were now both invited to Twenty's show at the rally near Cité Soleil. I wanted to take a driver. She wanted to go by motorcycle. Somehow I won out, and we headed down in the car of a Haitian driver nicknamed Sleepy.

Twenty and his girlfriend, Kettelie, were waiting for us next to Trazelie. Twenty looked fresh, his braids tucked into a black ball cap and matching shirt. "*Sak pase*," he greeted me, clasping his hand to mine. "I'm glad you came." The couple climbed in and greeted Claire warmly, the three chatting in Kreyòl. The clear, genuine depth of their friendship struck me. There was no pretense at all. In nearly three years in the country, always on the clock, I'd seldom been able to let my guard down with Haitians. They were subjects first, potential friends second. As we sped by the metal concert stage, Twenty explained that we were going to pick up his friends. "Cool," Claire replied. I noticed we were going into the slum.

Under a darkening sky, our headlights traced the cinder blocks of the narrow side street. The block just past us had been wiped out in the quake, but for some reason, this one had stood. We got out and followed Twenty into a blind alleyway until we hit a set of crumbling stairs. Smiling, he motioned for us to climb.

On the roof, some guys from his crew were knocking back beer and rum. Twenty's friends chided him—"I can't believe you brought the blan to Cité Soleil! Don't you know this place is dangerous?"—but he waved them off. "Don't worry," he told Claire. We were offered crates to sit on and handed the passed-around bottle. Twenty's friends discussed their plans for the show, their favorite new bands, and the latest innovations in their rhymes. A debate broke out about which was harder: living in a camp or a house in Cité Soleil. One of Twenty's friends, who had learned excellent English in school, told us that despite never having been a drinker, all he did after the quake was sleep during the day and drink at night. He asked if I could get him a job. Maybe, I said, trying to be polite.

As the hours and warming beers ticked by, the cloudy night upon us, we still hadn't left for the show, which was supposed to have begun at eight. Then a few drops of rain started to fall. Everyone moved downstairs into the breeze-block shack. Thunder cracked, the sky opened, and suddenly sheets of rain were battering the curtain blocking the paneless windows of the outer wall. We crammed in the dark room with two dozen others, the only light from cell phones and a candle. After a while I pulled back the curtain and looked out the glassless window. A flood half a yard high was lapping at the door. It was close to midnight.

Twenty sadly conceded that the show wasn't going to happen. I called Sleepy, who had been waiting in the street. His U-turn sent a wave of water crashing into the house. I waded through the surf, and Twenty's friends carried Claire to the car. We would learn the next morning that ten people drowned that night in Port-au-Prince, a small disaster that would pass unnoticed by the world.

We were both thankful to be in Sleepy's SUV, and not on a motorcycle, cutting through the high water on Maïs Gâté like a slow-
moving boat. We passed the abandoned blacked-out stage and the
mud-filled tarps of Trazelie, hearing only the music of the storm.

ON AUGUST 20, THE CEP RULED Wyclef Jean ineligible to run for
president. No explanation was given. His fans were furious, but
not surprised—after all, Jean didn't live in Haiti. He had also
taken a beating in the foreign press, including revelations that he
pocketed money from his own NGO and owed $2.1 million in back
taxes in the United States.[12] Finally, though Préval denied it, many
Haitians believed the president had urged the CEP to cross him off,
recognizing the threat Wyclef posed to any Unity candidate.

Unity chose the opposite of a pop star: Jude Célestin, the
head of the state-run construction company. As head of an in-
government contractor, he was already indebted to Préval. The
party also hoped his position would associate Unity with the
key postquake theme of jobs, rebuilding, and power—if not the
company's white dump trucks, which after the earthquake had
carted away tens of thousands of bodies to the mass graves outside town.

Nineteen were on the final ballot; Célestin, backed by Unity's
unparalleled organization, was the presumptive front-runner. But,
as had been proven over and over throughout the year, Préval's
backing was a mixed blessing. Given the discontent with him,
the race could be wide open for the challengers, such as Mirlande
Manigat, a constitutional law professor whose husband, Leslie,
had been president in the late 1980s and lost to Préval in 2006.
Leslie Voltaire made the ballot too. And while Wyclef was gone,
Sweet Micky had made it through. Months before, the landowner
with whom I'd discussed the elections had given me advice on pick-
ing a winner. "When the people vote," he told me, "they will think
about only one thing: Which candidate has never betrayed them?"
I wondered who fit that bill best, or at all.

After his disqualification, Wyclef Jean would go back to music,
releasing an album with a diss track about the CEP. But his candidacy had opened a door. During his moment on the political stage,
the young population had realized that it didn't have to stick with

the old-guard politicians who had let so many down. The young people of Haiti could turn to someone they felt they could really connect with—someone they felt they knew. After a year of misery, the race was open to anyone who could change the subject. Or, better said, the tune.

CHAPTER ELEVEN

A GUT FEELING

THE HORROR WAS IN THE STOMACH, AN EMPTY, DRAINING PAIN. ALL the way up the highway, Rosemond Lorimé had felt it running out of him. It was like the river running out of him, getting worse with every turn around the mountains.

Rosemond lived in a thatch-and-mud house in Meille, a small village on Haiti's central plateau, built along a little river of the same name. For a young man of twenty-one, there wasn't much to do there among the bean plants and banana trees. You could swim or take a bath in the river. You could help the older folks raise pigs and turkeys, or plant cassava. Rosemond and his cousin would sell rum and *kleren* moonshine to the blan soldiers at the UN base and introduce them to the neighborhood girls in exchange for a few dollars. But that was about it. Even the earthquake had been boring in Meille. The ground had just groaned, rumbled, and stopped.

The sickness came nine months after. Rosemond's father fell ill first. A low, hard pain formed in his gut and radiated all over his body. Then the diarrhea began, then vomiting, torrential like a fall storm. Soon everyone in the house was sick: Rosemond, his four brothers and sisters, his mother. The illness then moved into the neighboring houses. The family gathered up its money and sent Rosemond's father to the hospital in the nearby town of Mirebalais. But it soon became clear that Rosemond's sickness was the worst. The pain gripped his gut, and heat rose in his head and cut his intestines as if he'd eaten a stick of thorns. His stomach became a rejecting vessel. The water he drank would come back up or go straight out. Rice did the same. Even the garlic tea and cotton leaf that the women in the village gave him to settle his stomach ended up vomited or run out onto the ground. The diarrhea kept flowing; Rosemond became thirstier and thirstier. Neighbors whispered that it must be a spell.

The family looked for money to send Rosemond to the hospital too, but it took days to find enough. The day after his father returned home, weary but alive, Rosemond's brothers put the young man on the back of a motorcycle taxi to go to Mirebalais. He could barely move as the driver sped over the mountain bends. Under an arid sky, arms carried Rosemond into the little hospital with green-painted walls. A voice cried out in the room. Struggling for air, Rosemond closed his drying eyes and never opened them again.

It was Sunday, October 17, 2010.

WEDNESDAY, OCTOBER 20, WAS, for once, the end of a week. International interest in news about Haiti had bottomed out. Claire and I had decided to go away for a long weekend to the other end of the Caribbean, to an island without broken generators and harassing street kids, where no one was struggling to resettle a million people in tarp cities or clear the mounds of rubble blocking the streets. No one would notice four days without a feature from Haiti.

The day before Claire and I were set to leave, I was with Evens, grinding up Route de Delmas toward the AP bureau in Pétionville, negotiating stalled water trucks, stray goats, and overstuffed taxis. If I was taking off four days, he was saying, then he should be too. "I never get to see my boy," he complained, dipping his head and looking over plaintively, perhaps cribbing an expression from his toddler. But if I was leaving, I was trying to explain, someone needed to stay behind to mind the store. "Then you can take off—"

"Hold up," Evens said. He turned up the car radio.

". . . the hospital in Saint-Marc. The Ministry of Public Health and Population reports that forty-one people have died. Many are children. The patients arrive at the hospital with symptoms of vomiting, fever, and strong diarrhea. The Ministry of Public Health and Population urges all citizens in the Department of the Artibonite to watch for symptoms and report them. . . ."

I suddenly felt sick too. Though experts at the World Health Organization, the medical NGOs, and the Centers for Disease Control and Prevention had been emphasizing that a major epidemic would be unlikely after the quake, they pushed out vaccinations against diphtheria, tetanus, measles, and other communicable diseases to be sure. I'd dutifully chased down almost every lead, including May's diphtheria scare, increasingly joining the experts in their skepticism. But something about this—the number of people, the specificity of the symptoms, and the pinpointing of a locale—was different. This sounded real. We pulled out our phones, Evens dialing the health ministry to try to confirm the report. I did what I always did when major news broke in a place I couldn't reach immediately. I called the United Nations.

Yes, said a spokeswoman for the Office for the Coordination of Humanitarian Affairs in Haiti: There is a situation in Saint-Marc. Could be typhoid, flu, or cholera. An international team was making the sixty-mile trip north from Port-au-Prince to Saint-Marc to investigate. And yes, there were dead: nineteen confirmed.

THE NONSPECIALISTS' EXPECTATION OF AN OUTBREAK repeats a pattern: After natural disasters, survivors, responders, and journalists tend to assume that a disease epidemic may be imminent, due to the collapse of sanitation or simply the feeling that misery comes in bunches. After the 2005 earthquake in Pakistan, responders noted outbreaks of measles, respiratory infection, and diarrhea, and cases of hepatitis were reported in Indonesia after the 2004 tsunami.

In Haiti, thousands of corpses lay in the streets, the stench of their decomposition filling the air, so it wasn't difficult to imagine that their smell might prove a vector for disease. That was how a preacher convinced the people of a Port-au-Prince slum to give up their children to a group of U.S. Baptist missionaries that would, notoriously, be arrested for human trafficking at the border. "The pastor said that with all the bodies decomposing in the rubble there were going to be epidemics, and the kids were going to get sick," a stone mason who gave away his twelve-, seven-, three-, and one-year-old children and one of his nephews told my colleagues at the Associated Press.[1]

If the locals were scared of the dead, the foreigners were terrified of the living. Because Haiti's slums and difficult-to-reach rural areas had long suffered soaring rates of tuberculosis, malaria,
and hepatitis, the squalid camps frequently were portrayed by the
media as breeding grounds for infection, and the distribution of
clean water and vaccinations and the provision of mobile clinics in
the camps were central goals of the relief effort. After Sean Penn's
warning of impending mass death from diphtheria in May proved
overblown, the scares ended. Many of the aid groups began high-
lighting the lack of an epidemic as a rare victory for the humanitarian effort. Others called it a miracle.

CLAIRE AND I DECIDED TO GO AHEAD with our trip to St. Kitts. Evens
agreed to keep tabs on the situation; I'd already set up a stringer,
a recent American college graduate named Jacob Kushner, to be
on call. We were already boarding the American Eagle flight to San
Juan when my cell phone rang. The number of confirmed deaths
had jumped to fifty-two. I called Evens and told him to take Jacob
to Saint-Marc.

The town lies about an hour up the coast north of Port-au-
Prince, just below the Artibonite River delta, a hilly seaside town
where the air is a little cleaner than in Port-au-Prince on a good
day, and people stroll and cruise on motorcycles around the colonial downtown squares. Evens and Jacob arrived to find a city
in panic. The main hospital was overwhelmed with patients; more
than a thousand had flocked there from across the river valley.
The sick and dying lay on soiled blankets in the parking lot, nurses
darting around to put IVs in their arms. Police barricaded the hospital gate, letting only urgent cases through; relatives watched
helplessly as their loved ones went in. The policemen covered their
noses and mouths with surgical masks and bandannas, hoping to
ward off whatever it was the ailing were carrying inside the compound. Then a rain started to fall. Nurses rushed to carry people
inside.

By day's end, the death toll was 135.

From the beach, Claire kept calling Rosemide and Twenty. The
sickness had not reached the crowded encampment, they told her,
but the stories from Saint-Marc had. They were terrified, most of

all for their new nephew: Billy Chery had a newborn toddler named Prince, like the city. Rosemide asked Claire if she had gotten sick.

"We should be there with them," Claire told me as she put down the phone. I looked out on a windy hillside with real trees along a real goddamn paved road. "We'll be there soon," I said.

By the end of the weekend, cases of severe diarrhea, often terminal, had shown up in at least five hospitals in the Artibonite Valley and some in the neighboring Central Plateau. Health investigators took eight stool specimens to the national laboratory in Port-au-Prince. All tested positive for cholera. Health officials' phones lit up all over the capital, then at the CDC in Atlanta, at the Haiti desk at the State Department in Washington, D.C., and at the UN's WHO headquarters in Geneva. They all knew: Cholera was a remorseless killer, and it could move very fast. By the time Claire and I took off from St. Kitts at the end of the weekend, about two hundred people were dead.

The cameras were back on Haiti. Brian Williams set the tone on NBC: "It's what all of us worried about when we arrived in Haiti just hours after the quake . . . beyond the death toll, the inevitable spread of disease. Now it's happening in Haiti, an outbreak of cholera in that nation struggling every day, still, just to survive."[2]

But the narrative didn't make sense to me. If cholera was the inevitable result of the earthquake, centered fifteen miles southwest of the capital, why had the first concentration of cases appeared in the countryside, some forty-five miles to the north? And why had it taken nine months to appear?

In fact, despite the anecdotes from Pakistan and New Orleans, researchers consistently have found that the risk of epidemics following natural disasters is wildly overstated. After a 1976 earthquake in Guatemala, authorities scrambled to prepare for a surge of rabies, which is endemic there. Increased surveillance led to a spike in recorded dog bites, but no cases of rabies were reported. A week after the 2011 tsunami devastated the coast of northeastern Japan, a Self-Defense Forces captain fretted to the *Sunday Telegraph* about a flu epidemic, but none took place. In fact, a team of researchers from France has found that, out of more than six hundred disasters between 1985 and 2004, only three resulted in significant outbreaks of disease. The risk is only slightly larger, others have found, when large numbers of people are displaced. This was the reason the WHO and other health organizations had attempted at every turn to tone down the alarm raised by Sean Penn and the media.[3]

Moreover, if a disease was going to spread, it would have almost certainly been an infection that was already present before the disaster struck. If not treated immediately, cholera, an intestinal infection caused by a rod-shaped bacteria called *Vibrio cholerae,* can lead quickly to severe dehydration and death. Because it spreads through contamination of food or water by human waste, an emblem of bad sanitation, it is often associated with poverty. But poverty doesn't cause cholera. You can have the world's poorest people, the worst sanitation, hurricanes, earthquakes, and frogs falling from the sky. If you don't have *Vibrio cholerae,* you will not have cholera.

And there hadn't been cholera in Haiti for at least a hundred years.

THE FIRST PANDEMIC OUTBREAK OF CHOLERA erupted in 1817, when a disease long endemic to India spread ferociously across Asia. It struck and killed thousands as far east as Japan and as far west as the Arabian peninsula, before burning out by 1824. The next global outbreak, five years later, once again ravaged Asia before spreading to Europe and the Americas and then running out of fuel. This was the pattern for the rest of the nineteenth century: Cholera would erupt in India and spread around the world, killing tens or hundreds of thousands, before receding to South Asia.[4] The speed, ferocity, and ruthlessness with which the disease upended whole cities and nations inspired scientific advancement and literature. "In the first two weeks of cholera, the cemetery overflowed, and there did not remain an available place in the churches, despite having passed into the common ossuary the worm-eaten remains of our nameless national heroes," writes Gabriel García Márquez in *Love in the Time of Cholera,* a novel whose title would supply generations of headline writers with an easily detachable cliché.

The last of the old pandemics was over by 1923, and although the disease would appear with regularity in South Asia, it no longer spread. Then, in 1961, a seventh pandemic began. This one started in Indonesia and featured a different type of bacteria. While the first six epidemics exhibited what is now called "classical" *Vibrio cholerae,* the seventh was caused by a strain called El Tor.[5] Occurring in the era of mass globalization, it would spend the rest of the twentieth century spreading through much of the world, hopping continents as it hitched rides on ships and airplanes. In 1991, El Tor cholera appeared in plates of ceviche on the coast of Peru. It exploded across South America and ran up through Central America and Mexico, with cases as far north as Canada.

Yet El Tor spared the islands of the Caribbean. Not a single case was recorded in the Dominican Republic, Anguilla, Cuba, or anywhere else in the archipelago, including Haiti.[6] While there is debate as to whether classical cholera ever reached Haiti even in the nineteenth century, there is certainty regarding El Tor. Modern laboratory techniques to confirm the presence of *Vibrio cholerae* came into being around the same time as the seventh pandemic. As of the 2010 earthquake, not a single case had been documented in Haiti. As late as February 2010, a month *after* the earthquake, amid rampant fears of epidemic, the CDC could insist that cholera wasn't a candidate: "Cholera is absent from the Caribbean . . . [and] extremely unlikely to occur."[7]

Almost immediately, it became clear that the nascent Haitian outbreak was centered along the Artibonite River, the nation's largest and most important. At least 1.5 million people depend on its waters, many of them to drink, cook, wash, bathe, and carry away their waste. Many of those stricken earliest either worked or lived in rice paddies along the river between Mirebalais and the Caribbean Sea. Two-thirds of those surveyed by the CDC reported drinking untreated water from the river or canals before falling ill.[8]

Some experts wondered if the Peruvian outbreak had somehow spread to Haiti, twenty years late—if Haiti's *Vibrio cholerae* closely matched the South American outbreak's genetic structure, it was a possibility. Other scientists suspected the weather, hypothesizing that a rise in temperature and salt levels in river estuaries might have caused a previously unknown colony of dormant cholera bacteria to multiply.

On Monday, October 25, Jon Andrus, the deputy director of the Pan American Health Organization—the hemispheric office of the WHO—mentioned during a press conference that the out-break was the first of its kind in Haiti for "perhaps more than a century." A ripple of surprise ran through the room. A *British Medical Journal* reporter listening remotely submitted a question: How, despite "the appalling conditions of the people in the capital," had there not been a cholera outbreak in Haiti before?

Andrus let out a bewildered laugh. "That's a million-dollar question," he said.

HAITI HAS ALWAYS BEEN A TALKING PLACE. Rumors spread at moun-tain crossroads, the corner lottery stand, and across pressed shoul-ders in the back of a jammed city bus. The country's television and radio stations carry names such as Tele Ginen and Tele Caraïbes. But none can rival the speed, content, and predictive capacity of *teledjol*—"the mouth channel." Sometimes teledjol is valuable in-telligence, word of a coming riot or the resignation of a top official. Other times it's everyone swearing that a peasant woman in the southwest has given birth to a fish. You can't do any serious re-porting in Haiti without an ear to teledjol. The only way to know the value of a particular rumor is to check it out.

As word of the cholera epidemic spread, teledjol lit up. Some said they heard the sickness had begun when a UN soldier emptied a latrine into a water source. Others swore a white UN helicopter was seen dumping black powder into the Artibonite—shades of Haitian folk sorcery, where a *kou d poud,* or powder attack, is said to cause death or zombification.

Rumors about the UN were nothing new. The troops comprising the UN Stabilization Mission in Haiti (MINUSTAH), which ar-rived in the wake of the 2004 coup that overthrew Aristide, came from around the world: Chileans in the Haitian north, Sri Lankans covering the southeast, Brazilians running much of the capital, and so on. Their units first went about arresting the ousted presi-dent's partisans, preventing the rebels who had dispatched him from taking power, and attempting to disarm both groups. As the years went on and the coup faded into history, the mission's goals and reason for staying became vague. Some locals called the UN soldiers "TOURISTAH." For Haitians, who had overthrown slavery along with brutal colonial rule and repelled the empires that sought to take its place, the presence of foreign soldiers was a daily insult. Abuses soured the pot: A Sri Lankan contingent was dismissed as a result of a sex-abuse scandal; other units were accused of excessive force. Teledjol claimed that a group of Jordanian soldiers had once stolen and raped a farmer's goat. For years, many Haitians had been greeting blue helmets with a laughing "baaaaaaa."

All the same, the UN peacekeeping mission was the vanguard of international aid and relief in Haiti—the most visible emblem of the international presence in the country. From 2004 through 2012, the UN spent more than $4.75 billion on the military and police mission alone, about a quarter of that paid by the United States. Despite MINUSTAH's vague and ever-changing goals, the Security Council often advertised the Haiti mission as a positive example of its works, at least by comparison to allegations of sexual exploitation against peacekeepers in the Balkans or the catastrophic failure of the UN ahead of the Rwandan genocide. If the UN were discovered to have caused the epidemic in Haiti, its credibility would be catastrophically compromised, Haitian lives destroyed by the very people sent to protect them.

What stood out about the teledjol on cholera were the rumors' focus and specificity. Nearly all focused on a UN base outside Mirebalais and contained key elements in common: something deadly, usually waste, going into the Artibonite River. Some accounts were more specific: The outbreak was caused by a UN sewer dug too close to a river.

As Claire and I were getting ready to leave St. Kitts, a friend living in Port-au-Prince sent me a link to an epidemiology blog. It said: "Nepal: Cholera Outbreak in Kathmandu."[9]

The post linked to an article from the previous month in the *Himalayan Times*. Although Nepal is a cholera-endemic country— the disease is always present—there had been recent flare-ups, and now, as the article reported, one had reached the capital. Doctors at a Kathmandu hospital had warned that an outbreak was under way.[10]

The UN soldiers stationed along the Artibonite River were from Nepal.

EVENS PICKED US UP AT THE AIRPORT. We dropped Claire off at home and headed directly to the Central Plateau. Traffic was terrible as always and Evens' shortcuts less lucky than usual. On the radio, the talk was all cholera. Rice farmers called to ask if they should stop working their paddies. Urbanites worried about how long they had until the disease arrived, the slums and displacement camps lying in wait. I tried to talk to Evens about the epidemic, but he wanted no part. Finally he turned off the radio and put on a kompa CD instead. Past traffic, on the high ridge of Morne à Cabrit that marks the beginning of the plateau, the car stopped. Smoke blew in from the gear box. "We can make it," I protested. But Evens was already turning around.

That evening, a UN press release arrived in my inbox. It was composed in the ultraformal diplomatic French of all UN memos in Haiti, but I could imagine it read in the bouncy Dominican-Italian lilt of its sender, Vincenzo Pugliese. The MINUSTAH press office was in flux—the last spokesman off to Darfur and the new spokeswoman not yet arrived—leaving Pugliese, the deputy, in charge. A teddy bear–shaped man with a receding hairline of brown, closely clipped hair, he talked with high animation and a general amiability that seldom concealed his disdain for the press. Communiqué No. PIO/PR/423/2010 read:

> The United Nations Stabilization Mission in Haiti (MINUSTAH) seeks to clarify rumors circulating in certain media that human waste spilled into a river in Mirebalais by MINUSTAH is the cause of the cholera epidemic in Haiti.
>
> A Nepalese military contingent is currently based near Mirebalais in the village of Meille, on the river that carries the same name.

Why was the UN answering the rumors? Was there something to them? The release went on: It said the Nepalese base had "seven septic tanks" built to "construction standards of the [U.S.] Environmental Protection Agency," emptied "every week by four trucks from a private contractor." They were "250 meters from the river . . . representing more than 20 times the distance required at the international level." The management of the waste was "consistent with established international standards."

This may have seemed like damage control to Pugliese, but to me it was the equivalent of waving a bloody shirt at a pack of dogs. The UN was acknowledging the rumors and backing them up with a list of claims anyone could prove or disprove simply by heading to the base.

"We're making it this time," I said to Evens the next day as we raced back toward the Central Plateau. He answered with a roar of the engine. I waved off smoke from the gear box as we sailed over the ridge.

THE VILLAGE OF MEILLE IS A COLLECTION of concrete houses and thatch shacks thinly spread alongside National Road No. 3. The homes stretch out over the rolling knobs of earth along the road, peeking out through the trees. The UN, in contrast, built its base in Meille to be seen. In a wide clearing the size of an entire quartier of homes, wedged between the highway and the Meille River, the soldiers had installed a high white gate and a series of even higher watchtowers, surrounded by walls topped with concertina wire. The words painted on the gate read:

> UN
> NEPALESE BATTALION
> MINUSTAH HAITI
> ANNAPURNA CAMP

Some young men from the village were standing in front of the gate wearing backpacks and ball caps. "*Kouman nou ye la!*" Evens greeted them, approaching with open arms. Their eyes gazed up at the big man as he made small talk about food aid. Then he dropped the bomb. "We heard someone dumped kaka in the river. Know anything about that?"

Heads nodded.

"Can you show us where?"

All at once they turned and walked toward the base. We followed. Nepalese soldiers in green-and-brown camouflage and sky-blue helmets watched us from a guard tower. Just before the gate, the young men shifted right and walked toward the back, where only a steep, narrow slope of mud and rock separated the compound from the river. As we neared, they covered their noses and mouths. A second later, I realized why. The smell was debilitating. We held our breath and crossed a concrete embankment along the ridge. Standing at the end was a UN solider with a blond ponytail sticking out of her blue cap, a Guatemalan flag on her epaulet. At her feet was a thick-sided black plastic case topped with security clasps.

"This isn't good, is it?" I asked her in Spanish.

"No," she replied. She opened her mouth to say more, then looked away.

Down the ridge, exposed, lay a broken PVC pipe. Running from near what looked like a building of latrines inside the perimeter, it leaked a foul-smelling black liquid toward the river. More Guatemalan military police were standing farther down the ridge, about three-quarters of the way to the end of the compound fence. They took a sample of waste, put it in a jar, and sealed it with a sky-blue lid. Then they brushed past us and left.

The Nepalese soldiers were staring through the base's chain-link fence. One leaned over and took a concrete lid off an underground tank, releasing a blast of stench.

"WHOA! KAKA!" one of the villagers shouted. They started laughing.

Another villager tapped Evens on the shoulder. He was slightly older than the others, in a polo shirt, blue shorts, and galoshes speckled with what I hoped was mud.

"You and the blan should come with me across the road," he said.

His name was Jean-Paul Chery. He had lived in Meille his entire life, growing food, mining sand from the river, and, for the past six years, watching the soldiers come and go. He led us past the concrete house he shared with his wife and five children; his wife held the youngest in her hands on the porch. Up a small hill, past a bony mule and some pigs, the smell returned. Ahead were two shining pools of feces, filling pits dug directly into the ground. "This is where MINUSTAH leaves their kaka," he said.

A truck would come every few weeks from a Haitian company called SANCO, Chery said—the contractor that Pugliese, the UN flak, had referred to. The truck would go into the base, suck out the septics, and then drive across the street and dump the waste into the pools by Chery's house. When it rained, the pools overflowed. Sometimes they ran down the hill into the river. Sometimes they flowed the other way, toward Chery's house, and the smell would get so bad the family couldn't sleep.

Then Chery led us down the hill to what looked like another pit full of human waste. This one had pigs and ducks swimming in it. A few weeks before, he explained, a new SANCO driver had shown up and dumped the excrement from the base in the wrong spot. Some of it had run down here. He said he wasn't sure exactly when—the days tend to run together in the countryside.

It did not take long for most of Chery's story to check out. About an hour later, a green tanker truck marked SANCO Enterprises S.A. appeared at the base. The company vice president from Port-au-Prince followed in a white luxury pickup. I watched the truck hose up the contents of the UN's underground tanks, drive across the street and up the hill, and stop at the pits. A worker jumped out of the truck, opened a valve in the rear, and took a big step back as a stream of black liquid surged into the open pit. Then, using an orange canister outfitted with a spray nozzle, he doused the surface of the new pool with bleach.

SANCO is one of the main waste disposal contractors in Port-au-Prince—the U.S. Department of Defense had contracted the company to handle some of the postquake detritus too. I learned later that SANCO had acquired the contract at the Nepalese base several months before by underbidding the preceding contractor. The truck driver beside Chery's home said that MINUSTAH had not called him to come in a month.

Could the septic tanks at the base have overflowed because they weren't emptied on schedule? I tried to talk to the SANCO executive in the pickup, but she wouldn't get out, rolling down the window only long enough to say: "It's a very difficult client."

I called Pugliese and told him what I'd seen.

"I'll check it out," he said and hung up. Minutes later, he called back. He focused on the broken PVC pipe we had seen behind the base. The black fluid running out of it, he said, was from the kitchen and showers, not the toilets.

"But are the Guatemalans checking for cholera?" I asked.

"Yes," he said. "To be absolutely certain."

"Trust me, Vincenzo, this isn't what you described in the press release. And it doesn't smell like a kitchen."

"I hear what you are telling me, Jonathan, but I don't know. I'm not there."

"I'm not making this up," I answered.

He paused. "Well. I don't know."

My blood pressure rose. "Vincenzo, let us get into the base and talk to the commander. Someone needs to explain what's going on here. It will be better if it's now."

He said he'd see what he could do and hung up. It was the last time we'd talk for two days.

We asked Chery if people had gotten sick drinking from the river. Some had, he said, days before. But the river had been fouled ever since the Nepalese had arrived there six years ago. Many in Meille had stopped drinking from the river, and those who could had stopped using it altogether. "You can't even wash in it," he explained. Millions of people downstream hadn't known that.

"EXCUSE ME," I SAID, KNOCKING on the base's painted gate. "I'm a reporter with the Associated Press. We'd like to speak with the base commander."

Through gaps in the metal, I could see the Nepalese soldiers, some smiling and staring back, others scowling and waving us off. Evens got back in the car and started honking. Finally, a speakeasy-style flap opened, and a soldier asked for my credentials.

An eternity passed. One of the village men started singing a song: "Ko-ko-kolera. Ko-le-ra MIN-U-STAH." His friends laughed. Finally, a door opened, and a soldier beckoned us through. The base commander, slightly older, with stringy black hair and a camouflage uniform, was standing under a gazebo. He handed back my badges and motioned for us to sit down. He did not look pleased.

I asked him when his unit had arrived at the base.

He paused. "We came in shifts—three shifts. The first October 9. Then October 12. Then October 16."

The unit had been in country for less than a month, which meant that its members had been in Nepal during the cholera outbreak. And the base would have been in the midst of rotation—with more personnel on hand than usual—right before the Haiti epidemic began.

"Could you show us around the base?"

"It is not possible today. You must go." He pointed to the digital recorder I was holding next to my notebook. "Put that away."

"It's not on," I said. It wasn't. I turned it on.

The commander had every reason to be nervous. UN peacekeeping is a cornerstone of the Nepalese defense budget. In late 2010, Nepal—with roughly the population of Texas and almost the same per-capita gross domestic product as Haiti—was the world's sixth largest troop contributor to UN missions. The UN pays countries more than $1,000 per peacekeeper per month, eight times the base pay for a private in Nepal. The soldiers are paid so well that Nepal obliges them to pay nearly a quarter of their UN salaries into a general welfare fund for the country's soldiers and their families.[11] By letting us inspect the base, the commander would be endangering that relationship.

Evens and I took turns making our case. Each time the commander grew more insistent that we leave. I told him we had photos and video of the dump pits and leaking pipes, and that an Al Jazeera English crew that showed up after we did was filming too—that he should tell us what he knew, now, before the images went out. Evens chimed in with the hard sell: "You'll look very bad today. Today you'll look *very* bad. Tell us the truth. We'll put out the truth."

The commander shook his head. "What can I do?" he muttered to no one.

"Is anyone at the base sick?" I asked.

"No. You must go."

"Has anyone here been sick? Are there cases of cholera at the base?"

The commander rose to his feet. "I do not know cholera."

"You know cholera. There is cholera in Nepal, right? In Kathmandu?"

Now, I will never be able to prove this. But if you ask me, right then, there were tears in his eyes.

"No. There is no cholera," the commander said. "Only dengue."

BECAUSE HAITI HAD NEVER SEEN THE BACTERIA before, the people had no immunity against it. It bred prolifically, among the population and in each person infected. Symptoms typically began with an upset stomach or fever. Within hours, the victim could be unable to stand or eat. In another few, she might be dead. By the time I put out my story from Meille, 303 people had died and 4,722 had been hospitalized. For the second time in a year in Haiti, bodies were being piled into mass graves. The most important river in the nation had become an artery of disease, and, as people fled the valley, the infection spread with them to every corner of the country.

The NGOs leapt into action, calling for donations and setting up mobile treatment centers ahead of the outbreak. But the people in the communities did not trust the foreign NGOs. Because the clinics would arrive just before their families grew ill, many thought the clinics themselves were spreading the disease. Foreign doctors, few of whom spoke Kreyòl, tried to explain that immediate treatment was the only hope. "But the blan brought cholera in the first place!" people replied. Furious men pummeled aid stations with rocks and Molotov cocktails, burning tires and slashing the clinic tents. UN soldiers were sent to disperse them. Anger in the street—over officials' blithe reaction to the stalled reconstruction, over Préval's term extension, over sheer hunger—had been building for a long time. Until now, it had remained suppressed, as people focused on looking for housing, scraping together a living, hoping they or the scores of foreigners who'd come to their aid would find a durable way forward. Now the anger seemed ready to boil over.

In this atmosphere, our story from the base was bound to be explosive. For readers abroad, it was the first time that the UN had been named as a possible source of cholera and the first eyewitness account that human waste could have run into the river. To most of the Haitians who saw it or heard it read over the radio, it would bolster what teledjol had been saying for days, showing that even a blan could see that something was wrong.

The next day, CNN.com posted a story, citing Pugliese, that claimed all the Nepalese soldiers had tested negative for cholera before taking up their posts.[12] It took me a day to reach him.

"When were the tests done?" I asked. "How many soldiers were tested? How were the results verified?"

Well, he said—CNN hadn't gotten it quite right. It wasn't that the soldiers tested negative. It's that none of them tested positive. Because they had never been tested.

On investigation, this turned out to not be unusual. The *Medical Support Manual for United Nations Peacekeeping Operations* lists neither diarrhea nor cholera as conditions precluding service.[13] Worse, the examination that all arriving blue helmets have to undergo has to take place only within three months of deployment, leaving plenty of time between the last exam and deployment to be exposed to the disease, which can also be transmitted by those without major symptoms.

On October 29, hundreds of protesters marched from Mirebalais to the Nepalese base carrying tree branches, banners, and Haitian flags. "The Nepalese brought this disease to the center of Mirebalais," a student protestor shouted through a megaphone. "We have no water to drink. We have no choice but to drink the water from the river!" "*Vle pa vle, MINUSTAH fok ale!*" the crowd chanted. "Like it or not, the UN must go." Among the marchers were cousins of Rosemond Lorimé, the first cholera victim to die in a hospital.[14]

As terrified people demanded answers, the UN stonewalled or deflected inquiries. "It's not important right now," one WHO spokesperson said about the epidemic's cause. Focusing on its origin would be a dangerous distraction. It's "not a priority," said another. "The question of how it came here is not central in Haiti," a CDC official insisted.[15] In the space of a week, the WHO's own million-dollar question had lost its appeal. But if figuring out where an infection comes from isn't critical to containing an epidemic, what is?

AFTER THE MARCH, THE UN BRIEFLY RELENTED. On Halloween Sunday, our four-man AP team—photos, video, text, and Evens—was allowed to take a guided tour of Annapurna Camp of the Nepalese battalion.

Pugliese greeted us at the gate alongside their chief officer, in from Port-au-Prince. There was no sign of Commander Dengue.

Young soldiers fresh from the Himalayas milled in polyester work-out shorts and T-shirts. Evens and I had worn our worst shoes and pants, ready to wade into whatever muck to get evidence. Pugliese, I noticed, wore black leather loafers. The officers led us into an air-conditioned building, its walls decorated with green-hued mountain scenes and portraits of prominent Nepalese. A soldier brought over a metal tray carrying glasses of tea and juice. Evens stepped away. I took a juice and set it on the table.

It was immediately apparent that the soldiers had literally covered up the most incriminating evidence, most notably the smell. Pugliese tried to keep things moving, but he knew he couldn't prevent the soldiers from answering our questions. He stood by helplessly as they admitted to having undertaken repairs on the eve of our visit, including replacing the broken PVC pipe from the back of the base and scrubbing a drainage canal that emptied into the river. Yet the repairs had been superficial at best. When we went out back, we noted that a series of cracked aboveground pipes that originated at the latrines still ran over the drainage canal, cracks showing. One pipe was held together with what looked like electrical tape. In the river below, where the canal let out, a soupy brown mixture bubbled along the bank. Flies swarmed over it.

"What is that?" I asked Pugliese.

"That . . . that could be anything."

I didn't say a word. A villager was swimming a few yards away.

"It—it does not mean it is from the base," he said. "The people here, they swim in the river. They bathe in it." He pointed to the swimming man. "They—you know how they are!"

That was the end of the tour. The UN team refused to go across the street with us to see the dump pits by Jean-Paul Chery's house. "I don't need to go there," a UN engineer who'd come up from Port-au-Prince replied.

"Have you ever been?"

"No."

"It's worth seeing," I said.

The next day, the CDC put out the results of an analysis it had undertaken: The *Vibrio cholerae* in Haiti matched strains circulating in South Asia, including Nepal. It refused to investigate further.

The death toll passed four hundred.

ON NOVEMBER 8, THE FIRST CASE OF CHOLERA originating in Port-au-Prince was confirmed. Cases multiplied quickly, and the fear even faster. The body of a dead woman was left in her Champ de Mars tent for hours, neighbors and Haitian responders refusing to enter for fear of getting infected. But in fact the camps were not the most dangerous place to be—thanks to all the postquake concern about disease outbreaks there, the NGOs had already set up clean water provisions for many living under the tarps. The risk was greater for those not getting help, in the slums left standing by the earthquake.

The vast, densely packed shantytowns of Cité Soleil lie on the northern periphery of the capital, the first part of metropolitan Port-au-Prince one reaches coming down from Saint-Marc, and close to the highway from Mirebalais. Doctors Without Borders set up shop in the slum's main hospital and immediately struggled to find room for all the patients streaming in. Those too weak to turn over were placed in beds with holes cut out in the middle, and buckets were placed underneath to catch the runoff. Their bony faces showed no panic, but their eyes had no light.

Every few minutes another would arrive at the narrow entrance corridor, on foot, in a taptap, or in a wheelbarrow. As I stood out front, a man named Jedson Regis walked in carrying his two-year-old daughter, Clercilia, wrapped in a yellow blanket.

The Regis's church had a water-purifying machine, but without a job, Judson could no longer afford the price of 14 gourdes, or 38 cents, a gallon. Instead the Regises had been drinking from a tap in the slum. Their pastor had advised them to mix in some lime juice and bleach. On Sunday, Clercilia had lost control of her bowels during the morning service. Her mortified parents ushered her out and carried her home. Because the quarter's rancid latrines were too far for the constant trips necessitated by cholera's unyielding flow, the little girl was forced to do her business on the floor of their shack. The Regises dumped her waste into an abandoned home across the narrow alley, seven feet from their door.

The evening before I saw her, Clercilia had taken a turn for the worse. Fearing he'd get mugged if they went out in the dark, her father waited for morning. After the sun rose, he wrapped her in a yellow blanket and set out for the hospital.

He emerged from the hospital a short time later, his eyes narrow and his cheeks pulled in tight, Clercilia in his arms. Her lifeless body was stiff and sealed inside a plastic bag. He had wrapped the yellow blanket around it.[16]

No one was immune from fear. In an emergency meeting with his health officials and foreign aid workers, President Rene Préval stood suddenly and asked, "And what should I do if I get diarrhea?" Cabinet officials shouted back conflicting answers. The foreigners sat in silence, horrified.

As the epidemic's death toll soared past five hundred, life in Haiti changed. Small farmers suffered as terrified buyers turned to imports, demand for their rice and vegetables plunging even further. Some fishermen stopped going out to sea, no longer able to sell their catch and fearful of catching something from the water.[17] Children made cholera jokes, mocking the sound of a person losing his guts and falling dead. Cholera became the new swear word of choice. Opponents of the president spray-painted "Préval = Cholera" on rubble walls. With the presidential election a few weeks away, denouncing the UN, or foreigners in general, for bringing cholera to Haiti became a standard applause line on the stump.

Foreigners like me had less to worry about, with access to vaccines and ample supplies of antibiotics. Hand sanitizer became a social tool and mark of status. At better restaurants in Pétionville, waiters would offer a spritz of clear alcohol gel as patrons sat down. A sign at a UN cafeteria reassured diners: "All food is imported."

THE AUTHORITIES DEFENDED THEIR REFUSAL to investigate the origin of the outbreak on public health grounds—pursuing the source would detract from fighting the epidemic. On November 3, I decided to ask one of the most prominent public health experts in Haiti, if not the world, if he agreed.

Paul Farmer's medical NGO, Partners in Health, was taking a leading role in tackling the cholera outbreak. Farmer was also chair of Harvard Medical School's global health department, in addition to his work as Bill Clinton's deputy at the UN Office of the Special Envoy for Haiti. I reached him on the phone at a conference in the United States. Was there was a public health rationale not to investigate? I asked.

"That sounds like politics to me, not science," Farmer told me. "Knowing where the point source is—or source, or sources—would seem to be a good enterprise in terms of public health."[18]

John Mekalanos, a cholera expert who chairs Harvard's microbiology and immunobiology department, concurred. CDC analysis had showed the *Vibrio cholerae* in Haiti was a more virulent strain than had previously existed in the Western Hemisphere. Dealing with it meant getting as much information as possible about how it arrived and how it had spread, he said.

Health officials look into the source of cholera outbreaks all the time. In fact, the modern practice of epidemiology was built on the disease. In 1854, as cholera ravaged Britain, a physician named John Snow set out to find the source of one of London's worst outbreaks. By mapping out the infection, he managed to trace it to a single water pump. Henry Whitehead, a local cleric who knew the community, figured out that it had been infected by a sick baby's diaper. The pump's handle was removed, and the outbreak waned.

Such investigation is still the practice. In a 2004 guide, the WHO recommended investigating each outbreak's origin "so that appropriate control measures can be taken." The CDC says, in its guide to handling food-borne outbreaks: "Two activities are critical when an outbreak occurs. First, emergency action is needed to keep the immediate danger from spreading, and second, a detailed objective scientific investigation is needed to learn what went wrong, so that future similar events can be prevented."[19]

There are plenty of examples:

Australia, 1977: Researchers pinpointed the woman who imported cholera and the first local man infected.

Los Angeles, 1993: The CDC investigated a forty-eight-year-old woman who had traveled from Hyderabad, India, to Los Angeles to describe the threat of a new cholera strain.

Zimbabwe, 2008: Researchers went town by town to show how cholera had spread—in one case down to the first individual who died and the others infected at his funeral.

What if the cause of the epidemic was still out there? What if it was in a shipment of cholera-tainted food now headed for Miami? The UN and the CDC insisted that finding out wasn't a priority. There was another possibility, of course: One reason not to investigate the origin of cholera in Haiti was that the origin was already known.

THOSE SEEKING TO PROTECT THE UN—the WHO and CDC, sympathetic journalists, aid workers and diplomats who depended on the UN for protection on the ground—kept coming back to a three-word phrase: "the blame game." As the journal *Science* would later note, cholera experts' "passion for traditional shoe-leather epidemiology [had] been tempered by diplomatic and strategic concerns."[20] A friend at a health agency was more blunt. "You clearly enjoy shit stirring," she said to me one evening in a GMail chat. "Do you realize you could start a civil war?"

Most journalists, particularly those not based in Haiti, seemed to feel the same way. They stayed away from the story until there was too much evidence to ignore, then did their best to beat it back. When the *New York Times* published a story about the UN defending its anti-investigation stance, three weeks after our visit to the Nepalese base, health reporter Donald G. McNeil Jr. wrote a Week in Review piece titled "Cholera's Second Fever: An Urge to Blame." He gave past examples of cholera "blame games," including nineteenth-century New Yorkers accusing Canadians and the Irish. Then he warned of danger: "Officials are dead set against announcing what they find, since scapegoating provokes violence. Angry Haitian crowds have already stoned Nepalese vehicles and the peacekeepers have shot back. . . . Any transfer of a disease from one place to another is unfortunate. But it often can't be foreseen. And the 'fault'—if that's the word—often lies just as much with the victims as with the vectors."[21]

You could hardly blame the Nepalese soldiers for carrying a disease any more than you could blame Haitian farmers for catching it. But that was never the point of calling for an investigation. Had the UN screened its soldiers and followed international standards of sanitation at its base in Meille, the disease would likely not have erupted along the shores of the Artibonite River. The Environmental Protection Agency, whose guidelines Pugliese cited in his October 26, 2010, communiqué, credits the virtual elimination of typhoid, dysentery, and cholera in the United States to the proper disinfection of wastewater and chlorination of drinking water supplies. The guidelines call for on-site treatment of wastewater in places where no centralized sewer system is present and, above all, for safeguards to ensure that infected wastewater can't drip through or overflow along the ground into drinking water. There was no on-site treatment for wastewater at the UN base. Once the outbreak began, the UN soldiers themselves drank water filtered through a "high-quality process chain including filtration, reverse osmosis, and chlorination," investigators would later find.

As for provoking the feared Haitian crowds, weeks of watching the mission stonewall bolstered most Haitians' already strong belief that the UN had imported cholera. By refusing to engage, the investigators ceded inquiry to agitators and xenophobes. Everyone lost an opportunity to get a scientific answer that could have calmed fears and furthered the fight against disease, and the powerful nations that had been working in Haiti lost an opportunity to demonstrate to the Haitian people that they took their lives and welfare as seriously as their own.

In fact, Haitians know better than most the danger of careless blame. In 1983, the CDC published guidelines about a newly discovered disease called AIDS. It identified four groups of carriers: homosexual men, intravenous drug users, hemophiliacs . . . and Haitians. There was no scientific basis for the assumption that Haitian nationality per se was a risk factor; researchers had struggled to communicate with infected Haitian migrants and did not understand that they had come by the disease the same way as other patients. But the result was devastating. Haitians suffered widespread discrimination. Tourism, then the country's second largest source of foreign income, collapsed. Even after the guidelines were rewritten and Haiti made progress against the disease—for years, it hasn't had the highest HIV infection rate even in the Caribbean—the stigma never lifted. As late as 2010, a New York disc jockey still felt comfortable saying on the air that he was not HIV positive because he didn't "mess with Haitian girls."[22]

IN MID-NOVEMBER, AS THE DEATH TOLL from cholera passed one thousand, the barricades went up. Rioters showered Nepalese soldiers with rocks and set cars ablaze in Cap-Haïtien. Some blocked streets with coffins, as the unrest spread into central Haiti and the capital.

At least three protesters were killed—at least one shot dead by the UN—and half a dozen MINUSTAH soldiers were injured.

The immediate result was that the epidemic became harder to treat. The UN canceled flights carrying soap and medical supplies. Préval took to the radio to plead with people to go back to their homes.

MINUSTAH refused to see its actions as a cause of the unrest. A statement from Vincenzo Pugliese's office said simply that the "incidents [were] politically motivated," the protesters "enemies of stability and democracy." That attitude only cemented in many Haitian minds that the UN was guilty, that it knew it was guilty, and that it was doing everything in its power not to be held accountable.

The Haitian government wanted answers too. Quietly, Préval asked the French embassy to send for an epidemiologist. For twenty days in November, a team led by Dr. Renaud Piarroux of the Université de la Méditerranée in Marseilles investigated. It determined that the UN base in Meille was the source of the infection. The team found that being downstream from the village increased victims' chances of getting cholera while merely being close to it did not. An outbreak at a prison downstream of Meille, whose only exposure had come from drinking river water, bolstered the conclusion.[23]

The report was supposed to be secret, at least initially, but as I was finishing a follow-up story of my own, I learned that Piarroux had told the UN country chief, Edmond Mulet, about his findings.

I left a message for Pugliese, who soon called back. There is no need for more stories, he said, rambling. "You sound tired," he said. "You should take a nap." But the brass overruled him. A growing number in the organization were realizing the toll that stonewalling was taking on the troops' reputation. Mulet called me to give his first interview on the subject. An investigation was absolutely necessary, he said, insisting that this had been his conviction all along. With a diplomat's confidence, he reassured me, "There has been no cover-up—there has been no cover-up from our side—and we have done everything we can to investigate."[24]

On December 17, the pressure went all the way to the top. UN chief Ban Ki-moon announced a full investigation into the source of the outbreak. It took three weeks to name the panel. "The Secretary-General has been deeply concerned by the cholera outbreak in Haiti since the first cases were detected. Determining the source of the cholera outbreak is important for both the United Nations and the people of Haiti," his spokesman declared as the panel's members were named.[25] By then, the death toll was nearing four thousand.

THE UN REPORT CAME OUT IN MAY 2011, seven months after the outbreak and almost a year and a half after the earthquake. The bulk of it was damning, building the most complete case yet against the United Nations system itself. The panel discarded hypotheses about ocean currents, cholera in Haiti's soil, and the 1991 outbreak in Peru. *Vibrio cholerae* in Haiti was from South Asia and nowhere else. In fact, the report said, the strain in Haiti was a "perfect match" with samples from Nepal. And it was imported—by people—into Meille: "The evidence overwhelmingly supports the conclusion that the source of the Haiti cholera outbreak was due to contamination of the Meye [*sic;* the report used the Kreyòl spelling] Tributary of the Artibonite River with a pathogenic strain of current South Asian type Vibrio cholerae as a result of human activity."[26]

The panel confirmed that the exposed dump pits were unsanitary. The EPA notes that there are precise ways in which former wastewater can be safely dumped into the ground, but only after comprehensive processing by a treatment facility, which the base lacked. The pits received waste from two other Nepalese MINUSTAH bases as well, increasing the number of soldiers whose waste could have contaminated the river and the risk that the pits would overflow. The investigators saw children playing next to the pits. On the base itself, the cracked pipes over the drainage canal had "significant potential for cross-contamination" into the river, the report said. Such conditions were "not sufficient to prevent contamination of the Meye Tributary System with human fecal waste." In great detail, the report then showed how the Nepalese soldiers were the likely vector. They had spent three months training in Kathmandu before their mid-October arrival.[27] After their medical exams, they had been given a ten-day free period to visit their families, wherever they happened to be located in Nepal. Within a day of their arrival in Haiti, they were sent to their bases.

The authors of the report—four cholera experts from leading centers in Bangladesh, India, the United States, and Peru—thus treated the Haiti outbreak as a cautionary tale about epidemics in the era of globalization. They recommended screening all UN and emergency personnel for cholera before missions and building on-site systems at UN installations to treat and properly dispose of wastewater.

But when it came to accountability, the report balked. Its conclusion, after noting once again that the Meille River had been contaminated by "human activity," listed nine factors that allowed the disease to spread. These included the facts that Haitians had no prior immunity to cholera, that the imported strain was particularly virulent, that people stricken with the disease fled to other areas, and that there had been poor sanitation in place when the bacteria arrived. All of those factors are self-evidently important for understanding how cholera *spread* in Haiti but say nothing about how the epidemic *began*. Yet in the very next paragraph, in boldface type, the listed factors in the spread were referred to as *causes,* in what has become the defining quotation of the report: "The Independent Panel concludes that the Haiti cholera outbreak was caused by the confluence of circumstances as described above, and was not the fault of, or deliberate action of, a group or individual."

Finally, the report observed: "The source of cholera in Haiti is no longer relevant to controlling the outbreak." While that may have been arguably true from a strictly medical standpoint, in view of almost any other criterion—prevention of future outbreaks, scientific advancement, and justice and respect for the victims—it read like an egregious oversight.

When the report was released, I called the lead author, Dr. Alejandro Cravioto, and asked him: Wasn't citing people's dependence on the river as a cause of the outbreak like saying that a release of poison gas into the air was partially the fault of the victims who breathed it in?

"I like that metaphor," he said with a laugh. Cravioto, a Mexican cholera expert who helps lead one of the world's leading centers on diarrheal disease in Bangladesh, agreed that all the evidence pointed to the UN. But there was no medical report proving soldiers had been sick. The samples I'd watched the Guatemalans take had been inexpertly collected and passed along to a lab under MINUSTAH contract in Santo Domingo, where an obesity specialist with no experience in cholera oversaw the testing, a delicate process that produces many false negatives, according to cholera experts. No one—not the CDC, not the WHO, and not better-trained experts in the UN system—had done the right kind of environmental testing around the base in October, when it would have mattered.

The panel was missing the smoking gun, and in this sense, the cover-up had worked. The initial refusal to investigate and the attempts to stifle inquiry had left researchers with no evidence of *Vibrio cholerae* at the base itself. Complete, accurate medical records for the soldiers would have to be released by MINUSTAH or the Nepalese army itself. Both say there is no record of a soldier having been sick, but neither has publicly released its records.

Of course, Dr. Snow never found the smoking gun in London either: With a primitive microscope and no idea what pathogen he was looking for, he never identified the *Vibrio cholerae* infecting the Broad Street pump. The strength of his argument was in the evidence around it.

ABOUT 8,900 MILES SEPARATE NEPAL and central Haiti. In the imperfect, ever-evolving annals of science, there is always the possibility that a cholera strain described as a "perfect match" for one circulating in Nepal made that trip on its own, only to appear downstream of a base housing 454 Nepalese soldiers that also happened to be leaking waste into the river.

But imagine that the UN had held itself accountable for a *presumed* contamination and, at a sum roughly equal to the MINUSTAH annual budget, financed national water and sanitation systems. Imagine that, playing the odds, the UN also compensated victims' families, dismissed those responsible for negligence, and issued a landmark apology. What would the price have been if it all turned out to have been a big misunderstanding? The UN would have fulfilled its humanitarian mission, demonstrating an overarching commitment to a core principle of all interventions: "First do no harm."

Instead, the world's preeminent humanitarian organization continued to dissemble. Middle managers continued to claim that the panel left open the possibility that the strain in Haiti "is the same as the one they have in Latin America and Africa."[28] MINUS-TAH spokespeople fantasized in communiqués that other investigations have presented evidence for alternate scenarios as to how the *Vibrio cholerae* strain arrived.[29] The panel report itself is consistently cited by UN officials, including the resident coordinator in Haiti, as an exoneration, because it blamed a "confluence of circumstances."

After Rosemond died, the Lorimé family left its home and moved farther away from the UN base. Neighbors burned their little house to the ground. More than 7,500 Haitians have been killed by cholera since the epidemic began, and at least 580,000 people—6 percent of Haiti's population—have fallen ill.[30] The contagion has spread to the Dominican Republic and beyond. Aid groups and UN agencies continue to raise money in the name of fighting the epidemic. But scientists fear that cholera has become endemic in Haiti. It will likely never go away.

CHAPTER TWELVE

CARDBOARD PALACE

AS OF NOVEMBER 2010, FORTY-EIGHT MEN AND ONE WOMAN HAD been Haitian heads of state. Twenty-two were overthrown. Two were assassinated, one was executed, and another committed suicide. Seven more died in office. Nine were figurehead presidents who lasted a year or so before being replaced by, or taken down with, the military regimes that installed them. Four were propped up by the 1915 to 1934 U.S. occupation (the last forced to resign after the Americans withdrew). That left three: a nineteenth-century general who resigned to cede power to another general, another general who abdicated under pressure in 1902, . . . and René Préval. In his first term, from 1995 to 2000, Préval had become the first Haitian leader to be democratically elected, serve a full five-year term, and peacefully transfer power to an elected successor. He now planned, nervously, on doing it again.[1]

In a memo titled "Deconstructing Préval," written seven months before the quake and uncovered in late 2010 by Wikileaks, then–U.S. Ambassador Janet Sanderson had offered a complex portrait of a reluctant leader who remained "Haiti's indispensable man. Legitimately elected, still moderately popular, and likely the only politician capable of imposing his will on Haiti—if so inclined." The international community had been counting on Préval to build a bridge from the 2004 anti-Aristide coup to political stability. But by 2009, the ambassador had become frustrated by Préval's preference for laying low. What some saw as pragmatism, the ambassador saw as distraction. The president's fixation,

Anderson reported with some sympathy, was "to orchestrate" the upcoming election "to ensure that whoever is elected will allow him to go home unimpeded."[2]

A year later, after nine months of stalled reconstruction, the sympathy was gone. Donors didn't want to discuss their failure to deliver their pledges; aid groups preferred not to discuss how much money had been spent, or on what. Préval's postquake paralysis was the one problem that everyone—foreign governments, aid workers, and most Haitian voters—could agree on.

Still, as Election Day neared, its date still highly tentative, the Unity Party and its candidate, Jude Célestin, remained front-runners by default. None of the other eighteen men and women on the presidential ballot had the backing of a machine like Préval's, which plastered posters of Célestin's mustachioed face across the country and could mobilize the vote, particularly in the vast rural zones where the effects of the stalled reconstruction were felt less directly. Célestin himself, strategically, remained a cipher. The party bosses were happy to keep him as a one-note candidate: He had run a construction company. It hired people and built things. Beyond that, the party would simply sell the party, its slogan painted on banners of green and gold: "A vote for Unity is a vote for stability."

The challengers' one hope was that if all the other candidates together could prevent Célestin from getting at least 50 percent in the first round, the top two vote-getters would enter runoff in January 2011. The major contenders included Mirlande Manigat, loosely affiliated Aristide ally Jean-Henry Ceant, and garment factory owner Charles-Henri Baker. Since Wyclef Jean had been kicked out of the race, some had been taking a shine to the last musician standing, Michel "Sweet Micky" Martelly. The candidates' smiling faces were plastered across the capital's rubble on yellow, pink, blue, red, and green rectangles that faded quickly in the sun, striping the ruins in a repeating pattern of washed-out, toothy grins.

IF HAITI'S RECONSTRUCTION STILL MATTERED to the world, then the election should have too. The winner would be head of state for the next five years, theoretically overseeing the spending of nearly $10 billion in still-pledged donor money, empowered with a nominal veto over the Interim Haiti Recovery Commission (which Préval never used), and to form the Haitian-run commission to replace it. But three weeks out, I couldn't interest my editors in an election story. Too many candidates, they said. Too many local issues. Without an easy-to-follow narrative—a pro-U.S. candidate versus an anti-U.S. candidate, corrupt dictator versus plucky underdog—there was nothing readers could be trusted to latch onto.

So my Caribbean bureau chief and I came up with a compromise story: a slice-of-life piece about campaigning during the cholera epidemic. Candidates were canceling rallies in the most affected regions, some proposing the election be postponed until the danger waned. Politicians refrained from kissing babies. Handshakes were replaced with fist-bumps.

I knew I needed a strong personality to carry the story, so on November 12, in a small hotel courtyard in Mirebalais—a few miles from the UN base in Meille—Evens and I met up with Michel "Sweet Micky" Martelly. I asked him if cholera was discouraging him from campaigning. "In order for them to trust you, to *believe* in you, you have to suffer with them," he explained in a syrupy baritone, his English flawless. "Take a *risk* with them. *Walk* with them. Because they have lost confidence with everything in this country. People have lost confidence in the system, in the street, in the institutions, almost in God!" They only trusted him, he explained, because of his music.

Martelly had become a much more polished candidate in the weeks since he registered. Some of that was the work of the Spanish consulting firm Grupo OstosSola, which had helped elect Latin American conservatives, including Mexico's Felipe Calderón.[3] Micky was confident, on message, and making a good point: Through his music, he had been with Haiti's young people for the whole of their lives—he was the one who made them laugh at Carnival, the low rumbling crooner in their homes as they made love. Most importantly, he'd never been a politician. He'd never betrayed them.

A few hours later, we arrived with Micky's motorcade at a rally in Croix-des-Bouquets, on the eastern edge of the capital. I tried to keep up with the singer as he ran through the dusty twilit streets with the drums and horns of a ra-ra band. Thousands were waiting at the nighttime rally, filling a park built during Aristide's administration, climbing an obelisk in the back, and sitting on the gates. Martelly's longtime bandmate, Ronald "Roro" Nelson, was on the stage, charging them up as before a concert. As their energy peaked, the singer ran out and raised his hand. The crowd erupted.

The candidate wore a white T-shirt, blue track pants, and Nikes with a matching blue swoosh. A trademark sweat towel was slung over his shoulder. Micky threw his head back and roared at the crowd: "Hello, *Croix-des-Bouquaaaaaaaay!*" Then he invoked the town's most famous native son. "This is the city of Wyclef Jean! I heard they took him out of the race! But this is a youth movement! And I will keep—it—going!" The young crowd roared back.

Just like that, he had the crowd in the palm of his hand. Martelly paced like a prize fighter, mopping his epic brow with the towel and stopping now and then for a crowd-pleasing pelvic thrust. He could not have been more different from Préval or Célestin. *Screw your stability,* his manner said. *Let's have change.*

"They don't want us to *laugh* anymore!" the candidate observed, the young crowd nodding. "I travel around the country and all I see are *seeeeriooooous faces.*" He pursed his lower lip, bulged out his eyes, and shook his head. The audience laughed. Now Micky addressed Préval. "Your country has problems! You'd think you would fix it, but instead you destroy it! You let all these foreigners come to our country and give us security. You're standing there looking at them and you're not *working.*" He was talking about the UN peacekeepers. He pointed at the applauding crowd. "All these young men in the crowd could be a force of order! Some of you could be soldiers! Sergeants! Colonels! But instead you're sitting and not *working.* You imported an army from overseas and paid them a bunch of money, instead of investing the money in our own people!"

The crowd shouted its approval. Micky egged it on. "You can't sit here listening to nice words," he instructed. "You have to watch all nineteen candidates and decide if they're thieves! And if they are thieves, then *rip their photos down!*" Now the park went wild, people pumping their fists, crying Micky's name and his slogan, the Kreyòl for bald head: *Tèt Kale! Tèt Kale!*

Just as at Micky's show in Pétionville in July, one attendee became so excited that he climbed on stage. I wondered what Micky would do this time. The candidate smiled, handed him the microphone, and stood back.

The young man had a goatee and wore a rosy pink shirt, a cruise-ship giveaway hat, and chinos too big for his waist. As Martelly looked on, he broke into a rambling speech about foreigners bringing cholera to Haiti—which got shouts of approval and some nervous titters from his friends. But when he started talking about Micky, the stammering stopped and the pulse of the crowd joined his. "Your father sent you out of the country to study, and you came back with a keyboard in your hand. The president is *here for life!*" Micky laughed and joined the applause. "You didn't pay us to be here. It's just your bald head that got the people to come! This is the park of Aristide! It is here for you! Do whatever you want with it!" "*Tèt kale! Tèt kale!*" the crowd cried, and Micky raised the man's hand in triumph. The candidate bowed to his No. 1 fan and awarded him the sweat towel.

ONE WEEK BEFORE THE ELECTION, a clean vote seemed impossible. Lines of new registrants snaked around the capital's quake-shattered blocks, waiting for voter ID cards that wouldn't be printed in time. The extreme centralization of the state meant that quake damage to the headquarters of the Provisional Electoral Council (CEP) was causing logistical headaches throughout all ten of Haiti's departments—which were also coping with the cholera epidemic and fallout from the anti-UN cholera riots, which had taken place just days before. There were thousands of earthquake and cholera dead among the 4.7 million on the rolls, some of whose IDs, suspicious citizens grumbled, would surely be used by others to vote illegally.

Political factions clashed, though the violence was exaggerated by the campaigns. In Haitian politics, it's widely said, you're nobody until somebody tries to kill you. On November 24, Unity reported an assassination attempt on Célestin's convoy in the southwest peninsula hamlet of Jérémie that left three dead, which the party blamed on factory-owning candidate Charles-Henri Baker. The Baker campaign retorted that two of its supporters had been shot dead nearby, "in reaction to the success" of a Baker rally.[4] On the other side of the southern mountains in Les Cayes, Sweet Micky's people said their man had been rushed under fire into a bulletproof car. They reported one dead. The motive: the Martelly campaign's momentum.

But with the international community's investment on the line, there was no delaying the election now. The European Union warned that doing so would "jeopardize political stability."[5] The man the Organization of American States (OAS) sent to oversee the process, an affable Surinamese diplomat named Albert Ramdin, was more candid. "We're looking at the best elections possible under the circumstances," he told me in what should have been the shadow of the Hotel Montana. He called the slow distribution of IDs, inflated voter rolls, and lack of poll-worker training "technical issues." "I think keeping the constitutionally set date of the twenty-eighth of November demonstrates that Haiti's democracy is becoming stronger."

Democracy, that byword of U.S. and European policy in Haiti, was often spoken by foreign diplomats in a confusing way. When U.S. forces under Bill Clinton put Aristide back into power in 1994, the mission was called Operation Uphold Democracy. A decade later, State Department official Roger Noriega praised Aristide's 2004 overthrow because the now-exiled president had "demeaned the word 'democracy.'" How could both the reinstatement and removal of the same man be praised as democratic, especially since popular will had not changed dramatically? Because when the Americans said *democracy*, they meant *elections*. The democracy being upheld in 1994 was Aristide's election four years before. The democracy Aristide had demeaned, according to Noriega, was a flawed parliamentary election, which had been condemned by the OAS.

"Well-intentioned observers," the Haitian anthropologist Michel-Rolph Trouillot has written, "reduce Haiti's problems to a matter of procedures of access to political power. In its humblest expression, this position suggests that once a president is selected through 'free' elections, Haiti will be on the road to democracy." But this was not true, Trouillot argued. Prioritizing elections in a weak state with no effective legal system, a lack of access to institutions for the poor majority, and civil society dominated by a tiny, self-interested power class would never create democracy in its best sense. Instead, it would create what another scholar of Haiti, Robert Fatton, has called "predatory democracy," in which those with wealth and privilege exploit the trappings of elections and parliamentary procedures.[6]

It isn't that Haitians didn't understand the concept of democracy. The country's independence was won in the same wave of Enlightenment revolutions that forged the United States and France (except that the Haitian revolutionaries who shouted "liberty or death," meant for everyone). Although many dictators and autocrats followed, Haitian society remained profoundly democratic, with an endless parade of peasant associations, community groups, and block committees discussing and coming to consensus. When American anthropologist Jennie Smith visited rural Haitian communities in the 1990s to learn how farmers saw democratic ideals, she received sophisticated answers: the right to speak without getting beaten up; the right to housing, education, and food. She quoted one man as saying: "American democracy, that's not real democracy! How can you have democracy if you don't have respect?"[7]

In the fall of 2010, Haitians were fed up with the whole system, from their own feckless leaders to foreigners who hadn't lived up to their promises to help. Two days before the election, Claire interviewed a young man named Echzechiel Guerrier, who told her that the only possibility for change was the emergence of a great leader who would spark a national dialogue about Haiti's future. Like Nelson Mandela, he said. Or Gandhi. "Gandhi showed everyone their own importance," he told Claire. "He showed everyone what they had inside."[8]

There were no such figures on the ballot. All the favorites were squabbling, and all had baggage. Célestin was saddled with Préval. Manigat, the constitutional law professor, had been first lady in a presidency propped up by the post-Duvalier military regime. Even Micky, whose newcomer status was winning fans, had ties to hard-right figures in Haiti's past. Under the early–1990s junta, when entertainers who had protested the regime's abuses went into exile, Micky ran a club frequented by allies of the military regime.

He had long acknowledged a friendship with Lieutenant Colonel Joseph Michel François, a former Port-au-Prince police chief who helped orchestrate the 1991 coup against Aristide and was later indicted in the U.S. for drug trafficking. (The Miami *New Times* wrote in 1997 that François took the nickname "Sweet Micky" in tribute to the singer.)[9]

Some voters were willing to gloss over the flaws in their candidates or were too young to know all the details, but disillusionment was high. With the campaigns handing out T-shirts and cash in the run-up to the vote, some saw the election as just another opportunity to make money and get out into the streets. Many planned to skip it entirely.

But the organizers pushed on. As the day came into view, Edmond Mulet, the head of the UN peacekeeping mission, dismissed the problems as minor and the violence between campaigns as "a tradition in Haiti." Voice of America summarized his remarks under the headline: "UN: Outlook Good for Haiti Elections."

ELECTION SUNDAY DAWNED WITH HIGH HEAT. Lines formed early, and the polls opened late. Problems quickly arose: Voting was halted at Camp Corail because too few had been registered. Witnesses reported that police had stormed into a polling place in Carrefour because of reported vandalism and prevented people from voting. Photographers rushed en masse to a school in Port-au-Prince where ballot boxes had been torn apart and ballots strewn all over the room. Their pictures of children playing in the flurry of paper circulated around the world.

Tempers flared over allegations of fraud. At a voting station at a Pétionville school that Evens, Claire, and I were staking out, dozens of people who couldn't find their names on the voter rolls were fuming in the school's courtyard. A man who'd put on a dress shirt for the occasion recognized my reporter's notebook and begged me to help. He had found his name on a list outside a classroom, he said, but the *mandataire*, the room's head poll worker, refused to give him a ballot. It took about fifteen minutes of questioning and line-cutting to find the answer: The mandatiare's list was missing a page, which had somehow ended up in the polling place next door. The man shook my hand gratefully and went to vote. In the hall, a man was pushing through the crowd shouting "Disorder! Disorder!" I couldn't tell if he was reporting it or trying to create it.

By noon, my BlackBerry lit up with an e-mail that Michel Martelly was planning a press conference to denounce widespread fraud. Similar messages came from Mirlande Manigat, then other campaigns. Every candidate with a grievance was heading to the same place: the nearby Karibe Hotel.

The hotel ballroom could have fit in at any American chain—yellow-and-brown patterned carpet to hide stains; a ceiling of recessed, faux-crystal chandeliers. Nearly every journalist in town was there, breathing the same uncertainty. Was it worth it to be here? Shouldn't we be at the polls? But then the candidates started to appear, one after the other. Supporters chanted the names of their candidates as they appeared on stage. Charles-Henri Baker came out in his shirt sleeves; Manigat in a floral dress with her hair in a schoolmarm's bun. Then Sweet Micky took the stage in tight stonewashed jeans and a white dress shirt, the left cuff folded to reveal a silver watch. Supporters were trying to shout their candidate's name over the others, until someone had an idea that spread, and the whole room began chanting: AY-YI-TI! AY-YI-TI! As the first strains of an a capella rendition of the national anthem rang out, I looked at the stage. Every major candidate except for Célestin was in the room. Even Leslie Voltaire was sitting there, smiling. What the hell was going on?

Evens emerged from the crowd at my side. "There's going to be a joint statement," he said. The role of spokeswoman was given to Josette Bijoux, a little-heard-from independent candidate who posed no threat to the front-runners. She spoke in Kreyòl: "We, the candidates to the presidency, declare before the Haitian people, the press and the international community, that have witnessed a great deal of fraud. . . . Therefore, we ask for the annulment of the election."

There was a palpable buzz through the room, and then a cheer. Bijoux went on. "We ask the Haitian people, we ask every woman and man who loves their country, for them to raise their voices to mobilize pacifically against the brigandry and antidemocratic act of the Préval government. They have the duty to protect and defend their vote. We call on them to mobilize immediately to demonstrate that they do not agree with the fraud that has been done here."

And with that, the wheels came off.

There were hollers from every corner of the room. A new chant erupted like a thunder among the Haitians in the room: "Arrest Préval! Arrest Préval!"

"So what happens next?" Claire asked Evens.

Someone overheard and answered: "Go home."

I ran after Manigat into the parking lot but was pushed back by her staff. "When you call people to go to the streets, what do you think is going to happen?" I shouted after her.

"I'm tired of talking!" she said in French, and left.

Ceant was running out of the building behind me.

"Are you afraid that the result of the declaration is going to be violence?" I asked him.

He scoffed. "Violence? The only one responsible for violence is President René Préval."

Reporters' phones were ringing: Bands of protesters were coming up the hill. Thousands were pouring into the streets downtown. A crowd of dozens of young men ran up to the Karibe gates shouting for Micky. I told them he'd left. Then another report went out: Micky was in the downtown protest. He had jumped on top of a big car and was driven slowly into the city, gathering a crowd wherever he went. To one side, on the roof, sat Baker, the garment factory owner whose supporters had attacked Célestin's. To the other was Wyclef Jean.

Evens, Claire, and I drove into the city and kept circling as darkness fell. This was the election now. A few stalwart polling places in the capital had tried to stay open after the press conference at the Karibe, but the lines had petered out quickly. There were reports of a polling place sacked and filled-out ballots burned in Cap-Haïtien, and of shootings in the Artibonite Valley and in the south. But there was a kind of exuberance in Port-au-Prince that was something other than mere chaos, a feeling that the balance of power had shifted from the Electoral Council to the streets. Everywhere we went, thousands milled, chanted, and danced—for Micky, for annulment, for Célestin to go "under the rubble," and often for nothing at all. There were reports on the radio of police firing tear gas, but the night felt like Carnival to me.

THE DAY AFTER THE DEBACLE, Michel Martelly returned to the Karibe. We followed him there and found someone else ready to speak first. Wyclef Jean had already shown up at the hotel before him, in a flat-topped military cap. In the hotel's banquet room, Jean showed his ink-stained thumb to prove that he had voted, then offered his prescription for solving the electoral mess. Instead of canceling the vote outright as the candidates had demanded the day before, he called for a "credible international" team to come in and review the votes that had been cast. Then he issued a warning: "In twenty-four hours if we procrastinate, the country will rise to a level of violence that we have never seen before."

Martelly spoke in the courtyard outside, standing before the Haitian flag in a suit. At first he denounced Préval and Célestin. Hitting the president's most vulnerable nerve, he told him and his anointed successor to leave the country. "Haiti doesn't *want* you anymore," Micky spat. Then he did a complete about-face. Instead of canceling the vote, he called for patience as the results trickled in over the course of the week. No, he had never wanted to annul the election, he said, despite everything said the day before. Word soon came that Manigat had announced a similar change of heart.

It soon became clear why: Mulet, the chief of MINUSTAH, had somehow gotten wind of the probable results—of what portion of the aborted vote, it wasn't clear—and called Martelly and Manigat to advise them not to drop out. "I think that in the three thousand years of history of democracy, it's probably the first time that we see candidates who could be among the winners claim there was fraud and ask for the cancellation of the elections," Mulet explained to Reuters.[10]

AS THE DECEMBER 7 DEADLINE for the results approached, dread fell over the capital. No one knew what would happen—was the CEP even going to find enough votes to count?—but no one expected it to be good. If Préval's heir, Célestin, was declared the outright winner, the country would probably explode. If Micky was left out of a second round, the election-night protests could turn violent. And if for some reason the members of the CEP broke with the president who had appointed them, there was no telling what Unity's leaders, who were as well connected to the capital's gangs as anyone, might do.

Evens insisted on taking a long-postponed vacation to the Dominican Republic.

"What if shit kicks off?" I protested.

"It'll be fine. I'll put you with my man Bruno if it's not," he said. He sounded confident only about the second part.

Bruno was cut from the same block as Evens, with a similar height and build, but a softer attitude and a little red Suzuki Sidekick even shittier than my Tracker. Claire and I piled in, and we headed over to Le Villate, the Pétionville social club where the results were going to be read. The choice of venue seemed no stranger than the atmosphere on the way there: It was not yet six o'clock, but the streets were disturbingly empty.

We arrived to find a room full of waiting reporters with no sign of anyone from the CEP. The bar was open, so Claire and I drank beer with Trenton, of the *Miami Herald,* and Emily Troutman, a freelancer. One of the popular terms trending on Twitter at the moment was "#Keepyourpantson," which, under the circumstances and after a few bottles each, seemed apt. "When are the results coming out?" #Keepyourpantson. "Are riots starting tonight?" #Keepyourpantson. "Hey Micky, it's OstosSola, some advice if you're going on stage tonight. . . ."

I got up for more beer. At the front of the club, I recognized the squat, balding man in the Roland Hedley vest as the CEP's official photographer. He looked like he'd been at the bar for a while.

"Think it's going to be much longer?" I said in English.

"I don't think anything is going to be much longer," he replied.

"That's cheery."

"It's long, you know, it's a long night. I don't have a car anymore. My car got flat in the earthquake. So I don't have a car, so I can't leave."

Someone who looked like he might have been the bartender showed up. I flashed three fingers in the air and said "Prestige."

"You know," the photographer said, "there are Marines here."

"U.S. Marines?"

"America. American Marines," he said and took a thoughtful drink. "There are Marines fifteen miles out to sea. They have orders to shoot to kill. They are always there when there is going to be trouble."

"You think there's going to be trouble?"

"No. I know."

"Tonight?"

"Now," he said.

I looked out the windows. It was dark, but quiet too.

"I don't hear anything," I said.

But he wasn't listening. "If I didn't work for the government I wouldn't be here. I would be at home. Home sweet home. Be careful you don't get killed. Journalists always get killed in elections, you know. You take one wrong step, you ask one thing, you press too hard. Be careful out there. I should be careful out there. This might be my last beer!" He erupted with laughter.

I paid for the Prestige and went back to my friends. Soon, there was a commotion, and the CEP spokesman appeared. He sat down at the end of the long table in the front of the room. The rest of the council had stayed home.

He apologized for the delay. Then he delayed some more, going through twenty-eight minutes of legislative results, all of which had Unity dominating. "Now, for the presidential results," he said. He stopped again, looked around, and swallowed.

"RDNP," he said, naming the first party. "Mirlande Manigat has received 336,878 votes for a percentage of 31.37."

There was a pause, and he uttered the next two results quickly: "Unity. Célestin, Jude. 241,462 votes. 22.48 percent."

"Repons Peyizan. Martelly, Michel Joseph. 234,617 votes. 21.84 percent."

He kept reading, but it didn't matter. Célestin was in the runoff. Micky was out, by less than 1 percent. Only 20 percent of Haiti's population has chosen, and managed, to vote.

Journalists jumped up, empty beer bottles skidding across the hard floor. Someone yanked a cord out of a speaker so hard that it sent a feedback roar. I kept typing and sending and typing and waiting for edits until nearly everyone besides Claire, myself, and Trenton was gone.

"They're on the street!" someone shouted.

Rocks started pounding the metal shutters on the windows. Claire kept trying to get a closer look. "Get back!" I shouted. There were probably only a few people out there, but we could hear more shouting from farther down the street. Another volley hit the front.

I called Micky's advisor at OstosSola, Damian Merlo. He said the press conference Micky had scheduled after the results were announced was canceled. Security reasons. There was a shotgun blast nearby.

"OK, well, can someone call these protesters and tell them to back off?" I yelled. "There's no one from the CEP here. It's just a bunch of fucking journalists."

Merlo laughed.

The pounding and shouting stopped, and we made a run for the car. There were low barricades made of rocks on the street; people were piling up trash and lighting tires on fire. As we tried to weave our way through, a tall man with angry eyes came walking toward the car. Thinking we'd need to negotiate to go by, I lowered my window. "*Tèt kale!*" I said. "Viv Micky!" Claire yelled.

"Yah yah, *TÈT KALE!*" he said, walking over. Then in one hard move he jabbed his hand through the open window, shouted "GIVE ME THAT SHIT!" and ripped the BlackBerry from my hand. We sped home.

THE THREE DAYS THAT FOLLOWED featured the worst upheaval since the earthquake, the fiercest unrest in Port-au-Prince since the food riots of 2008. Claire and I woke that first morning to the sound of concussion grenades in the Place Saint-Pierre. Fires from the night before were still burning, thick black columns of voluminous smoke that called demonstrators to the barricades. So we went out.

Intersections and plazas were packed with young, angry men brandishing sticks, rocks, and posters. Nearly all were yelling for Micky to go on to the second round and for Célestin—and Préval, their names now synonymous—to be thrown out of the race. The entrance to Saint-Pierre, a pine tree–lined plaza near the narcopalace, was barricaded with flaming tires and heaps of garbage topped with empty ballot boxes. UN soldiers in riot gear had set up nearby in a white armored personal carrier, guns at the ready. At first, it was hard to tell who was in the protest and who was simply living in the plaza under a tarp. Then I realized it didn't matter. The UN soldiers were advancing on them all. I slowly walked backward as the white armored carrier came toward us, flash-bang grenades and canisters of tear gas popping on the street. A fusillade of rocks from the direction of the camp showered down on the carrier, but the aim wasn't particularly good. I shouted for Claire to get down as a hunk of rock flew over her head. She kept taking pictures of the tank-like carrier.

Unity ratcheted up its rhetoric too. Senator Joseph Lambert, a party leader, stated bluntly that his party had armed gangs at the ready. "If we cannot hold them back, prepare yourself for civil war," he warned the *New York Times*. In the midst of the protests, a group of gunmen, some wearing Unity shirts, strode into the crowded camp at the Champ de Mars, found some apparent Martelly supporters, and opened fire.

By the end of the day, the Unity Party headquarters had been looted and burned down, Préval's dream of political stability somewhere in the ashes.

In the chaos, it was easy for the players to spin events as they pleased. Martelly's campaign called the riots proof of his popularity, but that alone could not explain the breadth of the unrest: His official vote tally and Célestin's combined added up to just over 5 percent of the population. Unity said the opposition was trying to hijack the election. There was some truth to both positions.

I was thinking about something else. For eleven months, since those ghastly hours after the quake, the international community had warned and watched for unrest. The specter of Haitian meltdown had fueled the command-and-control nature of the early response, justified hundreds of millions of dollars for military personnel and equipment, dissuaded responders from venturing into the slums and into the countryside, and imposed security restrictions that cut off officials and aid workers from the people they were supposed to help. Hillary Clinton's warnings of poverty-driven upheaval had been the threat leveraged at the donors' conference to urge the funding of a garment factory-centered industrial plan, and fear that Haitians would riot explained the UN's early refusal to investigate its role in the cholera outbreak. Through all of this, the unrest failed to materialize, the people patient, willing to work together, to wait and see. It was only after so many months of disappointment and heartache, mendacity and manipulation, promises made and broken—and the onset of an imported epidemic—that people began rising up. And it was only now, when President Préval's hubristic plan had clashed with the foreign insistence that a flawed on-time election would be better than none at all, that a full-blown political crisis was taking place and the quake-addled heart of Port-au-Prince was in flames.

What little of the capital that had not been broken by the quake was now in tatters. Even Bill Clinton's Interim Haiti Recovery Commission had to move its December meeting to the Dominican Republic because of the unrest. Yet the U.S. Embassy pressed on. Adding fuel to the flames, it issued a statement calling the announced results "inconsistent" with exit polling by the European Union–sponsored Haitian observers.

Préval took the statement as usurpation. As his party headquarters burned, he seethed in an address with uncharacteristically public anger that "the American Embassy is not the CEP." He called for calm, over and over, salting his Kreyòl with the French si'l vous plaît. "Stop burning tires in the middle of the street. Stop defacing public buildings. Stop attacking your own businesses," he said. "This is not an election. This is not democracy anymore."

On the afternoon of December 8, word rolled out that Martelly was going to make a statement. Would he echo Préval and call for the protest to end? Martelly called into a radio station, Signal-FM, from his house:

> People of Haiti! Thank you for the love you have for me, and I bow low to salute you, everywhere. Since last night, the CEP has left the country in a bottomless pit of trouble with its worthless results. Since then, the whole country has stood up to decry them and demand they respect the vote of the people. . . . I understand your anger. To demonstrate without violence is the right of the people. I am asking you to watch for infiltration and provocation, so that others cannot put blame on our backs. Look high. Look low. I will

be with you until the victory, *Tét Kale*. Michel Martelly, candidate for the presidency.[11]

There was something different in his voice, the way he appealed to both paranoia and pride, egging on the protesters even as he called, in the familiar nod-winking way of a politician, for a stop to the violence.

He pledged to stand with the demonstrators until victory— and no less. It was then that I realized that Michel Martelly, Sweet Micky, could come out of this as president. I had a vision of returning to Haiti sometime not long from then and seeing his face smiling back from a poster at the airport, the shining half-moon grin, welcoming me to a new Haiti with more than an echo of the old.

The riots continued through the week until the CEP, broken, announced that it would recount the votes. But Martelly and Manigat refused, saying the CEP couldn't be trusted. There was blood in the water, and the opposition candidates, as well as the international community, started pushing for something more.

On December 17, the OAS announced it would form an independent team to recount the votes itself. Préval's government agreed under pressure. The team was dispatched a few weeks later: four Americans, two French, a Canadian, a Jamaican, and a Chilean IT specialist. Their report, when revealed on January 10, set the election on its ear. First it recommended against holding a new first round, saying that doing so would be too costly and difficult. Then it recommended taking away, according to a complex calculation of probable fraud, a certain number of specific tally sheets, thus reducing each candidates' total by a certain amount. The argument was opaque and the reasoning behind it debatable. But the upshot was clear: The new calculation would move Micky to the second round and knock Jude Celestin out of the race. All that was left was for Préval to accept the report.

CHAPTER THIRTEEN

ALL TOGETHER NOW

THE STREETS WERE ALMOST SILENT. THERE WAS NO KOMPA, NO TAP-taps honking, no merchant women hawking their wares. In a quiet neighborhood off downtown, where the buildings were still broken and bowed, the only sound came from a small procession in white, the marchers' arms raised as they praised God, who had protected them for a whole year. Twelve months that began with the end of days. Through the coming of the rains, through broken promises of aid, disease, a hurricane, and riots, they had persevered and were here to see the sun shine over another January 12. The wreath they carried was for the dead, still being discovered in the rubble, 95 percent of which remained where it had fallen a year before. Three skeletons, one still wearing an impossibly clean white shirt, had been found in a fallen restaurant at the city's center just days before. In a large white tent beside the wreckage of the Cathédrale Notre-Dame de L'Assomption, a cardinal sent from Guinea said a mass for the countless dead before hundreds in the tent and outside. Although the marchers here, on the eastern periphery of downtown, honored the dead with their wreath, too, their humble hallelujahs were for another 365 days of survival.

Mèsi Bondye, the penitents sang. Thank you, God.

"TOO MUCH RUBBLE CONTINUES TO CLOG the streets, too many people are still living in tents, and for so many Haitians progress has not come fast enough," President Obama said in an anniversary statement. However, he reminded his audience, "as we have said all along, helping the poorest nation in the Western Hemisphere recover from one of the worst natural disasters ever to strike our hemisphere will take years, if not decades."[1] Obama was right on both counts. The year since the earthquake was surely too short a time span to build a city's worth of permanent new housing, improve the country's political stability, and relieve the suffering of the poor. But many, too many, far more manageable promises had been broken as well. More than two-thirds of funds pledged for the two years after the quake—more than $3 billion—was still undisbursed, including nearly nine-tenths of the money promised by the United States for 2010. The lack of funding and urgency had resulted in months lost fighting over land titles, roles, and dump sites, and passing the buck.

Obama observed with admiration that "countless lives [had] been saved" by the provision of medical aid and water in the weeks after the quake. But he neglected to mention that thousands had later been killed by a disease almost certainly introduced by the reckless negligence of United Nations peacekeepers, who continued to refuse responsibility. The American president also made no reference to the fact that the underlying structural circumstances that had allowed the earthquake to be so destructive had been largely shaped by policies emerging from the Oval Office where he sat. Obama was silent on the ways in which the meddling of his State Department had hastened the political crisis that Haiti found itself in one year after the destruction of the capital.

That crisis showed no signs of abating. Haiti's president was livid in response to the recommendation in the Organization of American States report that Jude Célestin be dropped from the race in favor of Michel "Sweet Micky" Martelly. Préval was angry that foreigners were interfering, frustrated by what they wanted, and insulted that the OAS had not notified him about the results before the report made its way into my story for AP.[2]

The OAS spoke for the international community—its findings endorsed now tacitly and soon explicitly by every major power. With no allies to speak for him, Préval's last line of defense, it seemed, was obstinacy. He gave a press conference in which he pretended not to know whether the report existed or not, then alleged—perhaps with cause—that foreign diplomats had offered to fly him into exile as the crisis mounted. He then petulantly refused to formally accept a copy of the report whose existence he had just disputed, a bureaucratic formality that nonetheless managed to grind the process to a halt.

With the scheduled date of the second round—still officially to be contested between Célestin and Mirlande Manigat—rapidly approaching on Sunday, January 16, the stalemate showed no signs of cracking. Another Haitian election was about to be delayed.

AS I SHOULD HAVE KNOWN FULL WELL by then, if you stop in a seeming pause to reflect on Haiti's last story, you are bound to get pummeled by the next. This is in part the consequence of covering a place so poor, where shoddy infrastructure means a sudden rain can be deadlier than a hurricane, a spike in global food prices existential. But after a while in Haiti, it starts to feel as if something else is in play too. It's as if the island was built with a kind of reverse *deus ex machina:* No sooner does a story begin to find resolution than something arrives to thoroughly unresolve it.

On January 16, the day the now-interminably delayed second-round runoff between Jude Célestin and Mirlande Manigat had been due to be held, impossible news shot through the country: Jean-Claude "Baby Doc" Duvalier—the man who had ruled Haiti for fifteen bloody years, master of the tonton macoute secret police, scion of the tyrannical François "Papa Doc" Duvalier, "president for life"—was ending a quarter century of exile to fly back to Port-au-Prince. It felt like a fever dream. The popular revolt that overthrew him in 1986 had been a seismic event to rival an earthquake, the singularity from which all politics since could be traced. No one had expected him ever to return, not least because it would make him a wanted man. But the rumor was real. Baby Doc was coming home.

Upon landing at the airport originally named for his father, Duvalier and his girlfriend, Veronique Roy, headed straight for Pétionville. As the ex-dictator's loaned cars sped through the shattered suburb, onlookers cheered, peered suspiciously, and mused about what this could mean. Old folks murmured in bewildered amusement and horror. Untold thousands had been killed and tortured, and far more driven into exile, during his and his father's rule. For the seven-tenths of Haitians under thirty, though, the man in the car was a figure from history books and old jokes; Richard Nixon back from the grave, King Tut in an SUV. For the former dictator, after an earthquake and decades of rot, the unlit streets of his former playground must have been unrecognizable.

The decades of hardship since Baby Doc's banishment had given birth to a kind of Duvalier nostalgia, fueled by a vague memory of law and order in his day (i.e., when theft, rape, and violence were monopolized by the state), and the fact that, two and a half decades before, food had been cheaper. But many also felt a kind of shame about the number of recent Haitian leaders in exile— including Jean-Bertrand Aristide, still in South Africa—and put there aboard U.S. planes. As a young man had told me amid the uncleared wreckage of the Bel-Air slum in March: "We have a lot of very important people in exile. Why can't they come here to help us? The number one is Jean-Bertrand Aristide. And the other is Jean-Claude Duvalier. They would come to put their heads together." This longing would have been incomprehensible to most non-Haitians. How could someone want the opposites of Haiti's political spectrum—the ex-liberation theologian and the quasi-fascist former dictator—not only to come back but to put their heads together? Yet to the young and disenchanted, it seemed natural to hunger for the return of Haiti's powerful men—anyone, really—who could contribute to reconstruction.

Duvalier's convoy wound up at the Karibe Hotel, where the election-stopping press conference had taken place eight weeks before. Reporters would not be allowed in unless they were guests, so AP had wisely booked a room. Claire and I moved in the next day. It was one kooky scene. Every hanger-on, wannabe, and has-been who'd ever willingly associated himself with the *famille Duvalier* showed up in the marble lobby wearing an ill-fitting suit. A gray-haired man falsely claimed to be a family spokesman and was taken as such by major news outlets, who quoted him until Duvalier's girlfriend publicly shamed him as a poseur. Another character, known simply as the Colonel, complete with military-style medals pinned to his wide lapel, shuttled elderly *makout* to the elevator to pay respect to their former taskmaster. At one point the management had to shut off Duvalier's room service bill—people all over the hotel were charging meals and drinks to the ex-dictator's room.

There were many plausible reasons for Baby Doc to return. One was money. The ex-dictator had blown through his reported hundreds of millions of dollars in state funds living the high life in Paris and on a messy divorce. His last $5.7 million was in a frozen Swiss bank account; on February 1, the new Restitution of Illicit Assets Act—known in Bern as the Lex Duvalier—was going to make it possible for the Swiss government to confiscate ill-gotten assets and return them to ex-dictator's countries of origin.[3] Duvalier and Roy might have thought that a show of his returning to Haitian soil without being arrested might win them access to the funds.

Another was political. Many Haitians thought Préval had allowed or engineered Baby Doc's return, to pressure the State Department to drop the OAS report. When Duvalier, who was wanted under Haitian law for assassination, extortion, and embezzlement, and a decade and a half of other crimes, entered Haiti without arrest, some observers took it as a sign that Préval might be threatening to let another leader return as well. Since 2004, a central plank of U.S.-led policy in Haiti had been discouraging the return of Aristide. Aristide was, in the basest epithet Washington could muster, a threat to stability: If he'd maintained his political muscle, he could corral opposition to the export-focused, low-wage industries the responders were trying to build; the English-speaking businessmen the U.S. Embassy trusted warned he would deploy gangs. When Aristide would announce in the coming weeks his desire to return, Obama would personally call South African President Jacob Zuma to argue for the ex-president to stay in Pretoria.[4]

Finally, then there was the matter of Duvalier's flagging health. The pudgy 1980s dictator with the trademark sideburns had become gaunt and sallow, his hairline fraying on all sides. Seemingly unable to move his neck, he walked with a shuffle belying his fifty-nine years—he had become president as a teenager, after all. The weird constellation of political officers, journalists, and rumored spies at the lobby bar whispered that he had simply come home to die.

Duvalier kept to his room on the third floor. Old cronies went in, empty trays of poisson grossel went out. Veronique Roy worked the starburst-decorated lobby in Dolce & Gabbana sunglasses and a black pantsuit, buttering us up—"Préval must be angry with you," Roy joked to me about my OAS scoop. "You must think you have good security!"—and making us compete for interviews with Duvalier that never happened. One of the few times Duvalier left was to be escorted by police to stand before a judge, who informed him that an embezzlement case against him had been opened. But in a sign that the case would likely go nowhere, Duvalier was quickly allowed to return to the hotel.

That night, Claire and I sat at the table next to the old tyrant's at the Karibe's outdoor restaurant. Surrounded by his cohort, a humid breeze flowing through the garden, he seemed to come alive. He smiled as sycophants whispered in his ears and muttered jokes greeted with hearty laughter. It was a man home for the first time in half his life. But as the salad course was cleared, Duvalier began to slump again, and Roy announced that the president needed to lie down. The old men grumbled their good wishes and rose slightly in salute as Duvalier was helped into the silent dark. The man was like a ghost, and there were ghosts all around him, in a country full of them.

THREE DAYS AFTER DUVALIER'S RETURN, the Provisional Electoral Council (CEP) officially rejected the OAS report, again insisting on a second round between Célestin and Manigat. Then the real pressure began. At the UN Security Council, U.S. Permanent Representative Susan Rice demanded that Préval implement the OAS recommendation, stating that the delivery of billions in promised aid required "a credible process that represents the will of the Haitian people." Préval dug in.

The State Department then ratcheted up the pressure, revoking the U.S. visas of a dozen officials with ties to the Unity Party and the president. Washington was clearly fed up. U.S. officials blamed the failures of reconstruction on Préval, seeing years of tolerating him as having gone nowhere. They were right to view the election as a sham—there was no credible reason to think Célestin should have gone to the second round. But there was no credible reason to count the votes of Manigat or Martelly either, both of whom had headlined the call for annulment that had ground voting to a halt. If the election was fatally flawed, they were responsible too. But they offered the international community a clear change from Préval. While expressed in sharply contrasting ways—Manigat's professorial, motherly diligence versus Micky's aggressive, boisterous showmanship—their platforms were nearly identical: Both embraced a rightist vision of nationalism rooted in law and order, happy above all to court massive foreign investment with tax breaks and allowing companies to take all their profits out of Haiti, the "Haiti open for business" that the U.S. telecom executive Brad Horwitz had asked for at the donors' conference as Bill Clinton looked on approvingly. In this view, a second round without Célestin was a perfect do-over, a chance to redeem the marred vote without sinking another $29 million from the international community, with the result guaranteed to be acceptable either way.

Unity went mad. Its leaders issued a confusing statement in which they appeared to push Célestin from the race but concluded that "the political battle has just begun." Leftists and Aristide supporters at home and abroad, who had spent the last four years or so deriding Préval as a Washington-appeasing turncoat, rallied to his and Célestin's cause. They raged against what they saw as a U.S.-sponsored effort to install Martelly, whose past friendships with pro-Duvalierist putschists they saw as portents of a hard tack to the right. Meanwhile, Martelly's supporters blasted what they saw as a corrupt, fixed election and threatened to again set fire to the streets if he was not given a berth in the second round. The singer prodded them on. "We are ready to fight for justice for everyone," he told a news conference in the garden of the Hotel Oloffson. "We won't accept an electoral coup."[5]

Only Manigat stayed out of the fray. Although the seventy-year-old law professor's supporters had clashed with UN peacekeepers immediately after the election, she had come out of the December 7 tallies as the only one certain to be in a second round—if it ever took place. So she sat back and maintained her image as the dignified choice while the men brawled.

The CEP had set a deadline of Wednesday, February 2, to resolve the crisis and confirm or revise its announcement about which two names would appear on the second-round ballot. This was, even for Haiti, nonnegotiable. The constitution said Préval's term was to end five days later, on February 7. The mere possibility that the president might prolong his term had sparked protests eight months before; if he stayed on now, with no clear succession plan, political riots could break out again—this time with the nation's former dictator looking on from Pétionville and one of its most rabble-rousing presidents in history now openly plotting his return from South Africa.

So on Sunday, January 30, three days before the deadline, the big gun came to town. In the middle of the crisis in Egypt, where Hosni Mubarak's regime was unraveling, Hillary Rodham Clinton arrived in Port-au-Prince to break the deadlock herself. She set up shop at the mansion of the U.S. ambassador's mansion adjacent to the Pétionville Club. Her schedule was tight: brief meetings with the three major candidates and major constituent groups from Haiti. When the time slot for her meeting with "civil society" arrived, Reginald Boulos pulled up to the gate and walked through, alone. "There goes civil society," one of the reporters said with a smirk. Then Clinton went to President Préval and laid down the law: There would be no new recount. The OAS report was to be implemented, as is.

As the evening of the final announcement arrived, Haiti held its breath. Bank tellers shut their windows, and merchants went home. Journalists gathered at a former Gold's Gym in Pétionville that had been gifted to the CEP by Préval and waited for the 6 P.M. announcement. Thirteen hours later, as reporters woke from naps atop their riot gear, the spokesman for the CEP walked in, sat down, and issued the final presidential ballot—without results, percentages, or explanation:

1. Mirlande Manigat
2. Michel Martelly

It was done.

The announcement unleashed a sigh of relief across Port-au-Prince, people now confident that no riots would break out. There were cheers in Pétionville, where Micky lived and enjoyed his strongest support.[6]

There was jubilation in Washington, too. That afternoon, State Department spokesman P. J. Crowley opened the daily briefing in Washington by introducing the U.S. Ambassador to Haiti, Ken Merten. "It was a good day in Haiti today," the envoy said. The CEP had been "very diligent" in following the OAS report. A second round between Martelly and Manigat would be held on March 20. Préval would likely stay on until his successor was chosen—but with a schedule to replace him in place, the opposition and protesters would stay calm. "We are pleased," the ambassador concluded.[7]

The news from Haiti was a counterpoint to the day's biggest story. Gunmen in Cairo had just opened fire on demonstrators calling for the departure of Hosni Mubarak, and the journalists at Foggy Bottom were pressuring the State Department spokesman to take sides. Crowley emphasized, "We're calling for an orderly transition that leads to free, fair, and credible elections." But he wouldn't say that the U.S. backed the pro-democracy protesters in Tahrir Square. There too, a preference for elections at all costs over less predictable forms of democracy was creating a contradiction. In Haiti at least, the benefits to the U.S. seemed clear. Under intense pressure, the incomplete, riot-wracked first-round vote would now be cleaned up with a runoff. No matter who won, Haiti and the international community would be guaranteed a leader who would play ball with Washington's vision of reconstruction, even if the bawdy singer emerging as the favorite to win would have been unimaginable as president just a few months before.

The runoff was hotly contested. But Martelly's increasingly polished campaign, managed by the experts at OstosSola, made huge strides. The CEP had done him the ultimate favor: By kicking him out of the race, it made the singer into a folk hero, someone to rally around for anyone aggrieved by the President Préval. Looking back, Leslie Voltaire, one of the first-round candidates, admitted he'd never thought Martelly could really compete for the presidency. "But I misread the Haitian mind," Voltaire told me. "As a Westerner, [you would think] that there is no way Martelly can be president, anywhere! Because of his—his way of life." But in Haiti, the architect explained, people love *Gede*—a mischievous family of Vodou gods who rule fertility and the dead, popular for their crudeness and their caring. "Martelly is a pure *Gede*," Voltaire continued. "He is effeminate. He curses a lot. He drinks a lot. He smokes a lot. He's wild! People like entertainment. So when I say that I misread, I misread the moment. The moment is that the people had suffered catastrophe. They are under tents, under the rain and the sun. They don't want to argue with you or to discuss with you. They want entertainment. And Micky's giving them entertainment. For a campaign it's good, but to govern it's another thing."[8]

Even the dropping of the last shoe—the long-awaited return of Jean-Bertrand Aristide—had no effect.

In the end, just one-fifth of the electorate cast ballots for either of the two candidates. But the results were not close. With 67.5 percent of the diminished vote, certified by the international community, the Prezidan Kompa became the fifty-sixth president of the republic. Quietly, the Unity Party nearly swept the legislative races (international observers said these were outside their purview), guaranteeing gridlock in the next government. But that didn't matter for now. On May 15, in the midst of a sweltering power outage, in a parliamentary building paid for by the United States, Michel "Sweet Micky" Martelly accepted the presidential sash. He then went to the collapsed National Palace and took the podium, standing before a bodyguard wearing a hot-pink tie. Dignitaries including Bill Clinton looked on as the new president spoke of rebuilding Haiti. Then, in English, so he could be understood overseas, the new president began to shout: "This is a new Haiti! A new Haiti open for business, now!"

I HAD SPENT THREE AND A HALF YEARS in Haiti, five on Hispaniola in all. My tour was about to end when the quake struck, and I pledged to extend it by a year. Exhausted, traumatized, still having to tell myself not to run out of a building every time a truck shook the street—it was time to go. In one of life's happy coincidences, Claire was going back to NYU. She had a pleasant apartment in Brooklyn, just south of Prospect Park, where I could move in, and where we could live in relative peace with working electricity and hot water. It sounded like heaven.

Evens drove me to the airport. My possessions fit in a suitcase and a backpack, including a pile of handmade lacquered wooden gifts that Joselin, one of the new house staff, gave me to start a new home with Claire. The ride down Route de Delmas and across the airport road could have taken place on any day in our new postquake world. The music pumped from overloaded taptaps, sweat-caked vendors shouted at passing cars, and tumbled-down buildings and camps flew past the window. The weather was hot and the sky crystalline, and the smells of gasoline and dung wafted in the air.

Haiti had given, and it had taken, and I suppose I gave and took too. A little over a year before, the Earth had almost taken it all. I was leaving behind friends and the memories of friends, far too many of whom had gone from the world. The island, in good times and bad, is not a place to which you adapt. It rewires you. To cope and not be torched by its energy, you have to change the way you think and feel and see the things around you. Even the illogic has a rhythm to get used to. But there's a limit to understanding. I had thought I'd known Haiti before the quake struck; I had thought I'd learned postquake Haiti when the epidemic hit; I had thought I could predict the direction of things when the election went sour. I had no idea. Haiti, like life, does not care what you want from it.

The year of earthquakes changed everyone. The disaster brought many closer, and then the hardship of the year that followed drove many apart. Our brush with physical reality took its toll on the mind. A late 2010 survey by the International Organization for Migration found that more than half of families in camps had members who suffered from anxiety and fatigue—thousands up thousands of people, perhaps a generation, with probable PTSD. A quarter reported that one or more members had suffered panic attacks, and about one in twelve had a member who had recently attempted suicide.[9]

The Cherys slowly grew apart. Billy, along with his wife and son, moved to a house in a neighborhood called Cazeau. Around July he'd found a job with the International Federation of the Red Cross, guarding the gate for its ex-pat workers. They were friendly but always coming and going. "I'll meet one and spend time with them, after six months I meet another one," he said. "They drink a lot. They smoke a lot. I don't understand it."

Rose moved into her boyfriend David's house off Delmas 33, with cinder-block walls and a metal roof that vibrated in the wind. The earthquake year had made her more open-minded—"cooler, less standoffish," she said—because she understood more than ever that everyone had to work together to survive. But while she felt more a part of her community, the hardship of the year had splintered her family geographically. "We don't feel so well because we don't live together anymore. We don't know how the other is sleeping, we don't know how they're doing, if they ate, if they even woke up," she said. "That hurts me because it's not the way that it was before."

Twenty remained under his tarp in Camp Trazelie, working on his music in the shade of a now-towering ash tree, but without the resources to make it far. Work was scarce. He could not afford school, he could not afford a new home. Thanks to his uncle, a boatman, he could sometimes go back to Île-la-Gonâve, the island off the northwestern coast of Haiti where the Chery clan had been born. When Twenty was stressed, he would close his eyes and think about the sea. "Initially everyone was uniting, everyone was participating, everyone was collaborating," he would say, looking back. "But after more time, the system changed back. We hoped the country would change, and we would have a different life. But we're still here without hope. You have to play around with your mind to take yourself out of the situation that you're in, because you still can't see a way out. Everything is hard."

For Evens and me too, the disaster had brought us closer, then the stress of the year drove us apart. In that car on the way to the airport we were still riding together, come what may, but I was about to board a jet for a place he could not go.

One of the last things I did in Haiti was to get rid of my car, the hunk-of-junk Geo Tracker. The steering was now shot and the brakes worn, and it had a hell of a time shifting into second from first—a problem on the capital's endless hills—but it could still qualify as a fixer-upper. I had asked Evens to help me sell it, but just about every potential buyer who popped up then backed off without explanation. Soon I was left with just one taker—Evens, holding a roll of cash amounting to a third of what I'd paid for the car two years before. Evens had plopped it on the desk with a smile. We both knew we weren't negotiating. His name was already on the title.

When we got to the airport, we hugged.

"I'm sure I'll be back," I said.

"I know you will," he said.

Before the earthquake, I'd opened a new folder to store pic-tures on my computer. I'd named it after an old sci-fi movie: "2010: The Year We Make Contact." I had no idea how true that would be. I didn't know that I'd meet Claire and fall in love. I didn't know the degree to which the worlds where I was born and where I lived would collide. I didn't know how much turmoil and absurdity it was possible for anyone to face in just over twelve months. Most of all, I didn't know what the Earth had in store, at that moment when the contact of two onrushing plates would send everything tumbling down. And I'm glad I didn't know. Because if I had, I wouldn't have been there.

EPILOGUE

MEMWA

THROUGH THE OPEN WINDOW OF OUR BROOKLYN APARTMENT, I CAN hear the greetings on Ocean Avenue: "*Bonswa.*" "*Ki jan ou ye?*" A "dollar van" group taxi honks at would-be passengers. The second-floor hallway blooms with the smell of scotch-bonnet peppers and grilled *pwason*. Last night, by the lake in Prospect Park, I biked past a jam session of *ra-ra* drums and horns. Haiti, never far from America, is so present on these blocks that if I closed my eyes I'd think I was in Port-au-Prince. But I open them and it's clear that I'm not. There are homegrown police on patrol, an ambulance driving to a functioning hospital, and a well-stocked supermarket where most anyone can afford to shop. The city will probably, eventually, get around to fixing that sinkhole. But most of all, I can feel confident that this big brick building where Claire and I live will continue to stand—that someone has inspected it, made sure it's up to a code—though one never quite knows what this Earth has in store.

Friends sometimes ask about the earthquake. Those conversations often turn to their feelings upon learning the news, their deep desire to help, and their deeper frustration with the outcome three years later. Usually, the discussion boils down to the same question: What should we do differently next time? Should we bother giving again? My answer is yes; but that by then, we will have waited too long. Donations toward immediate relief will bring doctors and rescuers when people are still pinned under concrete, stranded by floodwaters, or fleeing the firestorm. Still, it's important to give wisely. Dig deeper to find organizations with long experience in the affected region. Find people who speak local languages and have strong local ties that will help ensure they understand what is needed, what is available, and to whom the help should go. Best of all would be to send help to NGOs and organizations from the affected countries themselves, so that they can lead the way. All that is important. But it's now, in the ample time between emergencies, when the heaviest lifting has to be done.

The issue is less with some organizations having more know-how than others; it's that the whole system needs to be overhauled—and not just when it comes to aid. Poverty and a lack of local institutions create the shoddy conditions that make disasters deadlier than they have to be. Few of us ever do enough to prepare for disasters, even in places like New York that could afford to make necessary investments to guard against floods, hurricanes—and, yes, earthquakes—today. But in impoverished countries, the failure to plan, and to have institutions that can coordinate a response, threatens millions of lives. Supporting efforts to give aid directly to local governments, and the goal of building local institutions that operate independently of foreign control, will go exponentially further than cargo planes of tarps and bottled water. It's true that we don't always know what locals will do with that assistance, but that's the point. It's up to them.

It's also critical to be informed about how our day-to-day decisions can affect people in places we only think about when a big-enough tragedy strikes. The low-wage Haitian garment industry would not exist as it does today, nor would it have played so problematic a role in the reconstruction, if American consumers were willing to pay more for their clothes, for instance. It's not enough to say that underpaid jobs with a destructive track record are "better than nothing." We have to understand the assets people in countries like Haiti already have, and how best to protect them, even if doing so means making decisions that might be uncomfortable for us in the short run.

The enormous talent, money, and goodwill of the postquake response left an ironic legacy in Haiti. Having sought above all to prevent riots, ensure stability, and prevent disease, the responders helped spark the first, undermine the second, and by all evidence caused the third. Claire and I went back to Port-au-Prince in the spring of 2012. I knocked back beers with Evens, now working for the new guy at AP, still beaming about his son. We hung with Twenty on his tarp porch in Trazelie, the camp crowded as ever, and bounced in the studio while his clique put down a new track. A month before, Rosemide and David had a baby. They named him Clide. We cooed and took pictures while the little one slept under a mosquito net at their tin-roofed house.

Cholera still plagues the country, spiking when it rains as the bacteria spreads in overflowing wastewater. Aid workers have tried to roll out vaccines. More evidence has emerged that MINUSTAH peacekeepers introduced the scourge; by March 2012, Bill Clinton, still UN Special Envoy, was convinced, telling a news conference that a UN soldier from South Asia had "[carried] the cholera strain. It came from his waste stream into the waterways of Haiti, into the bodies of Haitians."[1] The Nepalese peacekeepers were removed from Meille. They were replaced by a Uruguayan contingent that dug a new path for the river, farther away from the base, where people still wash and swim. Publicly, the UN clings to doubt about the epidemic's origins.

The anger in Haiti clouds acknowledgment of any help the UN might provide. "They don't come and do real work," Rosemide said. "We're here under the hot sun working, and they're killing us." A group of Haitian and American lawyers has filed suit on behalf of 5,000 cholera victims' families, calling for the world body to apologize, pay reparations, and finance water and sanitation. They argue that the UN's immunity from prosecution should not mean impunity for negligence. The case has not moved forward to date.

Haiti changed politically. The first thing I saw as I stepped off the jetway into 2012 Port-au-Prince was the smiling face of Michel Martelly on a poster declaring: "Victory for the People! The Airport Is Being Repaired. Tét Kale." Pro-Micky propaganda decked the capital, hot-pink posters showing the president embracing the elderly, or advertising the number of children for whom his administration says it has paid school tuition. Micky is still Micky, singing at Carnival and entertaining delegations with piano renditions of "Haïti, Cherie." But his burgeoning cult of personality belies a continuing political unease. The flawed 2010 election resulted in a president with little institutional support, at loggerheads with a parliament dominated by Préval's Unity Party. In early 2012,

Unity leaders stoked allegations that Martelly was secretly a U.S. citizen—which could have him thrown out of office. Senators took to the radio warning of riots. Tension grew until U.S. Ambassador Ken Merten declared, in Kreyòl, at a press conference that the president was not an American.

Camps are being steadily cleared from visible places such as the Champ de Mars, but the evicted have nowhere to go. Making enough to eat and pay rent is no easier for millions of Haitians than it was before. Nearly all who return to standing homes, even the several thousand repaired with money from the aid effort, are back in buildings just like those that collapsed in the earthquake. The Interim Haiti Recovery Commission's mandate ended, having approved $3.2 billion worth of projects—a third of which were left unfunded. Neither a Haitian-led commission, nor anything else, replaced it. A U.S. Government Accountability Office review in April 2011 found the commission remained understaffed and "not fully operational," and said it had done a poor job in its central task of coordinating with the Haitian government—funding less than a fifth of the rubble-removal projects Préval's administration said were needed but four times the number of road infrastructure projects requested.[2] While T-shelters were finally built at Camp Corail, they are overshadowed by the 100,000 squatters now massed on the hills around it. The most significant building projects in the capital are high-priced hotels for foreigners, including a $15.7 million Best Western in Pétionville, and a proposed luxury hotel to be built and owned by the International Federation of Red Cross and Red Crescent Societies.[3]

In a nod to the international community, Martelly made Bill Clinton's chief of staff at the Office of the Special Envoy his first prime minister. After five months, the appointee quit under pressure, reportedly from Micky himself. Laurent Lamothe, a businessman and old friend of the president's, replaced him. Lamothe's nomination was accompanied by a wave of investment, including a $10 million stake by the World Bank Group's International Finance Corporation in a private-business investment fund whose three-man investment committee includes Lamothe's long-time business partner. Another former IFC advisor, Paul Altidor—who had left the IFC to be vice president of investments for the Clinton-Bush Haiti Fund—was named Haiti's new ambassador to the

United States. True to his inaugural address, Martelly was proving a far more reliable partner for foreign business than Préval.

Another well-known figure has emerged by Micky's side; the celebrity president has forged a firm and mutual friendship with Sean Penn. In January 2012, Martelly officially named the actor an ambassador-at-large of the Republic of Haiti. Penn has become a powerful Haiti advocate, an outspoken critic of the waste and ineffectiveness of many NGOs, who strongly advocates for Haiti's government and people to do their own rebuilding. But Penn is a complicated figure in Haiti. His powers as a foreigner, greatly bolstered by his international celebrity, have allowed the actor to gain a level of influence far beyond his qualifications or expertise. Credentialed as a diplomat less than two years after first setting foot in the country, he oversees one of the newest, if more effective, entities of the "Republic of NGOs." For many Haitians, he has become another symbol of compromised sovereignty. In August 2012, Martelly gave Penn's NGO the task of finally demolishing the long-lingering ruins of the presidential mansion. A Haitian journalist lamented: "Two hundred twenty-one years after the slave uprising [against the French], and we are incapable of clearing the ruins of [our own] house."[4]

The United States continues to be a dominant force in Haiti's reconstruction, its policies sharing the garment-industry and export-agriculture focus of Paul Collier's 2009 report. Much of the U.S. effort, $224 million, is focused on building infrastructure and housing for the Caracol Industrial Park near Cap-Haïtien. (A third of the U.S. projects approved by the IHRC in its first year had to do with the garment factory–anchored industrial park as well.)[5] Sae-A Trading Co. Ltd., the South Korean company Brun had eyed for Corail-Cesselesse, is the anchor of the new park. Because the park is 170 miles north of Port-au-Prince, reachable by paved roads, it represents a positive kind of decentralization, encouraging people from the ever-more deforested countryside to migrate somewhere besides Port-au-Prince. Proponents also say that the kinds of garment manufacturing planned for the park, including equipment-intensive knitting and dyeing, will provide better training and make it harder for manufacturers to bolt the country at will.

But just like the export zones of Jean-Claude Duvalier's "economic revolution," which left behind little but the massive slum of

Cité Soleil, the foreign factory owners at Caracol will not pay taxes to the Haitian government and will be allowed to take all their profits out of Haiti. The U.S. State Department-brokered deal with Sae-A is expected to create 20,000 jobs, making the South Korean firm Haiti's largest employer. However, proponents of the project consider the new $5-a-day minimum wage, delayed for three years by Préval's 2009 compromise with Parliament, a barrier to the factories' long-term success. In July 2012, the *New York Times* reported that Sae-A had closed a factory in Guatemala amid a union's allegations of severe abuse, including death threats and rape, by the company.[6] (Sae-A responded that it abides by international standards, and that those responsible were reprimanded or fired.) For Guatemalans, the story was clear: Sae-A found a cheaper, more pliable source of labor elsewhere.[7] Leslie Voltaire, the Préval's master planner, now helping design a gated community for the Korean executives, predicts a grim future as still-impoverished people, in conditions as bad or worse than those three years before, flock to the factories in hopes of finding work. "Caracol," he told me, "will be the biggest slum in Haiti."

In January 2012, a Haitian judge ruled that Jean-Claude "Baby Doc" Duvalier could not be prosecuted for the innumerable human-rights abuses of his reign; flouting protests from Human Rights Watch and Amnesty International, the judge found that the statute of limitations on crimes in the indictment had expired. Duvalier and his girlfriend, Veronique Roy, moved to a house above Pétionville and can be seen frequenting the neighborhood's restaurants. Duvalier's son and Papa Doc's grandson, 29-year-old François Nicolas Duvalier, is a consultant to President Martelly.[8]

Aristide reportedly stays mostly in his house in the neighborhood of Tabarre. There are rumors of his imminent arrest, and also that Aristide may be weighing a return to politics in the form of a Senate run. But they are only rumors.

When I went looking for Préval, I was told he'd gone to Miami.

—*August 2012*

NOTES

INTRODUCTION

1. UN Office of the Special Envoy for Haiti, http://haitispecialenvoy.org. Caroline Preston and Nicole Wallace, "American Donors Gave $1.4-Billion to Haiti Aid," *Chronicle of Philanthropy*, January 6, 2011.
2. Hillary Rodham Clinton, "Remarks at the International Donors' Conference Towards a New Future for Haiti," March 31, 2010, http://usun.state.gov/briefing/statements /2010/139309.htm
3. Manuel Orozco, "Understanding the Remittance Economy in Haiti," *Inter-American Dialogue*, March 15, 2006.
4. Interviews with current and former U.S. government officials, 2012.
5. *World Disasters Report 2011: Focus on Hunger and Malnutrition* (Geneva: International Federation of Red Cross and Red Crescent Societies, 2011), http://www.ifrc.org /publications-and-reports/world-disasters-report/.

PROLOGUE

1. U.S. Agency for International Development Mission to Haiti, "Education: Overview," 2006, http://www.usaid.gov/ht/education.htm (retrieved August 2012 from http://web .archive.org).
2. "Net ODA Receipts 1998–2008," Organisation for Economic Co-operation and Development, http://stats.oecd.org/ (accessed July 2012). That figure would have been larger, but the largest donor—the United States—withheld aid during a political dispute between the Bush and Aristide administrations.
3. UN Office of the Special Envoy for Haiti, *Has Aid Changed?* (New York, 2011).

CHAPTER 1: THE END

1. I was introduced to the phrase by the author Madison Smartt Bell.
2. Oetgen reconfirmed most of the details of this conversation in September 2012, including that security protocols barred Evens and I from entering the embassy or using the Internet. He said that his no-commenting was due to a lack of available information. He did not recall suggesting we sleep in the parking lot. Evens shared my recollection of the conversation.

CHAPTER 2: LOVE THEME FROM *TITANIC*

1. "Taíno" was apparently a name given to the people by Europeans. Scholars are divided on what they called themselves.

2.   Some scholars say it might also have been named for a string of forgotten nearby islands called "The Princes."

3.   "Lettre du Roi aux administrateurs pour établier au Port-au-Prince la Capitale des Îles Sous Le Vent," King Louis XV of France, November 26, 1749, in Georges Corvington, *Port-au-Prince a cours des ans, Vol. 1* (Port-au-Prince: Henri Deschamps, 1970), 444.

4.   A two-month-old baby was reportedly left in a collapsing house, saved at the last moment by an aunt. He grew up to be Alexandre Pétion, a founder and early president of the republic (and the namesake of Pétionville). Via Saint-Remy (des Cayes), *Pétion et Haïti* (Paris: Librairie Berger-Levrault et Cie., 1956 reprinting), 11–12.

5.   David M. Morens, "Epidemic Anthrax in the Eighteenth Century, the Americas," *Emerging Infectious Diseases,* October 2002, http://wwwnc.cdc.gov/eid/article/8/10/02-0173.htm.

6.   *Voyages: The Trans-Atlantic Slave Database,* Emory University, http://www.slavevoyages .org/tast/assessment/estimates.faces.

7.   As the historian Laurent Dubois put it, "It was cheaper to let slaves die and buy more from Africa," in *Haiti: The Aftershocks of History* (New York: Metropolitan, 2012), 21.

8.   This was more complex than it sounds. For instance, evidence suggests that after gaining his freedom before the revolution, Toussaint himself had become a slave-owner.

9.   Smedley Darlington Butler and Anne Cipriano Venzon, eds., *The Letters of a Leatherneck, 1898–1931* (New York: Praeger Publishers, 1992).

10. Robert Debs Heinl, Nancy Gordon Heinl, and Michael Heinl, *Written in Blood: The Story of the Haitian People 1492–1995* (Lanham, MD: University Press of America, 2005), 352; Dubois, 204.

11. Hans Schmidt, *The United States Occupation of Haiti, 1915–1934* (New Brunswick, NJ: Rutgers University Press, 1995), 10.

12. Dubois, 243–248.

13. Michel-Rolph Trouillot, *Haiti: State Against Nation* (New York: Monthly Review Press, 2000), 104.

14. Holland America Lines, "West Indies Cruise Mercury," January 9, 1963.

15. Matthew J. Smith, *Red and Black in Haiti: Radicalism, Conflict, and Political Change, 1934–1957* (Chapel Hill, NC: University of North Carolina Press, 2009), 183–185.

16. Smith, 174–177.

17. The name is a Kreyòl version of boogeyman—"Uncle Gunnysack," who abducts naughty children. He is often described as the opposite of *Tonton Noël*—"Uncle Christmas."

18. Trouillot, 196.

19. Heinl, Heinl, and Heinl, 617.

20. The term "Taiwan of the Caribbean" had been used by aid workers, investors, and journalists for several years before being made famous by the administrator of the U.S. Agency for International Development when he uttered it at a congressional hearing in 1982.

21. Yasmine Shamsie and Andrew S. Thompson, *Haiti: Hope for a Fragile State* (Waterloo, Ontario: Wilfrid Laurier University Press, 2006), 38.

22. World Bank, "Haiti: Public Expenditure Review," 1987.

23. Dubois, 351.

24. Transparency International, "Introduction to Political Corruption," 2004, http://www .transparency.org/publications/gcr/gcr_2004#download.

25. Dubois, 354.

26. The detention centers were named for letters of the phonetic alphabet. One of these, "Camp X-Ray," would become particularly famous after the September 11, 2001, attacks.

27. Stephen Engelberg, Howard W. French, and Tim Weiner, "C.I.A. Formed Haitian Unit Later Tied to Narcotics Trade," *New York Times,* November 14, 1993, http://www.ny times.com/1993/11/14/world/cia-formed-haitian-unit-later-tied-to-narcotics-trade. html?pagewanted=all&src=pm.

28. William J. Clinton, "Remarks at an Arrival Ceremony in Port-au-Prince," March 31, 1995, *American Presidency Project,* http://www.presidency.ucsb.edu/ws/index.php?pid=51170 #zz1l9idU2j4.

29. This general family of policies is widely known as the "Washington Consensus," but there is broad disagreement about what that term really means. The economist John William-son, who coined the term in 1989, has since disavowed the connection between the prin-ciples he originally laid out and later emphasizes on monetarism, supply-side economics, and minimal government. Indeed, key elements of the original Consensus did not seem to get a hearing in Haiti, including expansion of the tax base and the assurance of public property rights. (See John Williamson, "A Short History of the Washington Consensus," September 2004, http://www.iie.com/publications/papers/williamson0904-2.pdf).

30. International Monetary Fund, "IMF Approves Three-Year ESAF Loan for Haiti," October 18, 1996, http://www.imf.org/external/np/sec/pr/1996/pr9653.htm; "Executive Sum-mary of Emergency Economic Recovery Program," *United Nations International Report*, Vol. I, no. A1, April 3, 1995, http://www.hartford-hwp.com/archives/43a/050.html.

31. Average, 1998 to 2006. That's 72 percent of the cost of production and exceeds Haiti's national budget. The Washington think tank Center for Global Development also cal-culated that U.S. tariffs and subsidies made imported rice 27 percent more expensive than American-grown products, with similar trade barriers for wheat, corn, and sugar. (See Daniel Griswold, "Grain Drain: The Hidden Cost of U.S. Rice Subsidies," The Cato Institute, November 16, 2006, http://www.cato.org/publications/trade-briefing-paper /grain-drain-hidden-cost-us-rice-subsidies. Also David Roodman, "Rich Country Tariffs and Subsidies: Let's Do The Numbers," Center for Global Development, December 2005, http://www.cgdev.org/content/publications/detail/5350).

32. MINUSTAH stands for *Mission des Nations Unies pour la stabilisation en Haïti.*

33. Finance Ministry of the Republic of Haiti, "Etat d'éxécution des dépenses budgétaires par institutions et par secteurs exécutées à partir des fonds du Trésor Public, Octobre 2009 à Septembre 2010" (converted using historical rate exchange rate of October 2009), http://www.mefhaiti.gouv.ht/Budget%20Execution%202009-10.pdf; Board of County Commis-sioners, Dade County, Florida, September 18, 2009, http://www.miamidade.gov/budget /FY2009-10/Adopted/Final/Volume1/Final_Adopted_Budget_Ordinances.pdf.

34. International Monetary Fund, "Haiti: Debt Statistics and IMF Support," January 27, 2010, http://www.imf.org/external/np/country/2010/012710.htm.

35. In January 2008, I wrote a story about how some Haitians unable to consistently afford food were turning to a traditional hunger palliative—cookies made of dried clay—to sate their pangs. The story went viral around the world, and those cookies eventually became a symbol of the April protests for some outside of Haiti. As our story detailed, the cook-ies were made from a kaolin-rich clay found in the country's central plateau and had long been eaten for their mineral value by pregnant women. The story was newsworthy be-cause we found that some people who had formerly shunned the "dirt cookies" (*gato tè*) were turning to them as a last resort, a sign of increasing hunger, while others who'd used them once in a while were now depending on them regularly. Some criticized the story for sensationalizing Haiti. Others praised it, especially as the extent of the hunger crisis became clear over the course of the year. In an ultimate irony, thanks to high fuel prices and increasing demand, the price of the clay cookies rose beyond what many could afford (Katz, "Poor Haitians Resort to Eating Dirt," *Associated Press,* January 29, 2008).

36. Wikileaks, "Earthquakes, Aftershocks Shake Port Au Prince (05PORTAUPRINCE1449)," May 25, 2005, http://www.cablegatesearch.net/cable.php?id=05PORTAUPRINCE1449.

CHAPTER 3: BLAN AND NÈG

1. Corvington, 88 (translated from French).
2. A U.S. government review would find that one-third of U.S. Embassy workers evacuated after the earthquake.
3. "Dollar" can mean two things in Haiti: It might refer to U.S. currency or a way of counting Haitian gourdes. In 1912, the gourde was pegged to the U.S. dollar at a rate of five-to-one. Though the peg was removed in 1989 and the dollar and gourde began separating

precipitously (in 2010, U.S. $1 was worth roughly 39 HTG), the designation "one Haitian dollar" remained another way of saying "five gourdes." Most Haitians have continued setting food prices and counting out salaries in "dola ayisien"—Haitian dollars, or the price in gourdes divided by five—while big-ticket items such as cars are quoted in "bon dola"— good dollars or U.S. currency. This is as confusing as it sounds.

4. The preceding dialogue was re-created based on various accounts and interviews, especially my interview with Youri Latortue on January 13, 2010, and Claude Gilles, "Le Palais législatif tombe de son piédestal," *Le Nouvelliste*, Special Edition January 12 to February 12, 2010, 6–7.

5. Kim Ives, "'Mafia boss . . . Drug dealer . . . Poster-boy for political corruption': WikiLeaked U.S. Embassy Cables Portray Senator Youri Latortue," *Haïti Liberté*, July 2011, http://www.haiti-liberte.com/archives/volume4-50/U.S.%20Embassy%20Cables.asp.

CHAPTER 4: THE CROSSROADS

1. Barack Obama, "Remarks by the President on Recovery Efforts in Haiti," January 14, 2010, http://www.whitehouse.gov/the-press-office/remarks-president-recovery-efforts-haiti.

2. Nathan Hodge, "U.S. Diverts Spy Drone from Afghanistan to Haiti," *Danger Room (Wired)*, January 15, 2010, http://www.wired.com/dangerroom/2010/01/pentagon-shares-earthquake-images-from-high-flying-spy-drone/.

3. Amy Oliver, "1st SOW among First Military Units on the Ground in Haiti," *1st SOW Public Affairs, U.S. Air Force*, January 15, 2010, http://www2.hurlburt.af.mil/news/story.asp?id=123185682. Note: The airfield's name was changed from François Duvalier International Airport to Toussaint Louverture International Airport after the fall of Jean-Claude Duvalier in 1986. Both the airport and road leading to it are also widely known as Maïs Gâté, the name of the old farm field where it was built.

4. Charles Onians, "Scientologists 'Heal' Haiti Quake Victims Using Touch," *Agence France-Presse*, January 22, 2010.

5. Tom Fawthrop, "Cuba's Aid Ignored by the Media?," *Al Jazeera*, February 16, 2010, http://www.aljazeera.com/focus/2010/01/201013195514870782.html.

6. "Fox News Poll: Over Half of Americans Contributed to Haiti Victims," *FoxNews.com*, March 25, 2010, http://www.foxnews.com/story/0,2933,589986,00.html#ixzz27ug7LQfN.

7. Bryce Widom, http://www.brycewidom.com/ (accessed May 2012).

8. Ofer Merin et al., "The Israeli Field Hospital in Haiti—Ethical Dilemmas in Early Disaster Response," *New England Journal of Medicine*, 362:e38, March 18, 2010.

9. When the official death toll passed the 2004 Indian Ocean tsunami's estimate of about 228,000, I cautioned an experienced colleague about making too certain a comparison. She replied, deadpan, "And what makes you think they knew how many people died in the *tsunami?*"

10. "At the Epicenter of the Crisis" (interview with Lt. Gen. Ken Keen), *Dialogo*, April 1, 2010.

11. John Lauinger and Christina Boyle, "Haiti Earthquake: Joint NYPD-FDNY Rescue Team Pulls Two Miracles out of Rubble," *(New York) Daily News*, January 20, 2010; "Governor Schwarzenegger Thanks Urban Search and Rescue Team for Work in Haiti in Weekly Radio Address," *States News Service*, February 12, 2010.

12. Joe Lauria, "U.N. Bodyguard Rescued From Haiti Rubble," *Wall Street Journal*, January 14, 2010.

13. *Dialogo*, ibid.

14. *CNN Newsroom*, January 14, 2010.

15. They had little to fear from the police, other than a possible shakedown. During other fuel shortages I have seen Haitian police similarly buying siphoned fuel by the side of the road.

16. Parts of this and other reporting from Carrefour appeared in my story: Katz, "Despair and Suffering at the Crossroads in Haiti," *Associated Press*, January 15, 2010.

17. Interviews with Harmel Cazeau and Raynold Saint-Val, Coordination Nationale de la Sécurité Alimentaire, and Myrta Kaulard, UN World Food Programme, March and April 2012.

18. One of the most-used methods of indicating the intensity of a food crisis was developed by Paul Howe and Stephen Devereux of the University of Sussex. Their five-stage scale ranges from "Food Secure" to "Extreme Famine." To move from Level 2, "Food Crisis," to Level 3, "Famine," an area must see a breakdown in social structures, the collapse of markets, and large-scale adoption of survival strategies such as migration to areas with more food. At the worst of Haiti's recent food crises, including that of 2008, the country has never approached Level 3.

19. Joe Mozingo and Ken Ellingwood, "Food Aid Trickles to Haitians as Marines, Airborne Troops Join Effort," *Los Angeles Times,* January 19, 2010.

20. U.S. Southern Command (SOUTHCOM), "Comments to Haiti Lessons Learned Report," January 2011, in Debarati Guha-Sapir et al., eds. *Independent Review of the U.S. Government Response to the Haiti Earthquake* (Washington: USAID, March 2011), 126.

21. "Haiti Nears Breaking Point as Aid Is Snarled, Looters Roam," *FoxNews.com,* January 15, 2010, http://www.foxnews.com/story/0,2933,583084,00.html#ixzz27uZyOJnT.

22. Rebecca Solnit, *A Paradise Built in Hell: The Extraordinary Communities That Arise in Disaster* (New York: Viking, 2009).

23. Erik Auf der Heide, "Common Misconceptions about Disasters: Panic, the 'Disaster Syndrome,' and Looting," in Margaret O'Leary, ed. *The First 72 Hours: A Community Approach to Disaster Preparedness* (Lincoln, NE: iUniverse, 2004), 340–380. Republished by U.S. Centers for Disease Control and Prevention (CDC) at http://www.atsdr.cdc.gov/emergency_response/common_misconceptions.pdf.

24. At least five photographers won awards for pictures of the Fabienne Cherisma's body, according to the blog *Prison Photography,* http://prisonphotography.wordpress.com/2011/05/14/a-photo-of-fabienne-cherisma-by-another-photographer-wins-another-award/.

25. Katz, "Haiti Slum Residents Face Gang Threat," *Associated Press,* January 19, 2010.

26. St. Felix said that Reuters replaced his cameras.

IN LOUISVILLE

1. American Psychiatric Association. *Diagnostic and Statistical Manual of Mental Disorders (rev. 4th ed.)* (Washington, DC: 2000), via U.S. Department of Veterans Affairs, "DSM criteria for PTSD," http://www.ptsd.va.gov/professional/pages/dsm-iv-tr-ptsd.asp.

CHAPTER 5: SPOILED CORN

1. Some organizations and theorists differ on the names and sometimes even the number of phases. Other versions combine recovery and reconstruction into one long phase, for instance, while some add a specific phase for disaster preparedness.

2. International Organization for Migration, "Preliminary Internal Database," January 16, 2010. IOM, "Displacement Tracking Matrix V2.0 Update," December 2010.

3. Tamara Lush, "Haiti Earthquake: Just 2 Percent of Quake Debris Has Been Cleared," *Associated Press,* September 11, 2010.

4. *Maïs Gâté* is French for "spoiled corn."

5. Sourcing includes interviews and a review of cluster meeting minutes.

6. Wikileaks, "Haiti Post-Earthquake USAID/DART Overview of Shelter and Settlements Strategy (10PORTAUPRINCE100)," January 29, 2010, http://www.scoop.co.nz/stories/WL1001/S01299.htm.

7. See, for example, "Press Conference on Relief Efforts in Haiti," U.S. Department of State, February 10, 2010, http://www.state.gov/documents/organization/136866.pdf.

8. Dubois, 88.

9. Duke University Haiti Lab, "Founding of the Lakou and Lakou-Style Inheritance," http://sites.duke.edu/lawandhousinginhaiti/historical-background/lakou-model/the-founding-of-the-lakou-and-lakou-style-inheritance/ (accessed July 2012).

10. Dubois, 268.

11. Organization of American States, "Modernization of Cadastre and Land Rights Infrastructure in Haiti," May 2010.
12. World Food Programme, "Our Work: Special Nutritional Products," http://www.wfp.org/nutrition/special-nutritional-products (accessed May 2012).
13. William Booth, "After Massive Aid, Haitians Feel Stuck in Poverty," *Washington Post*, January 11, 2011.
14. Active Learning Network for Accountability and Performance in Humanitarian Action (ALNAP), "Haiti Earthquake Response: Context Analysis," June 2010 put the figure at 211. USAID, "Success Story: USAID Supports Urban Search and Rescue Operations in Haiti," used a more widely quoted overall number of 136. It is also the source of the U.S. figure. The latter is available at http://transition.usaid.gov/our_work/humanitarian_assistance/disaster_assistance/countries/haiti/template/files/usar_success_story.pdf.
15. Anthony G. Macintyre, Joseph A. Barbera, and Edward R. Smith, "Surviving Collapsed Structure Entrapment after Earthquakes: A 'Time-to-Rescue' Analysis," *Prehospital and Disaster Medicine*, January 2006, for example.
16. Auf der Heide, ibid.
17. Obtained email. Name withheld.
18. Colum Lynch, "Top U.N. Aid Official Critiques Haiti Aid Efforts in Confidential Email," *Turtle Bay (Foreign Policy)*, February 17, 2010, http://turtlebay.foreignpolicy.com/posts/2010/02/17/top_un_aid_official_critiques_haiti_aid_efforts_in_confidential_email.

CHAPTER 6: BON DOLA

1. A study of the program by one of the participating NGOs noted that trees became more important to peasants after a 1970s USAID swine-flu eradication program wiped out thousands of families' income by slaughtering their pigs and replacing them with a variety ill-suited for the environment.
2. Library of Congress, "Country Profile: Haiti," May 2006, http://lcweb2.loc.gov/frd/cs/profiles/Haiti.pdf, for instance.
3. Chemonics, "Chemonics Is Sold to Private Investors," March 1999, http://www.chemonics.com/OurStory/OurNews/Pages/Chemonics-International-is-sold-to-private-investors.aspx (accessed June 2012); U.S. Securities and Exchange Commission, "Erly Industries, Inc.," http://www.secinfo.com/dsVsb.aB1.b.htm; U.S. Securities and Exchange Commission ruling, 2003, http://www.sec.gov/litigation/admin/34-47286.htm; Diana B. Henriques and Dean Baquet, "Cozy Links to a U.S Agency Prove Useful to a Rice Trader," *New York Times*, October 11, 1993; USAID Financial Audits, "Audit of Chemonics International consulting division," *Federal Contracts April 1, 1990 to March 31, 1992 Report No. 0-000-94-005-N*, March 16, 1994, http://pdf.usaid.gov/pdf_docs/PDABI141.pdf.
4. This confused many donors. When the results were presented at a conference in London, participants kept asking about whether aid was lost to corruption and how much. (See Enzo Caputo et al., "Assessing the Impacts of Budget Support: Case Studies in Mali, Tunisia and Zambia," OECD, October 2011; Overseas Development Institute, "Chairman's Summary of the Budget Support Meeting on the Recent Lessons from Evaluations," March 22, 2011, www.odi.org.uk/events/docs/4629.pdf).
5. Marian Leonardo Lawson, "Foreign Aid: International Donor Coordination of Development Assistance," *Congressional Research Service*, April 15, 2010, 14.
6. Quote from cable is a paraphrase of Rice's words. See Wikileaks, "Haiti: U.S. UN Permrep Ambassador Rice's Meeting with President Preval (09PORTAUPRINCE320)," http://filtradas.org/cables/cable.php?id=198354.
7. UN Office of the Special Envoy for Haiti, http://www.haitispecialenvoy.org.
8. U.S. Government Accountability Office, "U.S. Efforts Have Begun, Expanded Oversight Still to Be Implemented," May 19, 2011, http://www.gao.gov/products/GAO-11-415.
9. Senate Foreign Relations Committee hearing, March 10, 2010.

10. CARE, "Race to the Rainy Season in Haiti: CARE Calls for Mass Tarp Distribution and Sanitation Campaign," *CARE Newsroom*, February 2010, http://www.care.org/newsroom /articles/2010/02/haiti-shelter-rainy-season-sanitation-20100211.asp. (The press release also described installing toilets as "fighting the latrine battle in the sanitation war.")

11. The Sphere Handbook, "Shelter and Settlement Standard 3: Covered Living Space," http://www.spherehandbook.org/en/shelter-and-settlement-standard-3-covered-living -space/ (accessed August 2012).

12. Not his real name.

13. Mike Melia, "Heavy Rains Swamp Camps Holding Haiti's Homeless," *Associated Press*, March 19, 2010; James G. Pinsky, "NMCB 7 Air Detachment Seabees Improve Conditions in Petionville for Displaced Haitians," *Naval Mobile Construction Battalion 7 Public Affairs*, April 5, 2010, http://www.navy.mil/submit/display.asp?story_id=52412.

14. Bill Clinton has said that Edwin David Edwards, a Citibank executive who'd just made national headlines blowing the whistle on alleged currency fraud at the bank, paid for the couple's trip using frequent-flier miles.

15. Bill Clinton, *My Life* (New York: Knopf Publishing Group, 2004), 238.

16. More on this in my article of March 20, 2010, "With Cheap Food Imports, Haiti Can't Feed Itself," *Associated Press*.

17. Jessica Desvarieux, Haiti: A Visit from Two American Presidents," March 23, 2010, *TIME.com*, http://www.time.com/time/world/article/0,8599,1974422,00.html#ixzz1z9 hIULZn.

18. Hillary Clinton's remarks (see Introduction, note 2).

19. See especially Paul Farmer, *The Uses of Haiti* (Monroe, ME: Common Courage Press, 1994).

20. L'Unité de Lutte Contre la Corruption (ULCC), *Governance and Corruption in Haiti (Final Report)*, January 2007.

21. Chambre de commerce et d'industrie d'Haïti (CCIH), "La corruption: un obstacle au développement et à la démocratie," December 2, 2004, cited in ULCC, *Etat des lieux de la lutte contre la corruption 2004–2011*.

22. Fintrac Inc. for U.S. Agency for International Development, *USAID Office of Food for Peace Haiti Market Analysis*, August 2010, 118.

23. In November 2010, Lucke sued the consortium for $492,483.33 in back fees. A judge threw out the case. When I interviewed Lucke for this book, he declined to comment on the lawsuit other than to reiterate his denial of a conflict of interest.

24. Wording from 2011 Transparency International (TI) CPI. In 2009, TI put it this way: "It is difficult to assess the overall levels of corruption in different countries/territories based on hard empirical data, e.g., by comparing the amount of bribes or the number of prosecutions or court cases directly related to corruption. In the latter case, for example, such data does not reflect actual levels of corruption; rather it highlights the extent to which prosecutors, courts and/or the media are effectively investigating and exposing corruption. One reliable method of compiling cross-country data is, therefore, to draw on the experience and perceptions of those who see first hand the realities of corruption in a country."

25. Theresa Thompson and Anwar Shah, "Transparency International's Corruption Perceptions Index: Whose Perceptions Are They Anyway?," World Bank, March 2005.

26. Dilyan Donchev and Gergely Ujhelyi, "What Do Corruption Indices Measure?," *Social Science Research Network*, August 13, 2009.

27. Lower-bound estimate comes from 2009 USAID "Port-au-Prince Urban Baseline" survey, which estimated that families at the level above "poor" and "very poor" needed roughly $530 a month for basic needs. A March 2011 survey by the AFL-CIO Solidarity Center reported that a family of four in Port-au-Prince needed about $749 a month to afford food, clothes, school, healthcare, and transportation to and from work, along with an apartment with two bedrooms, a kitchen, and a bathroom.

28. Deborah Sontag, "Panel on Haitian Prison Deaths," *New York Times*, May 27, 2010.

29. "But what are they for?" Alice asked in a tone of great curiosity.
30. Lesley Clark, "Haiti's Preval Seeks Renewal of Direct U.S. Aid to Government," *Miami Herald*, March 10, 2010.
31. Editorial, "Haitian President Drops the Ball on Addressing Corruption Concerns," *Washington Post*, March 11, 2010.
32. "Haiti PM Criticises Post-Earthquake Rebuilding Efforts," *BBC News*, December 27, 2010, http://www.bbc.co.uk/news/world-latin-america-12082047.
33. Center for Responsive Politics, http://opensecrets.org.
34. Countries could also qualify by pledging $200 million in debt relief, but no country did so without also pledging the minimum in new funds.

CHAPTER 7: THE GOVERNOR

1. "Haiti Has Achieved 'Small Miracles': Bill Clinton," *United Nations Radio*, April 2011, http://www.unmultimedia.org/radio/english/2011/04/haiti-has-achieved-small-miracle-bill-clinton/.
2. Examples: Letter to Clinton Foundation, December 2010: "Haitians have the best chance in my lifetime to build the country they want to become." April 26, 2010, remarks to Clinton Global Initiative University: "I believe they have the best chance in my lifetime to build a self-sustaining state." Remarks at White House Rose Garden, January 16, 2010 (also cited in Chapter 6): "I believe before this earthquake Haiti had the best chance in my lifetime to escape its history. . . . I still believe that." First press conference upon becoming Special Envoy, June 2009: "Haiti, notwithstanding the total devastation wreaked by the four storms last year, has the best chance to escape the darker aspects of its history in the thirty-five years I have been going there."
3. The "catastrophe" in the report's title referred to the 2008 hurricanes and tropical storms, but Collier also saw other disasters on the horizon—he referred to Haiti's population growth as a "youth tsunami." On Collier's newness to Haiti and dates of trip, see Carlo Dade, "Haiti's Economic Prospects 'Hopeful': Carlo Dade interviews Paul Collier," *FOCALPoint*, March 2009, http://www.focal.ca/pdf/focalpoint_march2009.pdf; Security Council Report, "March 2009 monthly forecast," February 26, 2009, http://www.security councilreport.org/site/c.glKWLeMTIsG/b.4990005/k.64A8/March_2009brHaiti.htm.
4. Nathan Associates Inc., "Bringing HOPE to Haiti's Apparel Industry: Improving Competitiveness through Factory-level Value-Chain Analysis," November 2009.
5. J. F. Hornbeck, "The Haitian Economy and the HOPE Act," *Congressional Research Service*, March 16, 2010.
6. Vikas Bajaj and Julfikar Ali Manik, "Bangladesh Arrests 21 After Rallies," *New York Times*, August 17, 2010.
7. Krista Mahr, "Garment Worker Riots in Bangladesh Continue After 4 Killed," *TIME.com*, December 13, 2010; Manik and Bajaj, "Killing of Bangladeshi Labor Organizer Signals an Escalation in Violence," *New York Times*, April 10, 2012.
8. "Captain America Infant Toddler Boys Short Sleeve Tee, blue," *Target.com*, http://www.target.com/p/captain-america-infant-toddler-boys-short-sleeve-tee-blue/-/A-14028585, August 2012 (accessed September 1, 2012). Shirt is advertised as "imported."
9. Corey Flintoff, "In Haiti, a Low-Wage Job Is Better Than None," *All Things Considered (National Public Radio)*, June 14, 2009, http://www.npr.org/templates/story/story.php?storyId=104403034.
10. Simon Fass, *Political Economy in Haiti: The Drama of Survival* (Piscataway, NJ: Transaction Publishers, 1988).
11. Katz, "Can Low-Paying Garment Industry Save Haiti?," *Associated Press*, February 21, 2010.
12. Interview with Bill Clinton, June 16, 2009.

13. Wikileaks, "Haiti Anxiously Awaits Decision on Minimum Wage," 09PORTAUPRINCE 553, http://www.cablegatesearch.net/cable.php?id=09PORTAUPRINCE553.

14. Katz, "Ouster of Prime Minister Threatens Haitian Economic Campaign," *Associated Press*, October 31, 2009.

15. Katz, "New Haiti PM Inaugurated, Promises to Keep Trying to Attract Foreign Investment, Create Jobs," *Associated Press*, November 11, 2009.

16. Maura O'Connor, "Does International Aid Keep Haiti Poor?," *Slate*, January 4, 2011, http://www.slate.com/articles/news_and_politics/dispatches/features/2011/does_international_aid_keep_haiti_poor/the_most_dependent_independent_nation_in_the_world.html.

17. Cuba 78.6, Jamaica 72.4, Dominican Republic 72.7; Haiti 61.1. Those values stayed consistent through 2011. (See United Nations Development Program, *Human Development Report*, 2008, http://hdr.undp.org/en/data/map/)

18. Juan Forero, "Haiti's Elite Sees Business Opportunities Emerging from Reconstruction," *Washington Post*, February 15, 2010.

19. 2010 Lobbying Disclosure Report, filed with U.S. Senate and House of Representatives; Voila Foundation, "U.S. Secretary of State Hillary Clinton Presents Trilogy International Partners with Prestigious Award for Corporate Excellence," http://www.voilafoundation.com/images/imageRoot/files/trilogy_receives_ace_award_press_release_dec_2009.pdf.

20. Oxfam community survey, March 2010. The poll did not disclose its margin of error. Oxfam added in a January 2011 report titled "From Relief to Recovery": "In a separate focus group discussion with twelve representatives from four different civil society organisations in Port-au-Prince in December 2010, none of the participants felt that the government's Action Plan for National Reconstruction and Development (APNRD) was a Haitian document. 'The citizens of this country were not consulted,' said one respondent."

21. Paul Collier, "Haiti's Rise from the Rubble," *Foreign Affairs*, Vol. 90, No. 5, September/October 2011.

22. Ibid.

23. After media coverage highlighted the large number of fishing boats destroyed by the storm, NGOs rushed to provide new ones. But too many boats were provided, and they were of extremely poor quality; as it turned out, the local fishermen were much better at boat building than the NGOs. Critics pointed out that it would have been much smarter to use the funds for replacement housing instead. See, for example, "FAO Warns Indonesian Fishermen about Sub-Standard Boats," *FAONewsroom*, June 22, 2005, http://www.fao.org/newsroom/en/news/2005/103073/index.html.

24. The name was later expanded to the "Aceh-Nias Rehabilitation and Reconstruction Agency," following another major earthquake that struck Nias several months after the tsunami.

25. Tsunami Global Lessons Learned Project, "The Tsunami Legacy: Innovations, Breakthrough and Change," 2009.

26. BRR, "10 Management Lessons for Host Governments Coordinating Post-disaster Reconstruction," 2009.

27. Harry Masyrafah and Jock MJA McKeon, "Post-Tsunami Aid Effectiveness in Aceh: Proliferation and Coordination in Reconstruction," *Wolfensohn Center for Development, Brookings Institution*, November 2008.

28. Kuntoro laid the groundwork for the comparison in the article, telling the reporter, "I trusted that we were sent by God to do this job. We are the extension of the hands of God and it is our duty." Duncan Graham, "Kuntoro Mangkusubroto: Working as the hand of God in Aceh," *Jakarta Post*, December 26, 2008, http://www.thejakartapost.com/news/2008/12/26/kuntoro-mangkusubroto-working-hand-god-aceh.html.

29. Peter Gelling, "Clinton Sees Gains in Tsunami Zone," *New York Times*, November 30, 2005.

30. The other ninety-five representatives at the conference did not pledge. One of the most notable holdouts was the United Kingdom, which was rebuked by Oxfam for its lack of

giving and denied a chance to speak. The UK's development minister said that some of its funds were going through the European Commission, IMF, and World Bank. An official from Austria defended its decision not to pledge to *Foreign Policy*'s Colum Lynch, saying: "We are not such a big country: We have to prioritize our long-term aid."

31. Venezuela's official pledge was $1.59 billion, according to the UN Office of the Special Envoy for Haiti; $405 million of that pledge was debt relief, while 2 percent of the programmable funds were monies already pledged in other contexts.

CHAPTER 8: "WHEN I GET OLDER"

1. The 1987 Constitution called for the creation of a permanent electoral council, with the executive, parliament, and legislative branches each selecting three members, but it had never been implemented.
2. The framers of the current constitution had chosen February 7 because it was the anniversary of Duvalier's flight into exile.
3. Katz, "Protesters Blast Haiti President's Quake Response," *Associated Press,* May 10, 2010.
4. Katz, "Poor Get Better Health Care in Post-Quake Haiti Due to Foreign Aid Dollars, but Will It Last?," *Associated Press,* May 11, 2010.
5. Hospital records list his full name as "Oriel Lynn Peter," but it's possibly a mistake— neither surname is common in Haiti.
6. In fact, according to the CDC, the last recorded U.S. diphtheria case was in 2003, from an "elderly traveler returning from Haiti."
7. CDC, "Formulary: Products Distributed by the Centers for Disease Control and Prevention," http://www.cdc.gov/laboratory/drugservice/formulary.html#ib (accessed July 2012).
8. Not mentioned in the *Vanity Fair* profile was an underreported subplot: Penn's concurrent trial over an October 2009 altercation with a photographer in Brentwood, California. A week before his Senate testimony, Penn pleaded no contest to misdemeanor vandalism and was sentenced to three years' probation and 300 hours of community service—the latter servable in Haiti. It is not clear whether his NGO work was considered mitigation in the case. But in the judge's eyes, managing the affairs of an IDP camp home to tens of thousands of earthquake survivors while helping design and implement policy was a form of penance, to be completed while he underwent anger management counseling elsewhere. The case was a telling glimpse of U.S. attitudes toward Haiti and of possible alternate motivations for Penn's persistence in the quake zone. See Christie D'Zurilla, "Sean Penn Cuts a Deal over Altercation with Photographer," *Los Angeles Times,* May 12, 2010, http://latimesblogs.latimes.com/gossip/2010/05/sean-penn-no-contest-probation -anger-management-photographer.html; Douglas Brinkley, "Welcome to Camp Penn," *Vanity Fair,* July 2010.
9. Jay Newman, *The Journalist in Plato's Cave* (Madison, NJ: Fairleigh Dickinson University Press, 1996), 90–91.
10. Selected interviews online at http://haitimemoryproject.org. Interview with Chrispain Mondésir reprinted with permission of Claire Payton and the Louis B. Nunn Center for Oral History at the University of Kentucky Libraries.

CHAPTER 9: SUGAR LAND

1. Michael Norton, "Haiti Launches Land Reform by Giving Plots to Peasants," *Associated Press,* February 8, 1997.
2. Target is a member of the Retail Industry Leaders Association, which lobbied for the bill.
3. One of the most important tariff-reduction deals in the region was the Caribbean Basin Initiative (CBI), signed into law by President Reagan in 1983. The United States has benefited greatly under the deal, exporting more to the Basin than it imports, while becoming

the dominant trading partner for each—meaning that U.S. prosperity is a matter of national security to each of them. Seeking to reapprove the CBI in 2000, Senator Chuck Grassley told his colleagues, "The Caribbean Basin is one of the few regions of the world where the United States consistently—I want to emphasize consistently—maintains a trade surplus. In fact close to 70 cents of every dollar spent in the region is returned in the form of increased exports from the United States." See *Congressional Record (Bound Edition),* Volume 146 (2000), Part 6, Senate, 7407–7412.

4. Land reform in South Korea is credited with increasing peasants' wealth and forcing the children of former landowners to look for new kinds of work. See Michael J. Seth, *A Concise History of Modern Korea: From the Late Nineteenth Century to the Present* (Lanham: Rowman & Littlefield Publishers, 2010). On land, Seth cites John Lie, *Han Unbound* (Palo Alto: Stanford University Press, 2000).

5. Marcus Baram, "Camp Corail: Haiti's Development King Defends Role in Site Location of Huge Refugee Camp," *Huffington Post,* January 18, 2011, http://www.huffingtonpost .com/2011/01/18/camp-corail-haitis-develo_n_810038.html (accessed February 27, 2012).

6. Amy Goodman, "Sean Penn on Haiti Six Months After the Earthquake, Recovery Efforts, and Why He Decided to Manage a Tent Camp of 55,000 Displaced Haitians," *Democracy Now!,* July 13, 2010, http://www.democracynow.org/2010/7/13/sean_penn_on_haiti _six_months.

CHAPTER 10: FACE TO FACE

1. Wording of quote from Pooja Bhatia, "Dancing in the Dark," *The Caravan,* July 2011, http://www.caravanmagazine.in/Story/963/Dancing-in-the-Dark.html.

2. Maureen Taft-Morales, "Haiti's National Elections: Issues, Concerns, and Outcome," *Congressional Research Service,* July 18, 2011.

3. There should have been nine members, but one had just been dismissed for collecting his employees' paychecks.

4. Richard G. Lugar, "Haiti: No Leadership—No Elections: A Report to the Members of the Committee on Foreign Relations, United States Senate," *U.S. Government Printing Office,* June 10, 2010; Katz, "Preval Rejects US Advice on Presidential Election," *Associated Press,* June 30, 2010; Lugar, "Without Reform, No Return on Investment in Haiti: A Report to Members of the Committee on Foreign Relations, United States Senate," *U.S. Government Printing Office,* July 22, 2010.

5. UN Office of the Special Envoy for Haiti, "International Assistance to Haiti: Key Facts as of March 2012," http://www.haitispecialenvoy.org/download/International_Assistance/1 -overall-key-facts.pdf (last accessed August 2012); $12.30 billion in humanitarian and recovery funding to the post-earthquake response (excluding debt relief), $3.06 billion in private funding to international nongovernmental organizations, $971.9 million in debt relief for 2010 and 2011.

6. Amy Belasco, "The Cost of Iraq, Afghanistan, and Other Global War on Terror Operations Since 9/11," Congressional Research Service, 2011. Economic Development Research Group Inc., *Economic Impact of Maryland's Surface Transportation Spending* (Cambridge, MD: Cambridge Systematics Inc., 2005).

7. UN Office of the Special Envoy for Haiti, *Has Aid Changed?* (New York, 2011).

8. Data in this section is based on research in U.S. General Accountability Office's Federal Procurement Data System, along with interviews, investigations, and fact-checks with the State, Defense, and Homeland Security departments, and others.

9. "CVN-68 Nimitz-class Overview," Federation of American Scientists, http://www.fas.org /programs/ssp/man/uswpns/navy/aircraftcarriers/cvn68nimitz.html (accessed May 21, 2012). Inflation-adjusted figure based on 1996 US Navy Visibility and Management of

Operating and Support Costs (VAMOSC). Also Christine Clarridge, "Vinson Crew Proud to Be First in Fight," *Seattle Times,* January 20, 2002.

10. Agility contract first reported by Jake Johnston (Center for Economic and Policy Research), *The Hill,* December 21, 2011, http://thehill.com/blogs/congress-blog/foreign -policy/196851-blacklisted-contractor-continues-receiving-government-money-through -haiti-contracts. Interview with Harry Frazier, Fleishman-Hillard International Communications, on behalf of Agility, August 23, 2012. Further information from Agility Logistics Quarterly Report 2011, http://www.agilitylogistics.com/EN/GIL/Documents /Agility_PDF/InvestorRelations/QuarterlyReports/2011QuarterlyReports/Q1-2011.pdf (accessed May 2012). Also Excluded Parties List System, General Services Administration, https://www.epls.gov/epls/search.do (accessed May 2012).

11. Haiti Earthquake Response: Two Year Update, *American Red Cross,* http://www.redcross .org/images/MEDIA_CustomProductCatalog/m3640089_HaitiEarthquake_TwoYear Report.pdf (last accessed September 2012). As of the two-year mark, the American Red Cross had committed $330 million of $486 million raised.

12. "IRS Hits Wyclef With $2.1 Million In Tax Liens: Haitian Presidential Candidate Owes for 1040 Returns," *The Smoking Gun,* August 4, 2010, http://www.thesmokinggun.com /documents/celebrity/irs-hits-wyclef-21-million-tax-liens.

CHAPTER 11: A GUT FEELING

1. Frank Bajak, "Parents: All Haitian 'Orphans' Had Relatives," *Associated Press,* February 20, 2010.

2. Brian Williams, *NBC Nightly News,* October 25, 2010, http://video.msnbc.msn.com /nightly-news/39838181#39838181.

3. H. C. Spencer et al., "Disease-Surveillance and Decision-Making after the 1976 Guatemala Earthquake," *Lancet,* July 23, 1977; Julian Ryall, "Japan Earthquake: Survivors Battle Disease and Hunger," *Sunday Telegraph,* March 19, 2011; N. Floret et al., "Negligible Risk for Epidemics after Geophysical Disasters," *Emerging Infectious Diseases,* April 2006.

4. Christopher Hamlin, *Cholera: The Biography* (New York: Oxford University Press, 2009).

5. Oscar Felsenfeld, "Some Observations on the Cholera (El Tor) Epidemic in 1961–62," *Bulletin of the World Health Organization 28,* 1963, 289–296, http://whqlibdoc.who.int /bulletin/1963/Vol28/Vol28-No3/bulletin_1963_28(3)_289-296.pdf.

6. Pan American Health Organization, "Cholera: Number of Cases and Deaths in the Americas (1991–2001 by country and year)," http://www.paho.org/English/HCP/HCT/EER /cholera-cases-deaths-91-01.htm (accessed February 2012); J. P. Guthmann, "Epidemic Cholera in Latin America: Spread and Routes of Transmission," *The American Journal of Tropical Medicine and Hygiene 98,* December 1995.

7. CDC, "Acute Watery Diarrhea and Cholera: Pre-Decision Brief for Public Health Action February 2010," http://emergency.cdc.gov/disasters/earthquakes/haiti/pdf/watery diarrhea_pre-decision_brief.pdf. Note: This document was also the probable origin of a widely reported, incorrect assertion that Haiti had experienced a cholera outbreak in "1960," "the 1960s" or "50 years before" the 2010 outbreak. To bolster its assertion that cholera was unlikely to occur, the CDC wrote in the guidelines, correctly: "There have been no reports of cholera in Haiti since 1960 *or earlier*" [emphasis mine].

There was no cholera in the Americas in 1960. The sixth pandemic had ended in the 1920s, and the seventh pandemic was a year away from beginning in Indonesia. The WHO noted in 1966 that, four decades before, "cholera retreated to its Asian home." Hamlin wrote of the Peru outbreak in *Cholera: The Biography,* "In 1991 cholera popped up in the Western Hemisphere for the first time in more than a century." The most likely reason for including the date in the CDC guidelines was that around 1960 the scientific knowledge of cholera had vastly improved: William Burrows and Robert Pollitzer published their landmark paper on laboratory diagnosis of cholera in 1958, and their procedure became accepted soon after. That is why we can say with near certainty that there had been no cholera in Haiti from the beginning of modern laboratory diagnosis in 1960 until October 2010, a period that encompasses the whole of the El Tor pandemic.

The CDC report was opened for misinterpretation on October 22, 2010, when OCHA put out its "Haiti Cholera Situation Report #1." The report's author removed the "or earlier" context and wrote simply: "This is the first incident of cholera in Haiti since 1960." (This was sloppy, but the author wasn't trying to obfuscate, as it went on to say: "Since the disease is largely unknown in Haiti, resistance of the local population is low and the health sector unused to coping with this form of outbreak.") The OCHA report was widely distributed among journalists who then started reprinting the line out of context. On October 25, a BBC science writer used the "since 1960" line without explanation or source in an article about possible origins of the outbreak. Other journalists copied the error with a variety of phrasings. Bringing the game of telephone full circle, the CDC itself cited the erroneous BBC article as the source of the factoid in a March 2011 report, "Recent Clonal Origin of Cholera in Haiti."

Some public health specialists suppose that there must have been cases of classical (non-El Tor) cholera in Haiti during the circum-Caribbean epidemic of the late nineteenth century. But in 2011, a team of historians and researchers from Duke University led by Deborah Jenson and Victoria Szabo scoured the record from the early twentieth century back to 1804 and found that no instance of cholera had ever been documented in Haiti (*Emerging Infectious Diseases* November 2011). They attributed this to Haiti's abolition of slavery and the absence throughout the nineteenth century of foreign soldiers, who likely introduced the bacterium elsewhere. However, given the difficulty inherent in proving a negative, the remote possibility remains that some since-forgotten early outbreak will still surface.

8. Survey cited in CDC, "Update: Cholera Outbreak—Haiti, 2010," *Morbidity and Mortality Weekly Report,* November 19, 2010, http://www.cdc.gov/mmwr/preview/mmwrhtml /mm5945a1.htm.

9. "Nepal: Cholera Outbreak in Kathmandu," *H5N1: News and resources about influenza, infectious diseases, and the politics of public health,* http://crofsblogs.typepad.com /h5n1/2010/09/nepal-cholera-outbreak-in-kathmandu.html (last accessed September 2012).

10. Laxmi Maharjan, "Cholera Outbreak Looms Over Capital," *The Himalayan Times,* September 23, 2010.

11. United Nations data from "Financing Peacekeeping," http://www.un.org/en/peacekeeping /operations/financing.shtml; Nepalese Army data from "Salary/Ration Scale" and "Welfare In Nepalese Army," http://www.nepalarmy.mil.np/.

12. CNN Wire Staff, "U.N. Investigates Allegations of Cholera Source in Haiti," *CNN.com,* October 28, 2010. ("Preliminary tests on a suspected source of the cholera outbreak in Haiti were negative, U.N. peacekeepers said Thursday.") The article was later taken offline and stricken from CNN's archives, but an archived copy is available at http://web .archive.org/web/20101104091056/http://articles.cnn.com/2010-10-28/world/haiti .cholera_1_cholera-outbreak-cholera-cases-septic-tank?_s=PM:WORLD.

13. United Nations, *Medical Support Manual for United Nations Peacekeeping Operation, 2nd Edition* (New York: United Nations, 1999), 46–47.

14. Information in this chapter about Rosemond Lorimé, the first known hospital death in the cholera epidemic, and his family is based on interviews with his relatives conducted in March 2012. The credit for tracking down Lorimé's case goes to *Le Nouvelliste* reporter Roberson Alphonse. (See Alphonse, "Sur les traces du premier décès," *Le Nouvelliste,* November 3, 2010, http://www.lenouvelliste.com/article4.php?newsid=85268.) In January 2012, Louise Ivers and David Walton of Harvard Medical School and Partners in Health also found an earlier, nonhospitalized fatal case on October 12, 2010, in a 28-year-old Haitian man "with a history of severe untreated mental health disorder." (See Ivers and

Walton, "The 'First' Case of Cholera in Haiti: Lessons for Global Health," *The American Journal of Tropical Medicine and Hygiene,* January 2012.)

15. WHO spokesman Gregory Hartl to AP reporter Colleen Barry in Geneva, quoted in Katz, "Experts: Did UN Troops Infect Haiti?," *Associated Press,* November 3, 2010. WHO spokeswoman Fadela Chaib to reporters in Geneva, in "WHO: Probing Haiti Cholera Source Not a Priority," *Associated Press,* November 16, 2010. (In the same piece, UN spokeswoman Corinne Momal-Vanian called the suspicion about the Nepalese base "misinformation.") Robert Tauxe, deputy director of the Division of Foodborne, Waterborne and Environmental Diseases for the CDC, in Fred Tasker and Frances Robles, "Source of Haiti's Cholera Outbreak May Never Be Known," *Miami Herald,* November 20, 2010.

16. I first wrote about Clercilia's death in "Battle Rages in Slum, This Time Against a Disease," *Associated Press,* November 11, 2010.

17. Coordination Nationale de Sécurité Alimentaire (CSNA), "Rapport d'Évaluation de l'Impact du Choléra sur la Sécurité Alimentaire dans les Zones Bas Plateau Central et Bas Artibonite," January 2011.

18. Quote from "Experts: Did UN Troops Infect Haiti?," *Associated Press,* November 3, 2010.

19. Global Task Force on Cholera Control, *Cholera Outbreak: Assessing the Outbreak Response and Improving Preparedness* (Geneva: World Health Organization, 2004); CDC, "Foodborne Illness: Frequently Asked Questions," January 10, 2005, http://www.cdc.gov/ncidod/dbmd/diseaseinfo/files/foodborne_illness_faq.pdf.

20. Martin Enserink, "Despite Sensitivities, Scientists Seek to Solve Haiti's Cholera Riddle," *Science,* Vol. 331, no. 6016, January 28, 2011, 388–389.

21. Donald G. McNeil, Jr., "Cholera's Second Fever: An Urge to Blame," *New York Times,* November 21, 2010, http://www.nytimes.com/2010/11/21/weekinreview/21mcneil.html

22. DJ Cipha Sounds, *Hot 97,* December 18, 2010.

23. Later published as Piarroux et al., "Understanding the Cholera Epidemic, Haiti," *Emerging Infectious Diseases,* July 2011, http://dx.doi.org/10.3201/eid1707.110059.

24. Katz, "UN Worries Its Troops Caused Cholera in Haiti," *Associated Press,* November 19, 2010.

25. UN Department of Public Information, "Deeply Concerned from Outset by Cholera Outbreak in Haiti, Secretary-General Appoints Independent Expert Panel," January 6, 2011, http://www.un.org/News/Press/docs/2011/sgsm13338.doc.htm.

26. Alejandro Cravioto, Claudio F. Lanata, Daniele S. Lantagne, and G. Balakrish Nair, "Final Report of the Independent Panel of Experts on the Cholera Outbreak in Haiti," http://www.un.org/News/dh/infocus/haiti/UN-cholera-report-final.pdf.

27. The report differed slightly on the dates the Nepalese commander told me, saying the contingent's arrivals took place "between October 8 and 24." That includes the period of the rotation we were told about, but begins one day earlier and goes on for an additional week.

28. Mark Doyle, "Haiti's Cholera Row with UN Rumbles On," *BBC News,* December 14, 2011. Citations disproving Fisher's claim begin on page 26 of the UN report, including: "No relationship was observed between the South American isolates (indicating that this strain is not related to the early-1990's cholera epidemic in South America) or with the African strains isolated between 1970 and 1998. . . . The results of this study indicated that the Haitian strains were all identical and most closely related to strains of Vibrio cholerae from the Indian subcontinent and distinct from strains of Vibrio cholerae isolated in Africa, Bahrain, Germany, Indonesia, Vietnam, Malaysia, and South America."

29. For almost two years, this claim was made while citing no alternative evidence whatsoever (e.g., see MINUSTAH PIO/PR/453/2011 of July 1, 2011). Then in June 2012, a team, led by Rita Colwell of the University of Maryland, announced results it said proved a second strain of cholera had infected Haitians after lying dormant in the environment. Colwell built her career advocating the position that weather patterns, not person-to-person transmission, are the principal cause of cholera epidemics. Since the first days of the outbreak in Haiti, she

had been looking for evidence to bolster this point—and it seemed she and her colleagues had finally found it. (See Richard Knox, "Earthquake Not to Blame for Cholera Outbreak in Haiti," *NPR.org*, October 26, 2010; María Elena Hurtado, "Haiti's Cholera Epidemic Caused by Weather, Say Scientists," *SciDev.net*, November 19, 2010.) The study was taken by some observers as a ratification of the UN's continuing position that it was not possible to be conclusive about the epidemic's origins. But in fact, the study had little to say about that question: Nearly half the patients whose samples were tested were carrying the El Tor strain of bacteria circulating in South Asia, including Nepal—a transmission for which they could find no alternative explanation. The purported "second strain," meanwhile, was a type of non-toxigenic *Vibrio cholera* that had never been found to cause outbreaks. Other scientists, including Piarroux, noted a host of errors in the study, including a proposition that the November 5 arrival of Hurricane Tomas—a storm that had minor effects in Haiti and struck three and a half weeks after the outbreak began, when thousands were already infected—was one of the outbreak's primary causes. The study may, however, ultimately point to a more complicated hypothesis about how the known El Tor strain in the outbreak, most likely introduced by UN peacekeepers, proved so deadly.

30.   Ministere de la Sante Publique et de la Population, "Rapport de Cas," August 29, 2012, http://www.mspp.gouv.ht/site/downloads/Rapport%20journalier%20MSPP%20du%20 29%20aout%202012.pdf (last accessed September 9, 2012).

CHAPTER 12: CARDBOARD PALACE

1.   Because several Haitian presidents have served more than once and were double-counted, Préval was officially known as Haiti's fifty-fifth president (cf. Grover Cleveland, the twenty-second and twenty-fourth president of the United States). It's also worth noting that the last president under the U.S. occupation, Stenio Vincent, had been voted into office by the National Assembly in 1930 on an anti-occupation platform, in what Laurent Dubois calls "the most democratic [election] until the election of Aristide" (personal communication). In contrast to Aristide and Préval, however, he was chosen by a legislature and not a national plebiscite. He was forced out of office in 1941.

2.   Wikileaks, "Deconstructing Preval (09PORTAUPRINCE575)," June 2009, http://www .scoop.co.nz/stories/WL0906/S00116.htm.

3.   Micky was paired with one of OstosSola's most able consultants: Damian Merlo, an American who had worked in the past with John McCain, Otto J. Reich—the Bush administration's point man on Latin America, and the U.S. Special Interests Section in Havana. Merlo had also been a program officer at McCain's International Republican Institute, which the *New York Times* has reported provided political training for Aristide opponents in the early 2000s. (Merlo's activities with the IRI were all outside of Haiti, a spokeswoman told me.)

4.   Ben Fox and Jonathan M. Katz, "Skirmishes Raise Specter of Violent Haiti Election," *Associated Press*, November 25, 2010.

5.   "EU Wants Haiti Elections to Proceed as Scheduled," *Caribbean Media Corporation (CMC)*, November 23, 2010, in *Jamaica Observer*, http://www.jamaicaobserver.com /news/EU-wants-Sunday-s-Haiti-elections-to-proceed-as-scheduled#ixzz1tYNNtl8U.

6.   Trouilliot, *Haiti: State Against Nation*, 196. Robert Fatton, *Haiti's Predatory Republic: The Unending Transition to Democracy* (Boulder, CO: Lynne Rienner Publishers, 2002).

7.   Jennie M. Smith, *When the Hands are Many: Community Organization and Social Change in Rural Haiti* (Ithaca, NY: Cornell University Press, 2001), 4–5.

8.   Interview in Haiti Memory Project, http://haitimemoryproject.org.

9.   Elise Ackerman, "His Music Rules in Haiti: Sweet Micky's Provocative Music Moves Haitians with an Infectious Beat and Political Overtones," *Miami New Times*, May 29, 1997. Also see Trenton Daniel, "I DON'T CARE: A Conversation with Michel 'Sweet Micky' Martelly," *Transition*, Issue 91, 2002.

10. Pascal Fletcher, "Haiti Elections Process 'Stabilized' and On Track: U.N.," *Reuters*, November 30, 2010.

11. Signal-FM 90.5, Statement by Michel Martelly, December 8, 2010, online at http://bit.ly/R5QmGa.

CHAPTER 13: ALL TOGETHER NOW

1. Transcript by the White House Blog, "President Obama on Haiti, One Year Later," January 11, 2011, http://www.whitehouse.gov/blog/2011/01/11/president-obama-haiti-one-year-later.

2. Katz, "APNewsBreak: OAS Says Boot Haiti Gov't Candidate," *Associated Press*, January 10, 2011. ("You know, Jonathan," one of Préval's senior aides called to say after my story ran, "the polite thing would have been to share your copy with us first.")

3. Max Mäder and Olivier Longchamp, "La 'lex Duvalier' doit servir à Haïti et non profiter à des particuliers," *Le Temps*, June 8, 2010.

4. "Obama Tells Zuma of 'Deep Concerns' over Aristide Return," *Agence France-Presse*, March 17, 2011.

5. Fox and Katz, "US Revokes Visas to Pressure Haiti on Election as Candidate Warns of More Protests," *Associated Press*, January 21, 2011.

6. Later that week, one of the CEP's eight members said that only four had signed off on the final ballot, the other four having objected. But her argument that a split vote should have invalidated the process was by and large ignored.

7. U.S. State Department Daily Press Briefing, February 3, 2011, http://www.state.gov/r/pa/prs/dpb/2011/02/155950.htm.

8. Interview with Leslie Voltaire, March 2012.

9. Amal Ataya et al., eds., "Assessment of the Psychosocial Needs of Haitians Affected by the January 2010 Earthquake," International Organization for Migration, September 2010.

EPILOGUE: MEMWA

1. However, though Clinton added that the UN should take steps to prevent such transmissions in the future, he disagreed that the UN should be held directly accountable for Haiti's outbreak: "I feel terrible about what happened here. I was moved by the response . . . but I don't think this was a deliberate callous disregard for the lives of the people of Haiti" (source: audio recording by freelance journalist Ansel Herz, available at http://sharebeast.com/6daj5a5hdovm).

2. U.S. Government Accountability Office, "U.S. Efforts Have Begun, Expanded Oversight Still to Be Implemented," May 19, 2011, http://www.gao.gov/products/GAO-11-415, 31.

3. Daniel, "New Hotels Rise Amid Ruins in Haitian Capital," *Associated Press*, April 29, 2012.

4. Frantz Duval, "Penn avec peine," *Le Nouvelliste*, August 21, 2012. ("Nous cédons notre place à un ami. A l'ambassadeur Penn. S'interroge un journaliste senior . . . '221 ans après le soulèvement général des esclaves, nous sommes incapables de déblayer les ruines de la maison nationale.'")

5. GAO report, 41.

6. Sontag, "Earthquake Relief Where Haiti Wasn't Broken," *New York Times*, July 15, 2012.

7. Roxana Larios, "Cierra maquila y se va para Haití," *PrensaLibre.com*, October 29, 2011, http://www.prensalibre.com/economia/Cierra-maquila-va-Haiti_0_581341865.html (accessed July 15, 2012). Also cited in *New York Times*, ibid.

8. Daniel, "Haiti Gov't Links to Old Regime Prompt Scrutiny," *Associated Press*, October 13, 2011.

ACKNOWLEDGMENTS

THIS BOOK WAS WRITTEN IN MEMORY OF THOSE LOST ON A CLEAR January day and in the difficult year that followed. I hope it will serve in some way as a tribute to their lives. I remember Jan Olaf Hausotter, the memory of his wit and contagious optimism undimmed; the kindness of Andrew Grene; the friendship of Mamadou Bah; and Cleiton Neiva, whose generosity and professionalism saved my neck in Tropical Storm Hanna. I think of scores more friends, colleagues, and neighbors I am honored to have known. Ayiti pap peri.

All my work in Haiti was the result of collaboration with a team of creative, dedicated people. I refer first of all to Ramon Espinosa, a photographer of tremendous talent who was the first to welcome me to Hispaniola, guided my first forays on the island (including my first sortie into Haiti), and was a great partner when he joined me in Port-au-Prince. Gracias, pana, por tu amistad. I am equally grateful for the guidance of Pierre Richard Luxama, whose skill and unflappable bravery behind the camera are an inspiration to all who have the privilege of working beside him. And to Ariana Cubillos, who, after being the sharp and insightful eyes for millions through five tumultuous years photographing Haiti, came back when the earthquake struck. No word or frame any of us produced, meanwhile, would have been possible without the hard work and heartfelt care of Annette Pierre, Elias Gerasaint, and Joselin Herard, who powered our operation and made our bureau a home.

Thanks to Ben Fox, for patience and guidance; and John Daniszewski, Niko Price, and Marjorie Miller, for the many opportunities to work for and with them. Michele Faul, for bringing me to the Caribbean, then returning at the moment her advice was needed most; and Dan Perry, for his teaching, and a beer in Jerusalem where he asked what I wanted to do with my life. Thanks to all journalists who answered the call to come to postquake Haiti when most people were trying to get out—especially the AP team, for twenty-hour workdays, solace, support, and telling the story to the world. (And for the jeans, deodorant, and socks.) Thanks to Frank Bajak, Rukmini Callimachi, Paisely Dodds, Mike Melia, Danica Coto, David McFadden, Paul Haven, Andy Drake, Greg Bull, Rich Matthews, Tamara Lush, Kathy Corcoran, Mary Rajkumar, Maria Sanminiatelli, Chery Dieu-Nalio, Ron Bellafato, John Evens Darbouze, and scores of others from the Associated Press around the world.

Thanks to the whole gang in Port-au-Prince, for their wits, hard work, and above all friendship, starting with Trenton Daniel, Pooja Bhatia, Mischa Berlinski, Emily Troutman, Matt Marek, Stephanie Ziebell, Logan Abassi, Maria Civit, and many more. Special thanks to Ben Depp and Alexis Erkert for their epic hospitality. Mil gracias, Andrea del Angel. Thanks to all my friends on the island before, during, and after the earthquake, named here, elsewhere in this book, or otherwise. You know who you are.

Thanks to my agent, David Larabell of the David Black Agency, for believing in and shepherding this book. Also to my editor, Luba Ostashevsky, and everyone at Palgrave

Macmillan, including Victoria Wallis, Laura Lancaster, and Lauren Dwyer, for taking on a difficult project on such an extremely compressed timeframe. My tremendous gratitude goes to the J. Anthony Lukas Prize Project Committee at the Columbia Graduate School of Journalism and the Nieman Foundation for Journalism at Harvard University, including Linda Healey, Shaye Areheart, Dorothy Brown, Susan McHenry, Mirta Ojito, Jonathan Alter, Nicholas Lemann, and Ann Marie Lipinski, who honored me with their confidence, and whose generous financial support made this project possible. My ability to take off from daily journalism (and monthly paychecks) was also made possible by the family of Michel Kelly and Atlantic Media Co. And thanks of many kinds to the faculty, staff, and students at Northwestern University's Medill School of Journalism, which, in addition to being my alma mater, provided much-needed support through the Medill Medal for Courage in Journalism. Thanks also to Richard Stolley. Thanks as well to the students and faculty at Knox College, particularly Dan Beers, for hosting me and for a terrific and productive conversation about many of the ideas in the book.

Much gratitude and credit is owed to the dedicated, sleep-deprived hammering of prose, facts, and arguments by C. J. Lotz, Rob Ligouri, and especially the brilliant (is that the right word, Boris?) Boris Fishman. I shudder to think what would have been on the preceding pages if they hadn't been involved. I'm grateful for the research and fixing prowess of Evens "Bruno" Bruno, the translation expertise of Riva Precil, Erold Saint-Louis and the Kreyòl Lab of Chicago, and the exhaustive Haitian Creole-English Bilingual Dictionary from Albert Valdman at Indiana University. Mèsi (p. 480). Many thanks for the insightful comments, advice, and support of Kim Barker, Alex Kotlowitz, Marcel Pacatte, Jeremy Popkin, Bryan Curtis, Sam Eifling, J. P. Howley, Laurent Dubois, Kate Ramsey, Johnhenry Gonzalez, Grenville Draper, Rene Auborg, Louise Ivers, Paul Farmer, and Amy Wilentz. Thanks to the Duke Haiti Lab and Louie B. Nunn Center for Oral History at the University of Kentucky. Thanks to everyone at the Brooklyn Writers' Space and the New York Public Library (and, speaking of institutions, the taxpayers of New York City). Thanks as always to Frank X. Walker and Kelly Ellis, who I hope saw a touch of poetry here. And thanks to the programmers who designed the phenomenal word-processing program Scrivener, and to the people who built a Mac laptop that could survive an earthquake and then last long enough to write a book about it.

Mèsi anpil to so many in Haiti who have shared their lives and stories with me. Some of their names are in this book. Many more are not. My deepest gratitude and appreciation goes to the Chery family, who opened their homes and lent their trust, and have cared deeply for Claire and me. It is with the utmost measure of respect with which I have shared their stories and words here, and I hope to have done well by them in kind.

The man who bridges all these categories and more, of course, is Evens Sanon. No amount of gratitude would be enough, and no more words here can pay appropriate tribute. So here, all I can say is: Thank you.

To my mother, father, sister, and grandmother, for endless support I repaid with worry, and standing by me when the world seemed darkest. For love, guidance, support, and an unbreakable and hopefully hereditary sense of humor, all my love and thanks.

And, finally, to Claire Payton, whose name arrives at the end of these acknowledgments instead of woven throughout but for the tyrannical linearity of syntax. This book was born in our conversations and shaped by her help, intellect, and library. It is infused with her work and indomitable spirit, and it is made even plausible by the fact that I was lucky enough somewhere along the way to find that her path had joined my own. It is a fruit of, and I hope will bring more joy to, the life we share.

INDEX